THE ITALIAN LEGAL TRADITION

For
my family and my friends

The Italian Legal Tradition

THOMAS GLYN WATKIN
Senior Lecturer in Law
University of Wales, Cardiff

Ashgate
DARTMOUTH
Aldershot • Brookfield USA • Singapore • Sydney

BOWLING GREEN STATE
UNIVERSITY LIBRARIES

© Thomas Glyn Watkin 1997

All rights reserved. No part of this publication may be reproduced, stored in a retrieval system, or transmitted in any form or by any means, electronic, mechanical, photocopying, recording or otherwise without the prior permission of the publisher.

Published by
Dartmouth Publishing Company Limited
Ashgate Publishing Limited
Gower House
Croft Road
Aldershot
Hants GU11 3HR
England

Ashgate Publishing Company
Old Post Road
Brookfield
Vermont 05036
USA

British Library Cataloguing in Publication Data
Watkin, Thomas Glyn
The Italian legal tradition
1.Law - Italy
I.Title
349.4'5

Library of Congress Cataloging in Publication Data
Watkin, Thomas Glyn, 1952-
The Italian legal tradition / Thomas Glyn Watkin.
p. cm.
Includes bibliographical references and index.
ISBN 1-85521-759-7 (hb) 1-84014-062-3 (pb)
1. Law–Italy. I. Title.
KKH68.W38 1997
349.45–dc21
97-3354
CIP

ISBN 1 85521 759 7 (Hbk)
ISBN 1 84014 062 3 (Pbk)

Printed and bound by Athenaeum Press, Ltd.,
Gateshead, Tyne & Wear.

Contents

Table of Legislation

In the table which follows, references to the Digest and Institutes of Justinian are given by Book, Title and Section in that order. References to the Italian Constitution and other codes are by article, while references to other legislative enactments are given by the date of the Law followed by its number, laws being numbered consecutively during each calendar year. Decree-laws, *decreti-leggi*, are similarly cited, but preceded by the letters D.L. rather than L. Those preceded by the letters R.D. are decree laws issued under the monarchy. D.M. indicates a ministerial decree, a form of delegated legislation issued by a government Minister.

Table of Cases

Italian

Italian cases are cited by Court, followed by the date of the judgement and their number, judgements being numbered consecutively during each calendar year.

United Kingdom

Preface

Cardiff Law School was among the first university institutions in the United Kingdom to offer its students the opportunity not merely to study English law in conjunction with a second language, but to study both the language and the legal system of another country as part of a Law degree. Cardiff was certainly unique in commencing such integrated schemes of study with degrees in Law and Italian and Law and Spanish. French, German and Japanese followed, so that Cardiff has developed into a major centre of Law and Language teaching.

The present volume is the result of my involvement with those schemes of study and in particular the Italian Legal System course, which I have taught to students of Law and Italian since 1985. The course aims to prepare undergraduates for a year's study at the Law faculty of an Italian university. From the outset, one of the greatest difficulties was providing the students with sufficient appreciation of the context of the law and legal system of contemporary Italy to enable them to proceed to read the literature available in Italian not only with understanding but with confidence. These days, an English-speaking student comes to the study of a civilian system such as that of Italy without much if any knowledge of Roman law or European legal history to provide a basic ground plan, and without that due sense of the systematic nature of law with which continental legal discourse is suffused.. This book is meant to provide an introduction to Italian law and the legal system of Italy which will make good that particular deficit. It is not intended to be a detailed exposition of the rules of Italian law, still less a comprehensive history of that system. It is meant rather to give its readers sufficient information regarding the influences which have shaped and which continue to shape Italian legal development, together with a broad overview of the main areas and features of modern Italian law, to allow them to progress with confidence to literature which takes that context for granted.

My own interest in Italian law arises from several sources. There is my love of Italy and the Italian people stemming from visits paid over many years, beginning in childhood with my parents. There has been the inevitable interest stimulated by study of Roman law and legal history. To these must be added the influence of the many friendships I have made in recent years as a result of contacts with fellow academics in Italian universities. For their help and encouragement I am greatly indebted. In particular, I wish to thank Professors Rudolf Carpanini and Giovanni Cordini, both of the University of Pavia; Professors Andrea Padovani, Dario Mantovani and Giulio Ubertis, all of the University of Parma; and Professor Tullio Scovazzi, now of Milan. I am also grateful to those advocates and notaries who have so generously discussed their work with me and allowed me to visit their offices, and who have accompanied me on visits to the Law Courts; in particular, Professor A. Leoncini-Bartoli and Dottoressa G. Melegari of Parma. I also wish to express my thanks to the Rector of Parma University, Professor Nicola Occhiocupo, for the welcome and hospitality I have always received from him and his staff.

I owe a great deal also to the students to whom I have taught Italian law over the last decade. I am grateful too to my colleagues at Cardiff for their unfailing interest and encouragement at all times. In particular, I should like to thank Mr. James Young, Dr. Sotirios Manolkidis, Mrs. Rachel Fenton-Giglio and Miss Paolisa Nebbia for reading parts of the manuscript and offering me their comments and criticisms. I am very indebted to my wife Jane, not only for her constant support and help, but in particular for helping me compile the Index and Tables, as well as proof-reading the final draft. I am also very grateful to Mr. John Irwin and his staff at Dartmouth Publishing for their interest in and enthusiasm for this endeavour.

There are many others who have directly and indirectly inspired and aided the production of this book. With them in mind, as well as its future readership, the dedication I hope speaks for itself and conveys my heartfelt thanks.

Thomas Glyn Watkin
Cardiff
November 25, 1996

1 The Italian Legal Tradition

1 Justinian and the Corpus Iuris Civilis

Italy has a strong claim to being considered the cradle of European legal culture. This is so because it was in Italy that Roman civil law was first developed in the ancient world and also in Italy that that system re-emerged in the Middle Ages to become the foundation upon which the majority of European states chose to erect their modern legal systems. Indeed, the influence of Roman law stretches even farther afield in that it is the basis of the legal systems of all those nations across the world which have established their legal orders upon the tradition received when they were the colonies of European countries.

Roman civil law began as the legal system of a small city state upon the banks of the river Tiber in central Italy. As Rome grew from these modest beginnings to become the centre of the largest empire that the world had then seen, so also its legal system came to hold sway over the whole of southern Europe, much of Europe north of the Alps, much of the Middle East and North Africa. The Roman genius for law was closely allied to the great Roman feats in engineering. In both disciplines, the Romans were not great theorists like the Greeks, but rather endowed with a tremendous practicality, for ever conquering the problems they encountered with practical, workmanlike answers. Their system of private law endured the change of republican to imperial government under the Caesars, the rise and fall of a vast empire, the conversion of the people from paganism to Christianity, and finally the shifting of the centre of government itself from Rome in the west to Constantinople in the East. It is a remarkable tale of survival, and of the fitness of Roman law to survive and serve a much changed and much changing social order.

When the emperor Justinian ascended the imperial throne in 527 AD, the empire of which he became emperor was Roman mainly in name. Control of the western empire, including France, Spain and Italy itself, had already been lost, Rome herself having fallen to the invading tribes from northern Europe during the last quarter of the previous century. The empire which Justinian was to govern was centred in the east, his capital being Constantinople or Byzantium. Justinian set himself two great goals at the outset of his reign. Firstly, he wished to restore to his dominions those territories of the western empire that had been lost, and secondly to restore to his subjects the classical law of Rome as their rightful legal heritage. Justinian was well aware that the law by which the inhabitants of his Christian, mainly Greek-speaking empire now lived was but a poor reflection of the great system which had been developed in ancient Rome itself and which had reached its apogee in the first half of the third century AD.

In the first of these ambitions, he enjoyed but limited success. His generals did manage to reconquer some of the lost lands of the western empire, particularly in Italy, but their success was of short duration. Ultimately, the Byzantine emperors were only able to retain control of a relatively small portion of these reconquered territories. For many centuries, they did manage to retain control of the region around Ravenna in north-eastern Italy which to this day bears in its name the evidence of its reconquest for the Roman people, that is Romagna. However, not even Justinian could possibly have foreseen the extent of the success which he was to achieve in the pursuit of his second goal, the restoration of Roman jurisprudence.

The problems which faced Justinian with regard to this second goal were considerable. The sources of Roman law by his time were to be found mainly in two places: the enactments of his imperial predecessors and the works of the classical jurists. Both sources were vast and previous attempts at systematization had met with only very limited success. The array of source materials to be mastered must have appeared particularly daunting to those who were setting out upon a legal career in the law schools of Constantinople and Beirut. Justinian therefore determined to appoint a series of commissions to examine these voluminous sources and to extract from them those rules which were to remain valid, to amend those which required up-dating, to discard those which were no longer necessary or desirable, and finally to present their product in a systematized, accessible form. The immensity of the task confronting these commissions can be readily appreciated by a common lawyer were he to imagine being faced with learning or discovering his law from the assembled mass of all the statutes passed since Magna Carta together with all the reported cases from the Year Books onwards, the whole having no order other than the chronological and no really systematic guide to the contents being available.

Such was the task which faced the commissions appointed by the emperor Justinian. The first was appointed to examine the enacted laws in

529. Its work was probably aided by the existence of previous attempts at this task, which had produced the codex Gregorianus and the codex Hermogenianus, both in the third century, and also the Theodosian Code of the late fourth century. However, the task was still considerable and took them the best part of a year. The end result was the first code of the emperor Justinian, known as the codex Vetus, promulgated in 530.

Another commission was then appointed to examine the writings of the great jurists of Roman law. The work of this commission was much more onerous in that there were no previous attempts at systematization of any significance to assist it. Instead, the commissioners, six in number, were faced with having to wade through the whole range of juristic literature from roughly the third century BC to their own day, being assisted in their task by ten barristers from the Constantinople bar. When they completed their work in 533, it was said that they had worked wonders, in that the job had been expected to take ten years. Modern scholarship, however, suggests that they had worked from the outset to a strict timetable and that from this it was clear all along that the work would be done by 533.[1] The end product of their prodigious research, assimilation and ordering is known as the Digest or Pandects, both titles adequately describing the nature of their achievement: Pandects illustrating its comprehensiveness, while Digest points to the degree of assimilation achieved.

However, the work was far from being small. The Digest consists of fifty books, each divided into titles. By means of these books and titles, the various legal subjects are presented in a systematic, indeed scientific, manner. Thus, for instance, all the authorities on property are brought together and are then presented so that means of acquisition are dealt with first, then modes of transfer, and so on. The whole nevertheless is a massive work, being one and a half times as long as the Bible. Justinian quickly realized that whatever the merits of the Digest, and they were indeed considerable, the work was hardly one which could be placed in the hands of an aspiring law student in the hope that from it he could easily acquire the requisite legal knowledge. Accordingly, Justinian asked three of the commissioners who had worked on the Digest - Tribonian, Dorotheus and Theophilus, the last two being law professors at Beirut and Constantinople respectively - to produce a smaller work, suitable as an introduction for the "young desirous of learning the law" as he put it, and these three produced by the end of 534 a student textbook in four books, based largely on the second century Institutes of the Roman jurist, Gaius. This work was known as Justinian's Institutes, and has remained a basic textbook for aspiring civil lawyers to this day. This work, along with the Digest and the Code, was given the full force of enacted law, a somewhat remarkable fate for a student text.

Meanwhile, the changes to the law which had been made by way of up-dating during the compilation of these works had rendered the original Code out of date. It was therefore revised to incorporate the legal innovations and amendments of these jurisprudentially hectic years and republished as the Codex repetitae praelectionis. This revised Code, together with the Digest and the Institutes, was now to be the sole source of law in the Byzantine empire, all previous authorities being deprived of legal authority. It is these three works which a later age was to term the Corpus Iuris Civilis, but they did not bear this name in Justinian's time. Justinian's reign ended with his death in 565, but his legal codification was to survive to form by far the most important source of knowledge of Roman law for subsequent generations in western Europe.

2 The Dark Ages in Western Europe

While Justinian's great work of codification was taking place, knowledge of Roman law in western Europe was sinking to its nadir. Justinian had recognized that the jurisprudence of his age was but a pale shadow of that of the earlier classical age three centuries before. That is why he sought to revive those earlier standards through his codifications. However, the long-term failure of his other great goal, the reconquest of the western empire, meant that the sometime Roman citizens of western Europe had but little appreciation of the legal heritage that was theirs and the cause of which was being advanced at Byzantium.

In the west, Italy had been invaded during the fifth century by a tribe known as the Ostrogoths, or eastern goths, who moved down from the north to dominate the peninsula. Their leader, Theodoric, perhaps following the example of earlier Roman emperors such as Theodosius, promulgated a law code for his people, a code which is known as the Edict of Theodoric. Compared however to the compilations of the Roman emperors, let alone those of the emperor Justinian, Theodoric's enactment is crude and simplistic in the extreme. It consists in the main of lists of compensation payments, detailing the fixed amounts that had to be paid in compensation for wrongs committed - so much for a broken arm, so much for a broken leg, and so on. In terms of legal sophistication, the Edict of Theodoric marks a return to the level achieved at Rome in the XII Tables, promulgated by tradition in 450 BC. In other words, the clock of legal culture had been turned back nine hundred years.

In the following century, the Ostrogoths were themselves displaced by northern invaders, this time the Lombards, who settled Italy rather more permanently, giving their name to that portion of north central Italy, Lombardy, which contains the cities of Milan and Pavia. The sixth-century Lombard leader, Rothari, also gave his people a code of laws named after him the Edict of Rothari, a compilation which belongs in roughly the same category as that of Theodoric.

Similar codes of laws to those of Theodoric and Rothari were appearing at this time all over Europe. These codes were meant to be binding upon those who were the followers of the rulers in question, being tribal rather than territorial in nature. Thus, it was possible for more than one system of law to operate in a given geographical area if that area was occupied by more than one people. This was indeed the case in much of southern France and eastern Spain, lands which had been invaded by the Visigoths, or western goths, but which were still inhabited in part by those who regarded themselves as Roman by descent and cultural allegiance. While the Visigoths lived by their own customs and laws, these remnants of the Roman empire clung to what they were able to remember of the Roman way of life in their legal affairs. Their customs, codified for them by their Visigothic ruler, Alaric, in the so-called Breviary of Alaric, are in truth but a crude approximation of what classical Roman law had really been like. It is known for that reason as the Vulgar Roman law. Nevertheless, it gave Roman law a foothold for survival in the west, even if that foothold was really no more than a rough memorial.

The main vehicle for the survival of Roman values, and indeed of classical culture generally, in the western Europe of the post-Roman period was the Christian Church. It alone of the great institutions of the Roman empire survived the fall of that empire in the west and continued to govern western Christendom from Rome itself, the seat of the Papacy. What little was known of classical literature, history and philosophy in the Europe of the early Middle Ages was transmitted via the Church, the cathedrals and monasteries of which preserved and copied the classical texts which were to survive for posterity. These monasteries and cathedrals were the only centres of learning in Dark Age Europe, and the clergy and religious were the only learned class.

The main subject of study in the cathedral schools and monasteries was not however classics but theology, and the text for that study was the

Latin version of the Bible, translated from the original languages by St. Jerome in the fourth century and known as the Vulgate. Students of theology studied the Bible with reverence as the revealed truth of God, divinely inspired and divinely ordained. It would be difficult to describe the theological study of these centuries as critical in the modern sense, but the work of this age preserved the sources which were to form the basis of critical studies in later generations. As well as the Bible, the works of the Fathers of the Church - men like St. Jerome, St. Ambrose, St. Augustine and St. Gregory - were also studied, as commentaries upon and development of the Biblical text. These works too were thought to be inspired by the Holy Spirit, and therefore authoritative and beyond question.

As well as theology, the Humanities were also studied in the cathedral schools, particularly after that revival of learning which took place in the ninth century and which is known as the Carolingian renaissance. Law was also studied in certain centres, and during the tenth century, the cathedral school at Pavia emerged as a very important centre of legal studies, the law studied being primarily the feudal law of the Lombard kingdom. Modern scholarship has shown how the techniques developed at Pavia may well have formed the basis of the methodology which was to develop subsequently at Bologna in the revived study of the Roman law of Justinian.[2]

Before dealing with the revival of Roman law in eleventh-century Bologna, it is worth noting how the influence of the Italian cathedral schools was felt even in northern Europe. The career of Lanfranc bears eloquent testimony to this phenomenon. Lanfranc was born in Lombardy and educated at the cathedral school in Pavia. He may even have been active in the teaching of law in that city. He was a brilliant teacher who eventually left Italy to found a new cathedral school at Avranches in Normandy. There, once more, he enjoyed tremendous success. So successful was he that he is said to have become bored with his triumph and abdicated his control of the school at Avranches. Leaving that city, he crossed Normandy to the newly founded monastic community of Herluin at Bec. There, he became an influential figure, his talents again receiving recognition, becoming prior of the monastery. He came to the attention of Duke William, who invited him to become the first abbot of Duke William's new abbey of St. Etienne in the Norman capital, Caen. When William conquered England in 1066, it was only six years before Lanfranc was invited to follow his royal master across the Channel and assume the office of archbishop of Canterbury.

Lanfranc's career shows the pan-European nature of scholarship and ecclesiastical life at this time. It would be difficult even today to imagine such an 'international' career outside perhaps of science. Nor was Lanfranc's career extraordinary. His successor in the see of Canterbury, St. Anselm, was born in Aosta, also travelled to France and to Bec, where he was abbot before being summoned to his English archbishopric. One of the factors assisting this mobility of scholars and churchmen was the existence in Latin of an international language of the educated classes.

This international flavour to learning in the eleventh century makes it difficult to ascribe an important development of the period definitely to northern or southern Europe. The development in question was the use of a particular method in the study of authoritative texts. The method has become known as dialectic, and it was certainly used in the study of theology and philosophy in Paris by the end of the eleventh century, at which time it was also being applied to the study of the Corpus Iuris Civilis at Bologna. It is not possible to say whether the Parisians influenced the Bolognese or vice versa, or even whether alternatively the technique was developed independently at both places.

In Paris, the dialectic method is associated with the name of the gifted philosopher, Peter Abelard. He it was who had the temerity to confront the question of whether there were contradictions in the divinely inspired works of the Church Fathers. As has been said, the Bible was regarded as revealed truth and could not therefore contain error or self-contradiction. Abelard faced up to the awkward fact that there appeared to be passages in the Bible and in the works of the Fathers which contradicted each other. This, he argued, could not in fact be the case given their divine inspiration. Instead, the fault must lie in the defective understanding of the reader. Abelard therefore composed a book, entitled *Sic et Non* in which he presented one hundred and fifty pairs of apparently contradictory passages from the works of the Fathers and, by pitting them against each other in adversarial mode, sought to harmonize them, that is to show how by reason each could be shown to be correct in its proper sphere. Indeed, the proper understanding of each passage was increased as a result of this treatment. However, there was no disguising the fact that it was reason, and Abelard's personal reason at that, which was now responsible for this deeper understanding of the divinely inspired works. Not surprisingly, Abelard suffered criticism at the hands of the ecclesiastical authorities and was twice tried for heresy. The dialectic technique, however, was destined to triumph. It was to be one of the basic techniques of scholastic philosophy, and even in the twentieth century has been much used to resolve 'apparent' contradictions in the works of Karl Marx and other Marxist thinkers. It was at Bologna, however, in the eleventh, twelfth and thirteenth centuries that this method was particularly important in the development of European jurisprudence.

3 The Glossators of Bologna

Bologna, according to tradition, was the first university to be established in Europe. Although its claim to this title is sometimes questioned, particularly by rival Italian foundations, there can be no dispute that, like Pavia and others, the cathedral school of Bologna developed into a university during the great revival of learning that occurred in the Europe of the eleventh and twelfth centuries.

The Humanities were now the main subject of study for the students who flocked from all over Europe to the Italian centres of higher education. A course of study in the Humanities was becoming an essential precursor to more specialized studies in theology, law or medicine. The Arts faculty of the University of Bologna was without doubt the most distinguished of its time, and it was there that by tradition the question was asked which set in motion the revival of Roman legal studies in western Europe.

The question was asked of a scholar named Irnerius, or Guernerius. This latter rendering of his name as beginning with the letters 'Gu' in Latin, suggests that his name may actually have begun with a 'W', in the same way as William is rendered Guillelmus, the Latin alphabet having no 'W' in it. If this is true, then Irnerius, or Guernerius, was probably in reality called Werner, a German, thus again attesting to the international flavour of the scholarship of that age.

The question that was asked of Irnerius concerned the passage in the Gospel according to St. Matthew in which Our Lord asks the rhetorical question, "Are not two sparrows sold for a penny?"[3] Irnerius' text was the Latin Vulgate, in which the sum named is that of the Roman coin of least value, the *as*. Irnerius was asked about the nature and value of this coin, and he set about finding more concerning it. In the course of consulting various ancient manuscripts, he found one in which it was mentioned a great deal. It was a manuscript which had been little consulted previously, and its rediscovery altered the course of Irnerius' career and indeed of European legal history. The manuscript was the sole surviving copy in western Europe of Justinian's Digest. It had survived in the cathedral library at Pisa, where it remained until the thirteenth century when Pisa was captured by Florence and the manuscript taken to that city where it is housed to this day in the library of the church of San Lorenzo, from which it has become known as the Laurentian manuscript.

Irnerius was struck by the quality of the law which was described and discussed in this vast work. It was to his eyes, and to those of his contemporaries, vastly superior to the law codes by which they were governed. It was infinitely more sophisticated, and thereby more worthy of serious study. To the men, even the scholars, of the eleventh and twelfth century, the Digest, indeed the whole of the Corpus Iuris Civilis, to use the title which later generations gave to the entirety of Justinian's compilations, was a text comparable to the Bible itself. To the theologians, the Bible was revealed truth; to the jurists of Bologna, the Digest was written reason, *ratio scripta*, and thus they referred to it.

If the Digest was written reason, it followed that as a work of legal perfection, a work manifesting the highest level of law to which human society could aspire, there could be no imperfections in it. It could not, any more than the Bible, contain errors or self-contradictions. Accordingly, if there were passages in the Digest which appeared to contradict one another, the apparent defect must lie in the understanding of the reader and not in the text itself. Here, one finds a point of departure for jurisprudence almost identical to that from which Abelard had embarked upon *Sic et Non*. This time it was Irnerius who set off to reconcile the apparent contradictions within the ancient text, using reason as his tool and employing a method very similar to Abelard's dialectic. The technique which he adopted was to gloss the text, that is to interpret it. The interpretation was first of all written between the lines of the manuscript copies which had been made for Irnerius and his followers, but eventually these glosses became so long that they could not be accommodated interlinearly and were written instead in the margins. Finally, the glosses became so long that they dominated the manuscripts, the text itself sometimes being regarded as so well known that it did not merit inclusion.

The work which Irnerius initiated, that of glossing the Digest to remove all apparent contradictions and reveal the harmony of the whole, took two centuries to complete. Irnerius was followed in his work by the four doctors - Martinus, Hugo, Jacobus and Bulgarus - and the followers of Irnerius generally are known, from their work, as the Glossators. They worked at the increasingly important school or faculty of law at Bologna, where their effort reached its culmination in the 1260s, with the production of the complete gloss, the *Glossa ordinaria*, the end product being attributed to the work of the jurist, Accursius, whose tomb stands to this day outside the Franciscan church in Bologna.

The intervening two centuries had seen Bologna become the centre of European legal studies. Students from all over Europe travelled to that city for their legal education. Many famous teachers of the law were active there at this time. Among them, mention must be made of Azzo, whose lectures were so well attended that they had to be held in the vast central square before the basilica of San Petronio, from the steps of which the discourse was delivered. The students were expected to know the texts from the Digest by heart before attending, a vast feat of memory which astonishes those who have access to printed books as a system of information retrieval. Azzo was so influential that it was rhymed:

Chi non ha Azzo	If you don't know your Azzo
Non vada al palazzo	You won't get to the palazzo.

Another leading scholar from Bologna was Vacarius, who left that city for England, where in the 1140s and 1150s he was the first to introduce the study of Roman law. Significantly, he was invited to England by the then Archbishop of Canterbury, Theobald, who like Lanfranc and Anselm before him had come to Canterbury from Bec.

It was during the 1140s in Bologna that another very important development took place. In much the same manner as Roman law before Justinian's time had consisted of disparate authorities requiring the imposition of order, so too by the twelfth century had the law of the Church become needful of systematization. Although chronological collections of canons had been compiled together with collections which placed these canons under subject headings, there had been no attempt to systematize the whole law of the Church, harmonizing it so as to remove any contradictions. It was at Bologna that the body of ecclestical laws was first systematized in this fashion by the jurist, Gratian, who completed his great work of synthesis during the years 1140-1142. He entitled his work appropriately the Concordance of Discordant Canons, *Concordantium discordantum canonum*, emphasizing the harmony he had achieved. The work is also known as the Decretum and is the basis of the collection which eventually became known as the Corpus Iuris Canonici. This work was fundamental for the study of canon law thereafter, although it was never actually given authority as a source of canon law.

After the completion of Gratian's work, students at Bologna, particularly those who intended to make a career in the Church as lawyers and administrators, occupied themselves not only in the study of the civil law, the law of the Corpus Iuris Civilis, but also in the study of the canon law. They graduated therefore as Doctors of both laws, *Doctores utriusque iuris*, a formula which persists to this day in the degrees of bachelor, master and doctor of *laws* rather than just *law*.

4 St. Thomas Aquinas and the Commentators

The production of the Decretum by Gratian led to a challenging reflection upon the work of the Glossators and their students. True, Justinian had been a Christian emperor and therefore his compilation could be seen as a Christian code of law. However, the greater part of the texts contained in the Digest were the work of the classical jurists, men who had composed their works in pagan times. Why, it could be asked, were the laws of a pagan society accorded such importance in a Christian university, particularly when the law of the Christian Church itself was now available for study in its stead.

This question was a serious challenge to the jurists of Bologna and elsewhere. It was a challenge which had a particularly keen cutting edge in the thirteenth century, when several previously lost classical texts became available for study. The works of the philosopher Aristotle in particular fell into this category, many of which were found to have survived in Moorish Spain, having been translated into Arabic, and were now translated from the Arabic into Latin. The study of Aristotle was also challenged in the same manner. Aristotle, and pagan authors generally, found a great champion in the thirteenth-century philosopher and theologian, St. Thomas Aquinas.

St. Thomas was born in Italy in the little village of Aquino, situated on the plain overlooked by the great Benedictine monastery of Monte Cassino. Despite his Italian birth and geographical proximity to the Benedictine order, he spent most of his adult life in northern Europe and was a Dominican. In his two great works, the *Summa Theologica* and the *Summa contra Gentiles*, he defended the study of pagan authors in a manner that was eventually, after much controversy, to triumph in Christian Europe. St. Thomas argued that truth could be obtained from either of two sources: it could be directly revealed by God, as in Scripture, or it could be derived by man through the use of his faculty of reason. Reason, argued St. Thomas, was a divine gift, given to all of humankind, whether or not they were baptized Christians. Therefore, inasmuch as reason was a divine gift, knowledge which was derived from reason was also the gift of God, although in this instance God's truth was revealed indirectly. When pagan philosophers, such as Plato or Aristotle, reasoned, they used the gift which God gave for the purpose which God intended it should be used to serve, and to despise the fruit of their reason was therefore to despise the gift and the divine giver. Accordingly, St. Thomas argued, it was wrong to shun the works of the pagan writers, provided always that they were read in the light of what had been revealed by God. Revelation was a more reliable source of knowledge than reason, but in the absence of revelation, reason was the best available guide.

The influence of this argument upon the development of European culture can hardly be overstressed. At a stroke, St. Thomas had rendered respectable the study of the world in which human action occurred. Hitherto, the world was seen as a vale of tears, a place to be endured rather than enjoyed, whereas now it could be seen as a manifestation of God's goodness, a manifestation which through the use of reason upon its substance could reveal truth concerning its Creator and His will. In many fields, artists and writers responded to this outcome with a remarkable sense of release. In the paintings of the following century, although the subjects are still predominantly religious, the characters no longer inhabit a vacuous, heavenly space composed of gold leaf, but are represented in a world, a contemporary world, with buildings, birds, trees and flowers. Nature is celebrated as a manifestation of God's goodness. Natural motifs adorn the columns of churches erected at this time; music celebrates secular as well as sacred themes. In literature, the traditional Latin is supplemented by writing in the vernacular languages, no longer to be decried, the most potent illustration being undoubtedly the work of the Italian poet, Dante.

What was true of the Arts was no less true of law. The Glossators had studied the Digest as written reason, to present its contents as the highest law of which mankind was capable. Their study was an academic study, in the literal sense of a study undertaken in the schoolroom. They were not primarily practical lawyers, who undertook litigation on behalf of clients or who gave legal advice or who judged cases in the courts. Occasionally, they might perform juristic functions, but this was not their primary task in life.

Towards the end of the thirteenth century, this began to change. As the abhorrence of pagan thought diminished and such ideas were viewed instead as the fruit of the divine gift of human reason, so it became possible to contemplate using the results of pagan jurisprudence in the government of a Christian society. At this time, many of the city states and communes of north and central Italy were undergoing a considerable expansion in trade and commerce. These commercial developments required that they should possess laws, and indeed a jurisprudence, that would facilitate the growth in trade and prosperity that they were experiencing. The leaders of these communities began to turn to the university-trained jurists and to the university law faculties themselves for advice in the development of their laws and legal systems. The Digest after all contained highly sophisticated rules for the accomplishing of commercial transactions.

What tended to occur was that the jurists would be consulted when the law of a particular city or commune did not provide a solution for a problem which had arisen. The jurists would be asked to comment on the problem and supply an answer according to what the Digest provided in the like situation. If the Digest did not provide an exact solution, then the jurists could use their legal expertise to develop a satisfactory solution based upon the model of those provided in the Digest. For these purposes, the *Glossa ordinaria* was treated as being of equal authority to the Corpus Iuris Civilis itself. During the fourteenth century, the jurists who undertook this work came to be known as the Commentators. They are frequently said to have taken the revived Roman law out of the classroom and into the courtroom. Their comments were used in settling particular law suits, in advising upon satisfactory regimes for the governance of transactions - mainly commercial ones, and sometimes in actually framing laws for the emergent Italian communities. The most famous of these Commentators were Bartolus of Sassoferato and his pupil Baldus of Ubaldis. The latter lived to a considerable age and died in Pavia, reputedly after being bitten by a mad dog, his tombstone being preserved to this day in one of the courtyards of the Law Faculty of the University.

The Commentators, as has been said, not only produced Roman rules for incorporation into contemporary laws, but also adapted such rules for the same purpose by exercizing their own powers of reason. Whereas the Glossators had regarded the Roman rules as the zenith of legal development, the Commentators were prepared to allow for further development and improvement. In particular, they were prepared to examine Roman solutions in detail to discover underlying and unenunciated principles. It might be said that in doing this they were only discovering, or even uncovering, the hidden principles which had informed the Roman legal texts. However, it might equally be claimed that they were in fact inventing new legal rules, making rather than interpreting law.

There is a sense in which the different approaches of the Glossators and the Commentators continue to haunt the workings of civil law systems to this day. There are those who maintain that, in a country such as Italy with a civil law system, lawyers must work with the legal texts, the law codes, that they are given. Only the rules contained therein are to be applied. For them, the law is the law in the book. This view emphasizes that law-making is for those who legislate and not for those who interpret and apply the law. Indeed, some jurists concern themselves even today with the task of ensuring that apparent contradictions in the modern legal texts are harmonized and explained away. Others, however, believe that the legal texts are attempts to enunciate legal policy, which attempts are not always entirely successful. Accordingly, there must be space to allow for a reasoned approach to interpretation and application of the law. Sometimes, the text itself may not provide an answer to a specific problem. In such cases, the jurists of the latter persuasion argue, lawyers have the right if not the duty to use their trained powers of legal reasoning to uncover the principle underlying the text, which principle can be used to solve the instant problem. These latter exemplify the approach of the Commentators.

The impact of the work of the Commentators upon the Roman texts can perhaps best be appreciated by way of illustration, comparing a text from the Corpus Iuris Civilis with its counterpart in the modern Italian Civil Code. The text chosen is the well-known problem of *specificatio*.

> When a man makes a thing from another person's materials, the question is asked which of them is by natural reason the owner. Is it the man who made it or the owner of the materials? For example, suppose a man has made wine or olive oil or grain out of another man's grapes or olives or ears of corn, or has made some kind of vessel out of another man's gold or silver or bronze, or made mead by mixing another man's wine and honey, or compounded a plaster or eye-salve out of another man's drugs, or made a garment out of another man's wool, or a ship or chest or chair out of another man's timber. After prolonged controversy between the Sabinians and the Proculians, the law has been settled in accordance with the intermediate opinion, namely, that, if the finished product can be reduced to its original materials, it belongs to the owner of the materials; if not, then the maker is preferred.
>
> Justinian, *Institutes*, II.1.25

> (*Specificazione*) Se taluno ha adoperato una materia che non gli apparteneva per formare una nuova cosa, possa o non possa la materia riprendere la sua prima forma, ne acquista la proprietà pagando al proprietario il prezzo della materia, salvo che il valore della materia sorpassi notevolmente quello della mano d'opera. In quest'ultimo caso la cosa spetta al proprietario della materia, il quale deve pagare il prezzo della mano d'opera.
>
> *Codice civile*, art. 940

The Justinianic text is a collection of single instances, each of which begs for a solution. It is reminiscent of the "wilderness of single instances" that can be derived from reading a succession of common law case authorities. The modern definition, on the other hand, is a succinct statement of a general principle which should serve to solve not only all those instances in the Justinianic text but all others that might arise. Such was the result often achieved by the Commentators at the close of the Middle Ages.

The work of the Commentators allowed the rules of Roman law which had been studied in the universities in the preceding centuries gradually, in a piecemeal manner, to find a place in the legal systems of fourteenth- and fifteenth-century Italy. If there was a Reception of Roman law in Italy, it was through the work of the Commentators that it was accomplished.

5 The Reception of Roman Law

It is worth comparing the process by which Roman legal rules made their way into the legal arsenal of mediaeval Italy with the manner in which the same was accomplished in France and Germany. Some scholars wish to confine the term Reception to the German experience.[4]

France, in mediaeval times, indeed right up until the Revolution, was not a state with a centralized legal system. Instead, the law of France was localized, one's legal regime depending upon the area in which one lived. The southern third of France, that portion which had been most thoroughly Romanized in ancient times, was known as the *pays de droit écrit*, the land of the written law. The written law referred to in this designation was the codified version of the Vulgar Roman law, the law to be found in such compilations as the Breviary of Alaric. The northern two-thirds of France was known as the *pays des coutumes*, the land of customs. Here, folk lived by the custom of the region which they inhabited, and the customs could vary from region to region. Many of these customs were also reduced to writing, such as the famous Customs of Beauvaisis, described by Phillipe de Beaumanoir in the thirteenth century. In either part of France, when involved in litigation, the proper law by which to decide the case was the law of the region concerned.

However, with the growth of trade and greater sophistication in government, problems arose in the later Middle Ages to which the local custumals did not provide a satisfactory solution or sometimes any solution at all. In such circumstances, the French courts and jurists were not permitted to resort immediately to the revived Roman law to find an answer. Rather, they were expected to consult the customs of the Parlement of Paris, the chief court of that part of France around the capital which was ruled directly by the king and is known to this day as the Île de France. If the customs of that court provided an answer, then it was that answer which was adopted. However, if the Paris Parlement was not able to furnish a solution, then the Roman legal texts could be examined in search of an appropriate rule. Thus, in France, during the fourteenth and fifteenth centuries, Roman legal rules found a place in the legal order, but by a less direct route than that taken in Italy.

Germany, however, provided the most direct route of all. Germany, like Italy, in the mediaeval period was not a nation in the manner of England or even France. It was a loose federation of dukedoms, counties, free cities and lands, all owing titular allegiance to the Holy Roman Emperor. The Emperor, who claimed the ultimate sovereignty over all these lands, regarded his title as being in succession to the ancient Roman emperors in the west. The title of Kaiser by which the emperor became known was but a Germanicization of the Roman imperial Caesar. Insofar as the emperor was the successor of the Roman emperors in the west, he could claim that Roman law was the proper law of his subjects. Accordingly, in 1495, the German emperor decreed that henceforth the proper law of his imperial state court, the *Reichskammergericht*, was to be Roman law, the law of the Corpus Iuris Civilis and of the *Glossa ordinaria*. This was without doubt the most thoroughgoing Reception of Roman law in Europe, and it is perhaps not surprising that, in comparison with this, some scholars have been critical of the use of the term Reception to describe events outside of the German empire.

It is said that the Middle Ages in Europe ended with the three Rs - Renaissance, Reformation and Reception. To appreciate the next phase in the development of the civil law tradition in Europe, it is necessary to examine the consequences of an event that was for many years regarded as seminal to both the Renaissance and the Reformation. It occurred some forty-two years before the introduction of Roman law into the *Reichskammergericht*. It was the fall of Byzantium to the Turk in 1453.

6 The Humanist School of Civil Law

Byzantium, or Constantinople, had been the capital of the Greek, Orthodox east since the time of Justinian, and the compilations of Justinian had formed the basis of the law in the Byzantine empire throughout the intervening period. The west had occasionally come into contact with the exotic civilization of the Byzantine court during that time, particularly during the Crusades, but contact had been by no means close. The invasion of the city by the Muslim Turks in 1453 led to an exodus of Greek-speaking Christians from the shores of the Bosphorus to western Europe. Many of those refugees settled, at least at first, in Italy.

The upshot of their emigration was to bring the Latin west into closer contact with the culture of the Greek east than had previously obtained. Those with an interest in the classical age set themselves to learn the Greek language as the key to opening up their understanding of ancient Greek culture and civilization. The emigrants also brought with them manuscripts of ancient Greek texts which had previously only been known in the west in Latin translation. Moreover, some of those translations had been made not directly into Latin from the original Greek, but through the mediating influence of Arabic. This was true, for instance, of the west's knowledge of much of the works of Aristotle, which had been discovered in an Arabic translation during the reconquest of Spain from the Moors.

These works were now available to the west in the Greek original, and it was quickly realized that the Latin versions which had hitherto formed the focus of attention were often faulty in places, where either the translation or the manuscript tradition had been in error. Nowhere was this knowledge so shattering to western confidence as in the case of the New Testament. Written originally in Greek, it had been known in the west through the Latin Vulgate of St. Jerome. Now, the original Greek text was available for study and the results of the subsequent revision were social and political, as well as intellectual, dynamite.

In the Latin Vulgate, the Greek word, επισκοπος, had been translated as the Latin *episcopus* meaning "bishop". The meaning of the Greek word itself, however, did not designate a formal, authoritative office, but rather a seniority recognized by the people who conceded respect to the person, the elder, concerned. Thus, the Catholic Church's emphasis upon episcopal power was brought into question. Likewise, the very word taken to mean "Church", the Greek εκκλεσια, Latin *ecclesia*, was found to mean something more like "congregation" or "the people". Dissatisfaction with the Roman Church's practice of selling Indulgences for the forgiveness of sins was fuelled further by the discovery that the Greek word μεταvειv did not mean "do penance" so much as "change one's attitude". This new knowledge, the new learning of the Renaissance, provided the intellectual ammunition used to attack the power and prestige of the Catholic Church by men such as Martin Luther and John Calvin, as well as more moderate reformers like Erasmus and St. Thomas More.

The new learning exposed the weakness of the intellectual *status quo* in western Europe. The notion that the Bible, in the form of the Latin Vulgate, was revealed truth was shown to be unacceptable. The Vulgate was a translation, given to the defects and blemishes to which any other such work was prone. The scholars of the Renaissance were as prepared to tear down the old orthodoxies in religion in order to discover the truth as were their counterparts at that time who had demonstrated by geographical and scientific exploration that the world was not flat and that it did not lie at the centre of the universe. It is important to remember that all of these discoveries occurred at roughly the same time. Men were prepared to redraw the map of the world, to rechart the heavens and to redefine their religious and spiritual allegiances. The result was a fundamental reshaping of man's perspective of the world during the sixteenth century.

If the Vulgate of St. Jerome was not the revealed truth of God but rather an imperfect translation of the Bible, then the Corpus Iuris Civilis of Justinian was but a sixth-century redaction of classical Roman law and not the real McCoy. Respect for Justinian's compilation did not diminish any more than did respect for the Bible, but scholars were prepared to question how true a reflection it was of the classical age of Roman jurisprudence, particularly as the text itself spoke of amendments having been made. During the sixteenth century, scholars began for the first time to look behind the compilation of the Corpus Iuris Civilis (as it became known at this time) in an attempt to discover the rules of Roman law as they had been known in the heyday of the western empire, in the times of the Caesars and even earlier at the close of the republican period.

For the first time since the renaissance of Roman legal studies in eleventh-century Bologna, the focus of civil law studies moved outside of Italy. During the sixteenth century, the centre of this new Humanist school of Roman legal studies was in France, in the university city of Bourges. The two foremost scholars in this endeavour were Jacques Cujas and Hugues Doneau, both often referred to by the Latinized forms of their names, Cujacius and Donellus. Doneau was a Huguenot, that is a French Calvinist, and his religious beliefs eventually made France a dangerous country for him in which to reside. Accordingly, he moved to the freer atmosphere of the Low Countries, where his Calvinism was less objectionable, and where also the next important phase of civilian scholarship was to be inaugurated.

The leading figure in Dutch legal scholarship in the first half of the seventeenth century was Hugh de Groot, better known as Hugo Grotius. He it was who took the logical step of holding that if Justinian's Corpus Iuris Civilis was not written reason, *ratio scripta*, as had previously been believed, then it need not be either the highest form of law known or knowable to man. Indeed, the fact that it was not even a true reflection of classical jurisprudence pointed up this fact. Accordingly, there was no reason why man should not strive by his intellectual powers to achieve newer, greater heights in the field of jurisprudence and law making.

Grotius himself devoted himself to producing a system of law which would govern not the doings of individuals or groups within a particular nation state but rather the relations of such nation states one with another. He is recognized as the father of international law. In his great work, *De iure belli ac pacis*, concerning the law of war and peace, he attempted to set out the principles and rules that should govern the dealings of nation with nation in times of hostilities as well as during peaceful coexistence. An example will show, however, that he relied much upon the principles of the Digest.

Roman law had recognized the natural law mode of acquiring property called *occupatio*. One instance of acquiring by *occupatio* was where a new island emerged in the sea, by means of, for example, volcanic activity. Such an island would become the property of the first person to take possession of it. Grotius addressed the different question, a topical question in his day, of which nation had sovereignty over islands which were newly discovered and were not previously inhabited by Christian people. On analogy with the Roman *occupatio*, Grotius maintained that sovereignty over such lands would go to the nation whose citizens were first to take possession of it. Thus were whole continents taken by the Spanish, Portuguese, British and French, and many parts of the world by the Dutch themselves. By dint of reason operating upon the Roman legal heritage, Grotius initiated the idea and the substance of international law.

7 Reason and Codification : the Napoleonic Code

Grotius believed that, through reason, a legal system could be devised to introduce legal order among the nations of the world. Although he based many of his proposed rules of international law upon the norms of the Corpus Iuris Civilis, he no longer felt it necessary to follow those rules slavishly if his own reason suggested a departure. The influence of the Digest was still great, but it was no longer an unassailable, ultimate authority.

This was not only the case in relation to international law. In the sphere of national law also, the supreme place of the Corpus Iuris Civilis was sacrificed to the idea that Justinian's work was the fruit of the intellectual achievement in his age, but there was no reason to believe that the intellectual achievements of the current age could not match or even surpass those of sixth-century Byzantium. Jurists therefore began to aspire to the creation of a new legal perfection, based on reason rather than the written reason of the Digest or even revelation. The later seventeenth century and the eighteenth century have become known in intellectual and cultural history as the Age of Reason, a title which is both accurate and less tendentious than the alternative name given to the period, namely the Enlightenment.

Belief in reason at this time reflected the tremendous confidence of the age. It was a confidence which is perhaps as difficult for our own age to grasp as was the certainty of faith in the Middle Ages. The *savants* of the Parisian salons in the eighteenth century actually believed that by the use of reason the human mind could embrace all knowledge, everything that could be known. They initiated the great enterprise which sought to reduce all knowledge to writing and place it within the covers of a single, multi-volume work, the Encyclopaedia. The belief in reason, the confidence in the human intellect, fuelled scientific and technological development, bringing about in Britain the industrial and agricultural revolutions. Rational order was to be imposed upon chaos.

This belief in the imposition of order can be seen in the architecture and landscaping of the period. Houses were built in the classical style, reflecting the order of symmetry and proportion. Gardens were laid out formally, to modern eyes perhaps rigidly, in subservience to the rational ideal. Nature itself was to be tamed and indeed improved upon; landscape gardeners thought nothing of creating proportioned lakes, even hills, to produce a terrain which conformed to the dictates of an ordered sensibility.

The musical works of Bach and Handel, Haydn and Mozart reflect the same rational order, while in poetry the verse of Molière and Racine, the writing of Pope and the other Augustan poets, all indicate the same veneration for classical order and presentation. Painters such as Poussin, David and Ingres belong to the same school.

In law, the jurisprudence of this age reflects a certain contempt for the mediaeval inheritance. In France, in particular, this led to an abhorrence of the local, customary laws by which the kingdom was governed. Jurists were called upon to try to overcome the fragmentation which was the legal heritage of France. As Louis XIV abandoned the disorder of Paris, marred for him by his memories of the insurrection called the *Fronde*, in favour of the reasoned order of life at Versailles, so his jurists sought to lead his subjects from the darkness of their mediaeval legal heritage into the dawn of a new, rational legal age. Work upon this task had begun in the reign of Louis XIII, with the production of new codes of law which were to apply to the whole kingdom. These codes dealt with specific areas of the law, such as road transport, transport by canals, trade and other such topics, where local customary rules inhibited the growth of commerce and the free passage of goods. The production of such *ordonnances*, as they were known, continued until the Revolution. The ultimate goal, however, the legal equivalent of the Encyclopaedia, was the production of a code of law which would suit the needs of any nation at any time. Prominent in the jurisprudence of France at this time were jurists such as Pothier and Domat.

It was not until after the Revolution that a code in fact emerged. The Revolution fired the confidence and enthusiasm of the nation to achieve even greater things. For many it was the ultimate triumph of reason, democracy replacing the feudal order of kingship. Fresh starts were made in a bewildering number of areas. Nothing perhaps expresses the strident self-confidence of the period so well as the attempt to reform the calendar. No longer were years to be measured according to the age of Christ, but a new start was to be made for the new era. Thus, Year I began in September 1792. Likewise, the internal divisions of the year were no longer to be according to the names of Roman gods and deified emperors; new months were introduced with equal numbers of days, and with names reflecting the predominant weather - *Pluviôse*, *Ventôse*, *Brumaire* and so on. These departures did not meet with success in the long term, but some of the rational reforms did. Older notions of measurement were permanently swept away in favour of the new metric system, based on multiples of ten, in which the standard unit of measurement - the metre, the gram, the litre -

was established on a reasonable, scientific foundation. Decimalised currency also proved to be a lasting reform.

It was not until 1804, however, that a code of private law was produced and promulgated for the people of France. By that time, Napoleon had assumed control of the nation, and, although the code is in reality the fruit of many decades of juristic effort, its creation as well as its promulgation is usually accredited to the emperor. Nothing perhaps better illustrates the contemporary attitude to the *Code Civil* as the bas relief at the foot of Napoleon's tomb which celebrates Napoleon the law-giver, one of several relating the emperor's achievements. There sits the emperor in all his state, with the tomes containing the customs of the old French kingdom being suppressed like a serpent beneath one of his feet. At his left hand, a figure approaches offering him the Corpus Iuris Civilis of Justinian as a worthy replacement for the old French laws, but Napoleon disdainfully raises that hand to signal their rejection. In his right hand, he holds up to the gaze of his adoring nation his own great contribution to the jurisprudence of the world, the new *Code Civil*. The message cannot be in doubt. The *Code Civil*, or the *Code Napoléon* as it is sometimes known, is the summit of human, legal achievement. Napoleon is a new and greater Justinian.

Napoleon's legal achievement was not however limited to France. The new code, as a rational system of law, was suitable for all peoples at all times. Accordingly, wherever Napoleon's armies triumphed, their victorious general introduced his legal order. Thus, the French *Code Civil* came to be known in the territories which Napoleon conquered in Italy and in Spain. In those countries, the code replaced older systems of law and, although the subject nations, which had French jurisprudence forced upon them, were more than ready to cast off the legal mantle by which they had been forcibly covered as soon as the military yoke was removed, they could not deny that the *Code Civil* had been a better system of law than that which it had replaced. Accordingly, although national or civic pride forbade their adoption of the *Code Civil* itself, they set themselves the target of producing for their own lands law codes after the French model. In Italy, these were to come after the unification of the kingdom in the second half of the nineteenth century, but before that point is reached, attention must be given to one final and important influence upon the development of the Italian civil law system and indeed of civil law systems generally.

8 The Romantic Movement and the German Historical School

The emphasis that had been placed upon reason during the eighteenth century almost inevitably provoked a reaction. Man, it was thought, could not live by reason alone but required that attention be paid to other needs, notably the emotional and the spiritual. Those who reacted against the over-rational approach of the *savants* and *philosophes* of the Enlightenment wished to reassert the importance of the spiritual nature of man. This reaction to rationalism at the close of the eighteenth century and at the beginning of the nineteenth century is known as the Romantic movement.

Romanticism affected the cultural life of Europe quite profoundly. In the literature of the period, it produced in Britain poets such as Keats, Shelley, Byron and Wordsworth, all of whom responded to beauty and feeling rather than to reason. Wordsworth's outburst of joy and confidence at the French Revolution was emotional rather than rational, while Keats summed up the Romantic rejection of reason as the royal road to knowledge in the lines:

> 'Beauty is truth, truth beauty,' - that is all
> Ye know on earth, and all ye need to know.[5]

In music, the rational, classical models of composition gave way to the freer approach of Beethoven and Schubert, while in painting the classical gave way to the romantic in the works of artists such as Géricault and Delacroix. Architecture also responded to the romantic impulse; builders sought to emulate the gothic of earlier ages and in the nineteenth century there was not only a gothic revival but also a departure from Roman to Greek styles and even acceptance of models from the Orient and the Americas. People began to pursue the natural rather than the rational. Walking in beautiful countryside, climbing mountains for exhilaration and appreciation of fine views came into vogue. Romantic exploits were undertaken, such as Lord Byron's championing of Greek nationalism, the movement to rescue Greece from the rule of the Ottoman Turks who had remained in power in that country since Constantinople had fallen in 1453.

In law, it is hardly a surprise to learn that no school of jurisprudence has been dubbed 'the Romantic school'. Nevertheless, the same forces which produced the Romantic movement in the Arts were at work among the jurists of the period and with much the same results. The movement was most influential in the emerging state of Germany, for Germany like Italy underwent unification in the nineteenth century, and in Germany the juristic movement in question came to be known as the Historical school. Its leading exponents were jurists such as Von Savigny and Jhering. The motive force of the Historical school was the rejection of reason as the sole, appropriate basis for a system of law and thus the rejection of the French *Code Civil* as a system of law which was, as it claimed, a system of law suitable for all peoples at all times. In this rejection, one can detect a strong element of anti-French feeling, tied in with the growing spirit of German nationalism. Tensions between the two nations were to be present from the Congress of Vienna onwards, and were eventually to be manifested in the series of conflicts which began with the Franco-Prussian War and were to continue through the First and Second World Wars.

The German jurists, instead, postulated that every nation had a right to its own system of law based on its own customs and history, hence the title Historical school. This notion arose from the concept of the nation as an expression of the identity of the people which made up the State, and that their law was as much an expression of their nationality as their language. The law had to be an expression of the spirit of the people, the *Volksgeist*, and not just of a cold impersonal reason. Herein lie the roots of the Historical school in the Romantic movement. The same ideas influenced German writers and artists of the period, perhaps most notably the philosopher Nietzsche and the composer Richard Wagner. Wagner deliberately based his operas on German myths and legends rather than on classical sources. In the twentieth century, however, the concept of the *Volksgeist* has fallen into disrepute largely through its connection with National Socialism in Germany. In this, the concept has suffered through association with an extreme and unrepresentative form of the idea.

The idea that Germany should have a law of its known, expressing its own legal culture and tradition, emanated in a demand that Germany should produce a code of law which manifested the spirit of the German people. Work on this code culminated in 1900 with the publication and promulgation of the *Burgerlichesgesetzbuch*, the German Civil Code, more commonly referred to as the BGB. Although this code was meant to be the peculiar expression of German legal culture, its pedigree is as clear as that of its French counterpart; it is a descendant of the Corpus Iuris Civilis of Justinian. Indeed, much of the German code is indistinguishable from its French cousin. The family resemblance is apparent almost everywhere, although in the area of contract much is based upon Germanic rather than Roman concepts.

By the time that Germany produced the BGB in 1900, Italy too had become a nation state and had promulgated its own law codes. In the fifty years leading up to Italian unification, northern and central Italy especially had been subjected to alternating French and German influences. The aftermath of Napoleonic conquest had familiarized Italy with the advantages of a code on the French model, while the nationalist sentiments which anticipated and led up to the *Risorgimento* favoured a warm reception for the ideas of the German historical school, as did the exposure of this part of Italy to German influence as alliances were alternately formed with France and Austria during the struggle to regain control of the peninsula. At the end of the day, the French *Code Civil* had the greater influence upon its Italian counterpart, but German jurisprudence has probably held the greater sway in Italian legal thinking.

9 Conclusion : the Civil Law World

From France and Germany, the modern civil law codes, the latter-day successors of their great Byzantine ancestor, have gone out to conquer the world in a manner that the emperor Justinian cannot possibly have contemplated. Italy was not the only nation to adopt the French *Code Civil* as the model for its own codified legislation. Spain and Portugal did the same, and so did all those nations which were once colonies of those Iberian states. Thus, the whole of Central and South America is composed of countries with codes after the French model. The erstwhile colonies of France in North Africa - nations such as Morocco, Algieria and Tunisia - have the same basis for their law, as do the former colonies of Belgium, for the kingdom of Belgium adopted French civil law as its juristic base after achieving independence in 1830-31. The freed people of Greece also conformed to the prevailing fashion for French jurisprudence, and in the United States, Louisiana alone of all the fifty states has a legal system based upon the French *Code Civil*. In Canada, Quebec's legal system is also French in inspiration but its laws are based upon the laws of France prior to Napoleon's codifications.

The German BGB has also been influential on the world stage. The Austrian empire followed Germany in its legal ordering, as has the modern state of Austria. Neighbouring Switzerland also has a German-based code of laws. Somewhat remarkably, Turkey adopted the Swiss version of the BGB for its legal affairs and, even more remarkably, Japan assumed the legal tradition of the BGB when it was minded to westernize its legal system in the 1930s. Since the Second World War, Japan has adopted a body of public law based on that of the United States, thus making its legal system into a fascinating jurisprudential hybrid.

Italy therefore has a legal tradition which is related to those of a very large number of other countries around the world. Every one of those systems is ultimately a descendant of the civil law of ancient Rome as mediated by the Corpus Iuris Civilis of Justinian and the work of the Italian Glossators and Commentators of the Middle Ages. Thus, it can be said without exaggeration and with little fear of contradiction that Italy is possessed of a legal tradition which has given much of the globe its legal order. An appreciation of that legal heritage is essential if a proper understanding of modern Italian law is to be achieved.

Notes

---

[1] See A.M. Honoré, (1972) 88 *Law Quarterly Review*, 31, 530; *Tribonian* (Ithaca, New York, 1978) pp. 170-186.

[2] See Charles M. Radding, *The Origins of Medieval Jurisprudence: Pavia and Bologna, 850-1150* (New Haven and London, 1988).

[3] Matthew, x. 29.

[4] See, for instance, R.W. Lee, *Elements of Roman Law*, 4th Ed., (London, 1956) ss. 37-38.

[5] John Keats, *Ode on a Grecian Urn*, v. 9-10.

2 The Hallmarks of Civil Law Systems

1 Civilian Reasoning

The scholars in Bologna and the other Italian universities who first studied the Roman legal texts during the Middle Ages came to their legal studies having previously studied the liberal arts in the *studium generale*, a phrase which continues to be used of Italian universities which are to this day described as *Università degli studi*. The study of the liberal arts in the nascent universities of Italy and Europe consisted of two groups of subjects, the so-called *trivium*, consisting of three subjects, and then the *quadrivium*, consisting of four. The three subjects of the *trivium* were grammar, rhetoric and logic; the four of the *quadrivium*, arithmetic, geometry, astronomy and music. It is important to realize that the scholars in the law faculties of the Italian universities who were analysing and explaining the legal texts had first of all been trained in grammar and logic.

As students of grammar and logic, they would have approached the texts they were studying primarily as consisting, at different levels, of grammatical sentences and logical propositions. Thus, take the following excerpt from Justinian's Digest:

> An island arising in the sea (a rare occurrence) belongs to the first taker.
>
> Digest, 41.7.3

This sentence contains the proposition that the first person to occupy an island which arises in the sea owns it. The person who first takes the island is its owner. This means that if A is the person and X the island, the proposition that "A owns X" is valid if X is an island which has arisen in the sea and A is its first taker. There is a sentence, which contains a logical proposition which will be true if its concomitant parts are correct.

If this is taken further, a whole mode of analysing legal rules about property and ownership will emerge. If one begins with the sentence "A owns X", as a grammatical sentence it has a subject, "A", and a predicate "owns X". The predicate consists of a direct object "X" and the verb "owns". For the sentence to make sense, as a matter of logic its subject A must be someone or something which is capable of owning, that is being the subject of the verb "to own", and the X must be something or indeed someone who is capable of being owned. Thus, although the sentence, "The lawn owns the hippopotamus" may be perfectly grammatical and contain a logical proposition, it will only be a correct statement if as a matter of law Lawns are capable of owning Hippopotami.

Thus, the sentence "A owns X" leads logically to questions which are questions of law. For the sentence to be a correct statement as a matter of law, A must be capable of owning and X of being owned. Two legal questions arise: who is capable of owning? what is capable of being owned? These questions have to be answered with reference to legal rules.

A further example may be useful. Suppose the sentence is not to do with owning but with owing. "A owes B £*x*." Again, there is a sentence with a subject A, and a predicate "owes B £*x*". This time the verb is "owes", the direct object - that which is owed - is "£*x*", and the indirect object - the person to whom it is owed - is B. Logically, for the sentence to make sense, the subject A must be someone who is capable of owing and the indirect object B must be someone who is capable of being owed something. Likewise, the direct object, £*x* must be something which is capable of being owed to someone. One is left therefore with a series of legal questions which are to be answered, namely: who can owe something? who can be owed something? what can be owed?

Once the legal questions have been teased out of the sentences and the propositions in the texts, the task of the legal analyst is to answer those questions. The source from which the answers are to be obtained was evident to the mediaeval Glossators and Commentators; the source was the written reason of the Roman legal compilations. That this was the appropriate source of law was not in doubt. Therefore, the texts were examined to discover who, according to the written reason of Roman law could own or owe? Who could be owed something? What were the things which could be owned or owed?

This leads almost inexorably to a method of expounding a body of law. In order that legal rules such as that conferring the ownership of a newly arisen island upon the first taker can be properly understood, it is necessary that the meaning of owning be understood first. Thus, the civilian jurists developed a form of exposition by which they dealt with the questions of who could own, what could be owned and so on in an ordered sequence. In this, they were in part following the jurists of ancient Rome, who had set forth the law they were studying under three broad headings: the law of persons, the law of things and the law of actions. The law of persons was concerned with who could be the subject of rights - who could owe, own and be owed. The law of things was concerned with what could be owed and owned, while the law of actions was concerned with how persons who owned or were owed things could enforce their rights against others.

Modern civil law systems utilize this classification, but have developed it. Firstly, the question of how rights are enforced has been placed into a separate legal code, the code of civil procedure, and is thus nowadays treated separately from the substantive rights that are enforced. Most civil law systems today deal with the law of persons in the first book of their civil codes. However, the law of persons has changed somewhat in its meaning since it was first used by the Roman jurists.

2 The Law of Persons

Under the law of ancient Rome, the oldest living male ancestor in a particular family controlled all those of his descendants who were descended from him in the male line. Thus, all of his sons and daughters were in his power or *potestas*, as were his sons' sons and daughters. His daughters' sons and daughters however would be in the power of the oldest living male ascendant in their fathers' respective families. The oldest living male ascendant who was in control of his descendants was called the *paterfamilias*, and he was the head of the household which was in his power. Only he could own property, and only he could owe and be owed obligations. Accordingly, the law of persons was primarily about who was a *paterfamilias* and how that status was acquired. Thereafter, the position of children and grandchildren was described according to their relation with the only person who could be the subject of private law rights, namely their *paterfamilias*. Likewise, the position of slaves was discussed according to the methods by which they could become free and thus the subjects of legal rights. Depending on the type of marriage into which they entered, wives were either in the power of their husbands, in which case their husbands were their *paterfamilias*, or in the power of their oldest living male ascendant. If they had no living male ancestors, women were independent, *sui iuris*. Indeed, whether one was in one's own power, *sui iuris* or in the power of another, *alieni iuris* was one of the primary categorizations of the

Roman law of persons. Only males who were *patres familias* and females who were independent were *sui iuris*. Everyone else was *alieni iuris*.

From this it followed that if a child was left without a living male ascendant, that child was immediately *sui iuris* albeit that he or she was not yet old enough to manage his or her own affairs. Thus, the law of persons dealt with what was to happen in such circumstances, that is who should be the child's guardian or tutor and what guardianship, or *tutela*, entailed. Similarly, the law of persons dealt with what would occur if a *paterfamilias* who was in charge of the family property became unable to manage it effectively as a result of becoming insane or prodigal. *Cura* was the form of care into which such a person was entrusted, and the appointment and duties of the curator were also dealt with as part of the law of persons.

In as much as the power of the *paterfamilias* over his children and grandchildren depended upon their being born of a marriage recognized as lawful by Roman law, the question of what constituted a lawful marriage was also a matter for the law of persons, as what were the circumstances in which such a marriage could be terminated. In short, the Roman law of persons contained much that today would be classified under the heading of family law. However, it must be remembered that the unifying factor in this department of the law was the notion that only the *paterfamilias* could be the subject of private law rights, and the law of persons was therefore an analysis of this position. In modern civil law systems, it is no longer the case that this type of parental authority subsists until all one's living male ancestors are dead. Instead, children become *sui iuris* upon gaining what is termed the age of majority, in most modern systems the age of eighteen. At this age, they become capable of owning and owing on their own behalf; indeed, they are capable of having property rights vested in them in advance of reaching that age, majority being today more a matter of being legally entitled to deal with one's own property on one's own behalf. Likewise, wives no longer pass into the power of their husbands upon marriage, and marriage is increasingly being viewed by legal systems as a partnership rather than as an institution in which the husband is the head of the household containing his wife and their children. Nevertheless, despite the fact that wives and children are today capable of being the subjects of legal rights, the manner in which marriages are contracted, the respective rights and duties of parents and children, the institutions of guardianship - *tutela* and *cura*, are all still treated as part of the law of persons. The topics have remained under the heading which they logically occupied at the time when only the father of the family had any private law rights. To understand, however, why these matters are treated as part of the law of persons at the start of modern civil law codes, one must be aware of the meaning of the original classification and of its appeal to the mediaeval jurists who developed it.

3 The Law of Things

If one returns to the sentence "A owns X", the law of persons informs the jurist as to who is capable of owning, that is who may be A in this sentence. There is also the question of what may be owned, what may be X in the sentence.

Roman law already had a discussion of this issue. It dealt with the question of what things could be owned by private individuals and what could not. Thus, some things were the property of the gods, some the property of the State or of other communities, and some were the property of all people and thus not susceptible to being owned by individuals. Temples, for instance, were dedicated to the gods, roads and public buildings were the property of the State, and the air, the sea and the sea shore were common to all men. None of these things was capable of being owned by a private individual, A, and therefore could not be the direct object of a sentence of the type "A owns X". However, a road or a bridge was capable of being owned by the State, so that it could be the direct object of a sentence "A owns X" if the subject A was the State or a public entity. Thus, one is led to the distinction between public and private law to which the discussion will return.

Among those things which could be the object of private ownership, Roman law recognized various other distinctions. Thus, it distinguished immoveable property - land, buildings, crops, etc., from moveable property - animals, vehicles, furniture and the like. It also distinguished various economically important forms of property from less significant things - the distinction between *res mancipi* and *res nec mancipi*. Both of these distinctions were of importance to another question with regard to property rights, namely how did they arise. This also can be related to the grammatical and logical analysis of the sentence "A owns X", for if the subject A does own the object X, it can be asked what does it mean to say that he "owns" X, how did he come to have this relationship with the object, and how can this relationship be terminated.

Roman law did not have much to say about the nature of ownership. As a system, as has been said, it was practical rather than theoretical. The mediaeval jurists on the other hand were by their initial training in the subjects of the *trivium* primarily academic in their outlook. To understand the meaning of the sentence "A owns X" therefore they needed to know of what ownership as a concept consisted. This led them also into a consideration of the allied concept of possession and its meaning in law. Modern civil law codes continue this theoretical bent, and have sections of their books on property dealing with ownership and possession.

In answering the practical question of how property was acquired, the Romans drew a distinction between methods of acquiring immoveable and moveable property and also between the acquisition of *res mancipi* and *res nec mancipi*. Modern civil law also distinguishes between the methods by which immoveable property is acquired and the less formal methods normally required for the acquisition of moveables, but also places some moveables of especial economic value into a category requiring formalities for their acquisition, transfer or disposition. Italian law for instance treats of motor vehicles, boats and aeroplanes in this manner.

One important way in which the property owned by one person ceases to be owned by him and becomes the property of another is through succession on the death of the first person. This was treated in Roman law as being part of the law of things, which is strictly speaking correct, for, although the deceased's children had inheritance rights, it was only on his death in Roman law that they became capable of owning. Therefore, while their becoming capable of owning on the *paterfamilias'* death is a proper subject for the law of persons, the transfer of property to them by succession is a proper part of the law of things. In modern civil law, with the children now capable of owning during their deceased ancestor's lifetime, succession is perhaps more clearly a method of acquiring ownership, and thus part of the law of things. Thus, in the contemporary civil codes of France and Spain, succession is dealt with as a part of the law of things, relating to how things are acquired. Civil law also however insists upon the rights of the family to succeed to at least a certain portion of the deceased's property, thus suggesting that succession is closely tied to rights and duties which an English lawyer would place under the title of family law. Italian law, following this line, devotes a separate book to the topic, book two of the Civil Code, lodged between the law of persons and the law of things, thus recognizing that the law of persons today encompasses family law rights and duties, and that these issues are germane to an understanding of the law of succession.

France perhaps has stuck most closely to the Roman law categories, insofar as its modern civil code consists of just three books, dealing respectively with persons, things and the modes of acquiring things. Under this last head, it treats of methods of acquiring ownership, including in this the manner in which obligations arise, that is relationships in which one party owes something to another. While it is true that the right to what is due under an obligation is a form of property, a thing, nevertheless there are important distinctions between things which are owned and things which are owed. This is particularly evident when one of the parties to a transaction becomes insolvent, when the rights of an owner are considerably better than those of a creditor with regard to property in the bankrupt's possession. To recognize this distinction, Spain's *Codigo Civil* has created a fourth book, dealing with Obligations to follow the second book on Ownership and the third on Modes of Acquisition. Italy also deals with obligations in a separate fourth book. Its Civil Code now extends to six books in all, marking a further departure from the Roman origins of this method of presentation. The sixth book deals with the methods of protecting property rights under Italian law.

Despite these developments or departures, whichever way one cares to look at them, all of the modern civil law systems continue to demonstrate their basic adherence to the divisions which were first made by the jurists of ancient Rome. However, the modern presentation is much more logical and systematic than that of the Roman jurists themselves. Therein may be seen the particular contribution of the mediaeval lawyers, who, trained first of all in grammar and logic, approached their legal sources with questions and techniques honed in the service of those subjects of the *trivium*. Their contribution deserves to be recognized in the structure of the modern civil codes, and such recognition is important to a proper understanding of that structure. The order and method of presentation is the result of answering questions about who could be the subjects of rights, what their objects and what those rights meant, all of which was the handiwork of the Glossators and Commentators, a theoretical exposition greatly removed from the practical considerations of their Roman antecedents.

4 Civil and Common Law Approaches

The approach of the civil lawyers of the mediaeval period to the analysis and presentation of the legal system which was the object of their study was therefore grounded in their previous training in grammar and logic, two of the basic elements of the *trivium*. This mode of analysis was based however upon the study of texts, in the same manner in which the logical development of systematic theology and philosophy by the scholastics was also based upon the study of texts - in the case of the theologians, the Vulgate translation of the Bible; in the case of the philosophers, the surviving texts of Plato and Aristotle, also translated into Latin. That all of these disciplines turned upon textual study rather than an analysis of human experience as observed in contemporary society is what justifies their descriptions as being academic rather than practical subjects of study. Only with the Commentators of the fourteenth and fifteenth centuries did civil law begin again to have a practical application, and even then the scholars furnished answers to current problems by logical development of the extant texts.

There was however one major exception to this, and that was the work of the canonists. In the middle of the twelfth century as has been said, Gratian produced his Concordance of the Discordant Canons, his Decretum. This text was produced by a study of the decrees of Councils, Synods and of the Popes, including contemporary texts. However, the technique employed by Gratian and his followers was the same technique of textual analysis leading to systematic presentation of the answers to the questions raised by grammatical and logical enquiry that the contemporaneous Glossators were using in their study of the Digest of Roman law. In other words, textual study was also the method of working employed by the canonists. All therefore studied the law of the book. A written text was essential to their jurisprudential method.

Immediately, this points to a distinction between the developing legal literature of Italy and continental Europe and the legal literature of the common law which was developing in England. One of the problems for any hypothetical student of English law would be to identify the source of that law. Unlike the Glossators who took the Digest as their source, their ultimate text, in the same manner as theologians viewed the Bible and the works of the Fathers, and philosophers viewed the works of Plato and Aristotle, for the would-be student of English law, there was no obvious text to study. His first problem therefore would be to bring together the texts which were to form the focus of his study. This can perhaps be seen to have occurred, or rather an attempt was made to do this, early in the twelfth century when an anonymous author produced the work which goes by the name of *Quadripartitus*. *Quadripartitus* as its name suggests is a work in four parts, although only the first and second were actually produced to plan. The first part, *Quadripartitus I*, is a collection of all of the extant law codes of the Anglo-Saxon kings translated into Latin. It is just the sort of collection of laws that would have to be made before an ordered analysis on the Bolognese model could be made. Such collections of canons were already available to the first canonists at Bologna, in the works of such editors of canonical documents as Ivo of Chartres and Burchard of Worms. *Quadripartitus* however is the first such collection of English legal texts. *Quadripartitus II* then gathers together the laws of king Henry I, beginning with his coronation charter, to bring things up to date. Although Parts III and IV were never produced to plan, it is generally believed that the work called the *Leges Henrici* was from the hand of the same author, in which he gathered and to some extent ordered the prevailing customs of the various parts of England.

The next step should perhaps have been for someone to turn upon this corpus of collected laws the implements of textual analysis honed by the scholars of Bologna. However, events in England took a different turn. Although scholars from Bologna came, starting with Vacarius in the 1140s, the next legal text produced in England was of a different style. That work is known as Glanvill, after Henry II's famous justiciar, and was written between 1187 and 1189. Glanvill, unlike *Quadripartitus*, is an analysis of how law works in England, but only the law of the king's courts, and the raw material of its analysis are the writs which brought litigants and litigation before the court of the lord King. Moreover, the questions which this author asks of his raw material are not the academic queries of the Bolognese glossators, but practical questions. What cases are to be heard in the king's courts and what cases in the courts of lords? How does a case in the king's court commence? How are the parties summoned? What happens if one doesn't attend? What excuses are acceptable and with what consequences? What happens when both are present? It is a systematic analysis, but of a practical nature. The first major textbook on English law is concerned with practice not textual analysis and sets the tone for much that was to follow.

The work which is usually held up as being most influenced by Roman legal learning in mediaeval England is that which goes by the name of Bracton and which was written in the second quarter of the thirteenth century. Bracton attempts to present English law in terms of persons, things and actions. However, actions account for three-quarters of his work and his analysis is predominantly practical rather than academic. Moreover, the practical aspect of his work is highlighted by the manner in which he uses cases decided in the royal courts to illustrate his legal propositions, something which the civilian jurists, with their reverence for an ancient text, would never have dreamt of doing. It was to be Glanvill's writs and Bracton's cases that were to be the staple food of English legal study in the coming centuries with texts produced to show what was happening in the law courts so as to guide potential litigants and their advisers along the paths which led to obtaining legal remedies. The literature of the common law was to be about getting remedies, when and how they were available, and not about the elegant presentation along logical lines of the answers to expertly framed questions put to authoritative and believed-to-be comprehensive juridical texts. While the students of the civil and canon law studied and perfected legal systems, which were thought to be and which were shaped to be, complete and internally consistent, the students of the common law studied the doings of the law courts as reported in the Year Books to find out what was actually happening with little interest in developing systematic elegance or consistency within the subject of their study.

Only in the seventeenth and eighteenth centuries, in the Institutes of Sir Edward Coke and the Commentaries of Sir William Blackstone, does an emphasis upon orderly exposition again emerge. However, that is all there is - orderly exposition. Coke and Blackstone may borrow the end result of civilian learning to shape their treatises in the presentational headings they employ to expound their subject, but they do not utilize the methodology which produced those headings in the first place. It is therefore the form which civilians produced which shapes their studies not the method which produced the form. By this time, the gulf between civilian and common law legal reasoning has been opened. The civilian form is the product of how civilians treated the substance of their study. The form as well as the substance is the result of their methodology, based on grammar and logic. The method of the common law, on the other hand, was shaped systematically by the needs of practice not analysis, by practical study in the Inns of Chancery and the Inns of Court, not by academic study in the Universities. Until the late sixteenth century, students of the common law would not have studied the liberal arts first in the universities as would their counterparts in the law faculties of the European universities, and English law was not a subject of university study until the eighteenth century.

The mind of the common lawyers was shaped therefore in the arena of action and in the study of it. The mind of the mediaeval and modern civil lawyers on the other hand was from the first formed in the law faculties of the universities. The latter begin with a general theory which is the outcome of academic study; the former have no authoritative general theory. Those raised in one tradition therefore have problems in gaining an understanding of the other. To understand modern Italian law, the student already versed in English law must grasp this essential difference between the structures of the two systems, and understand that the different structure is itself the result of the very different environment in which each was shaped and of the different methodologies employed by those who first aimed at the orderly exposition of their respective legal orders.

5 The Divisions of Civil Law

The basic division of Roman law was into public and private law, and this dichotomy remains fundamental to modern civilian systems. Returning to the simple legal sentence:

A owes X to B,

if both A and B are private individuals and not State bodies, then the legal relationship described in the sentence is governed by private law, but if either A or B is a public body - the State, or any organ of State or local government, then the relationship is governed by public law.

Public law can be subdivided into two main types: public international and public domestic. Public international law applies to legal relationships in which both parties are nation States, while public domestic law pertains to legal relationships between a State and a private individual. Within the sphere of public domestic law, different headings of law can be identified. Constitutional law sets out the basic duties of the State to its subjects and *vice versa*, as well as defining the mode in which the citizens participate in the law-making activity of the State on their behalf. Administrative law regulates the manner in which the State and other organs of public administration prosecute the policies by which they seek to fulfil their duties. Criminal law defines the circumstances in which the State will be entitled to interfere with and curtail the rights of subjects which it should normally uphold, crimes being in effect the circumstances in which and for which the State is so entitled to interfere, and the extent of that interference constituting the lawful punishments the penal law justifies. Procedural law sets out the manner in which the judicial powers of the State are organized to provide civil, criminal and administrative justice, together with the procedures by which the tribunals so set up are to fulfil their tasks. Revenue law defines the State's powers to require contribution from its subjects so that it can finance the achievement of lawfully agreed policies. Ecclesiastical law pertains to those legal relationships which have the State as one of their subjects and the Church for the other.

Private law on the other hand is only capable of subdivision under two headings - civil and commercial law. Commercial law relates to those legal relationships in which both parties are entrepreneurs. If either party is not an entrepreneur, the transaction is governed by civil law. Basically, this subdivision recognizes that men of commerce, merchants, have traditionally governed transactions between themselves according to different rules from those which obtain between non-merchants. This was the meaning, for instance, of the rules called the Law Merchant in the mediaeval period. In some civil law countries, such as France and Spain, these rules are still set out in a separate Commercial Code, allowing commercial transactions to be treated differently from those which involve ordinary members of the population, thereby recognizing that they are motivated by different considerations. The businessman buys and sells for profit, while his ordinary customer seeks the provision of goods and services.

These divisions are familiar to those acquainted with modern civil law systems. Their application to Italy will be examined more particularly in the chapter which follows. It is important to realise that both the divisions themselves and the mode of reasoning which underlies and underpins them, link Italian law to its civilian heritage and its sister systems of jurisprudence.

3 The Sources of Modern Italian Law

1 The Italian Constitution and its History

When Napoleon was defeated in 1814, the Italian States that had been subjugated by him were returned to their own governments. Not surprisingly, they did not have any great enthusiasm for remaining under the governance of the French system of laws which had been imposed upon them as part and parcel of the Napoleonic occupation. Accordingly, they reverted to the laws which they had utilized before they were overcome by the force of French arms. However, it was not possible for them to pretend, even to themselves, that their native systems of law were equal to that which they had come to know while under French rule. There began therefore to be a movement for codification of the laws of the Italian States along the French model, although there was a growing feeling that the contents of those codes should mirror the historical traditions of Italy itself. The movement for Italian unity, the *Risorgimento*, only served to strengthen this nationalist dimension. It should also be remembered that the French codes themselves owed a tremendous debt to the Italian legal tradition.

The pattern of achieving unity within the peninsula virtually dictated the system of laws which would at first serve the new nation State. Italian unity was achieved by the annexing of one Italian State after another to the northern kingdom of Piedmont, more generally known as the kingdom of Sardinia. This kingdom, the prime minister of which was the wily but very successful count, Camille de Cavour, had been granted a written constitution in 1848 by its king, Carlo Alberto. The constitution had been granted following a popular insurrection and took its name from the monarch who granted it, being known as the *statuto Albertino*. Eventually, as the process of annexation was completed, the *statuto Albertino* became the first constitution of the united nation of Italy, remaining the basic law of the new kingdom until it and the Italian monarchy were rejected in the aftermath of the Second World War.

The *statuto Albertino* is generally regarded as a weak constitution. This value judgement reflects in fact the reasons for its rejection and replacement in 1948. It was and is regarded as weak because it was not a basic law in the sense that all other laws were inferior to it. Instead, it was of equal status with other enacted laws and could be amended or abrogated in the same manner. Its weakness, in other words, was one which it shares with, for instance, the current constitution of the United Kingdom, the substance of which can also be altered by ordinary legislation passed without any special majority in the two Houses of Parliament. Moreover, the United Kingdom constitution is not even reduced to writing as was the *statuto Albertino*. It is not easy therefore for British students of Italian constitutional history to accept these causes of weakness at face value, as do modern Italians.

The weakness of the *statuto Albertino* is also, however, attributed to the fact that it gave very large powers to the monarch. For instance, the monarch was able to select the prime minister under its terms. Here again, a British reader may gib at accepting this as a source of weakness for, under the constitutional arrangements of the United Kingdom, it is the monarch who chooses the prime minister. In the United Kingdom, however, there is a constitutional convention that the monarch chooses as prime minister the leader of that party in the House of Commons which has the largest number of seats. Such a convention did not exist in pre-war Italy, with the result that when in 1922 the fascists marched upon Rome, the King, instead of declaring a state of emergency as his ministers advised, chose to appoint the leader of the fascists, Benito Mussolini, as his prime minister. The disaster which ensued, culminating in Italy's alliance with Germany in the Second World War and defeat at the hands of the allies, sealed the fate of the Italian monarchy as well as that of the *statuto Albertino*. The prerogative powers of the king under that constitution had been too great, and when those powers were swept away, the constitution which gave them and the monarchy which enjoyed them were consigned to history as well. It is worth remembering also that the choice exercized by the king in 1922 was against the advice of his ministers, in contrast to the United Kingdom where again there is a convention that the monarch must accept the advice of her ministers.

Following the defeat of Mussolini's fascist government by the allies in 1943, Italy was a divided nation. The king, in Rome, appointed the army general, Badoglio, to be prime minister and to rule nominally that part of Italy which was under allied control. Mussolini meanwhile had escaped to the north, which part of Italy was now in effect occupied by Germany. There, *il Duce* established what is known as the Republic of Salò. Against this regime and the occupying German forces, the Italian partisans fought until Italy was finally liberated in 1944. The partisans were of various political persuasions, the majority being either communists or supporters of what was to become Christian democracy. With the defeat of fascism, a National Liberation Committee was set up, which was succeeded in 1946 by a Constitutional Assembly, which body paved the way for a return to democratic government. This body oversaw the drafting of the new Italian constitution, which came into force and effect on January 1st, 1948. Before that date, however, a referendum had been held on the question of whether Italy should remain a monarchy or become a republic. Virtually on the eve of the referendum, King Vittorio Emanuele, the king who had in 1922 appointed Mussolini as prime minister, abdicated in favour of his son, Umberto, and it was the unfortunate new king who was rejected at the polls and formally expelled from the Italian territory in conformity with the new political order.

The constitution of 1948, the first republican constitution which Italy has enjoyed, is still in force. Although at the time of writing, its future with that of the first republic is in some doubt following the scandals which have riven political life in Italy over the last years, there is no sign at present of a new constitutional order being in the offing.

2 The Italian Law Codes

In the same manner as the constitution of Piedmont extended to the whole of Italy through the process of annexation that led to unification, so also did the law codes of the Piedmontese kingdom furnish the basis of the legal order of the new kingdom in 1861. Tuscany alone at that time insisted upon keeping its own Criminal Code in force, believing it to be superior to the Piedmontese version. When Venice was annexed in 1866, it kept its own Austrian-inspired Commercial Code.

The first codes expressly promulgated for the new unified kingdom were issued in 1865. These were the Civil Code, the Code of Civil Procedure, the Commercial Code, the Navigation Code and the Code of Criminal Procedure. All were heavily reliant upon the French models which had formed the basis for most of the Italian codes that had been brought into force since the end of the French occupation. A new Commercial Code, also on the French model but incorporating the substance of much nineteenth-century development, was brought into force in 1882 for all of Italy including Venice, and in 1889 a Penal Code was introduced for the whole of the kingdom, replacing the previous arrangement which had accorded Tuscany the special privilege of its own criminal law. The 1889 Penal Code was particularly liberal in inspiration, abolishing the death penalty for all offences other than treason. Here may be detected a true expression of the historical identity of Italian jurisprudence, in that Italians, such as Beccaria, had contributed much to liberal thinking with regard to penal policy.[1] It was the felt need to preserve this element in their Criminal Code which had prevented the Tuscans abandoning their own code in favour of that of the unified State in 1865.

A liberal influence can also be detected with regard to the Code of Criminal Procedure that was introduced in 1913, replacing that of 1865. This code began a pendulum reaction with regard to criminal procedure in Italy, the last swing of which is a recent event. The 1913 Code was thought by many to be too liberal, favouring the rights of the accused above the interest of the State in the repression and punishment of crime. Not surprisingly, with the advent of fascist government in 1922, the 1913 Code was subjected to criticism and carefully scrutiny. It and the 1889 Penal Code were both replaced in 1931, and the new Code of Criminal Procedure, known as the Rocco Code, was manifestly more authoritarian in its attributes. This code magnified the importance of the State in the criminal process, emphasizing the discovery of the truth in relation to criminal accusations at the expense, so some felt, of the rights of the accused in the course of inquiries and indeed trial. The 1931 Penal Code too was noticeably less liberal than its 1889 predecessor.

The fascists also replaced the Civil Code and the Code of Civil Procedure, both in 1942. There is little however of fascist ideology to be discovered in either of these items of legislation, underlining the view that political change, even when extreme, has but little impact upon the development of private law in civil law countries.[2] The most important change wrought in this area was perhaps the abandonment in Italy of a separate Commercial Code at this time. French jurisprudence dictated that the contracts of entrepreneurs should be dealt with separately in law from those of other citizens. The 1942 Civil Code rejected this notion, bringing entrepreneurial dealings under the same rules as those of other contracting parties. Many of the changes in the codes reflect the influence of German jurisprudence upon Italian jurists since the time of unification. However, the Civil Code does not have the introductory General Part which is such an important feature of the BGB, such learning being supplied by juristic doctrine, the source of law called *la dottrina*, rather than by the code itself.

The Penal Code of 1931 together with the Civil Code and the Civil Procedure Code of 1942 remain in force, as amended, to the present day. The 1931 Criminal Procedure Code, however, has been superseded. This occurred in October 1989 as the culmination of the criticisms of the fascist code which were mentioned earlier. The new code has attempted to redress the balance of interest as between the accused person and the State. Most notably, the defence is now allowed to insist upon certain witnesses being called to give evidence, and has also acquired the right to cross-examine other witnesses called to give evidence. This introduction of Anglo-American, common law elements has not been without controversy, particularly as there was much initial confusion resulting from those who were arrested before the introduction of the new code being tried under the old system with the new code operating alongside for those arrested after its introduction. Some feel that the mix of adversarial and inquisitorial methods which the new code involves undermines the integrity of the Italian tradition in criminal procedure. Many advocates felt that their training and experience in the inquisitorial system had not prepared them for their new role under the 1989 code. It is probably as yet too early to assess the success or otherwise of this most recent change in Italian criminal procedure.

3 Other Sources of Legislation

The Constitution is the basic law of the Italian State, occupying the chief place in the hierarchy of legal sources. After it comes ordinary legislation, the codes being the main sources of this, as one would expect in a civil law system.

However, particularly in the years since the Second World War, there has been an increasing amount of ordinary legislation which has not taken the form of amendments to the codes. Instead, the Italian parliament has chosen to enact many items of legislation which are free-standing in the sense of being apart from the legislation contained in the five main law codes. Such items of legislation are similar in effect to the statutes which embody the legislative source of law in the United Kingdom. One of the most important instances of such free-standing legislation in Italy is the divorce legislation which was enacted and came into force during the 1970s. The amount of free-standing legislation has led some to speak of Italy being in the age of decodification, a process of the break up of law as being predominantly contained in codes. It is interesting to compare the condition of Italian law in this regard with that of England and Wales, a system which is meant to be based on common law or case law to the exclusion of codes. While Italy is experiencing a growth in legislation outside of its codes, the amount of statutory material forming the basis of broad areas of English law has increased enormously in the last century and a half. In effect, it is statute which forms the true basis of much of English law today and not the decisions in actual cases. Much case law is now confined to statutory interpretation and the filling of gaps. Furthermore, many of the statutes are in reality mini-codes. Criminal law is contained in many such enactments, for instance the Offences against the Person Act, the Theft Act, the Sexual Offences Act, and so on. This is even more the case in land law, where the 1925 property legislation amounts in sum to a code of real property law, while enactments such as the Sale of Goods Act and the like have fulfilled the same function in the field of obligations. This piecemeal codification of English law, which has significantly been taking place during the centuries which produced the law codes of continental Europe, has brought the English legal system to a position not unlike that of contemporary Italy as a result of its so-called decodification. This corrective perspective needs to be borne in mind when superficial comparisons are made of the differing sources of law in common law and civil law Europe.

The constitution, the codes and other national legislation are all enacted by the Italian parliament. It too is the final authority behind the *decreti-leggi*, or legislative decrees, issued by the executive. At first blush, these would appear to offend against the doctrine of the separation of powers. However, although issued by ministers, such decrees are only valid if ratified by the Italian parliament within sixty days. Failure to do so renders them void *ab initio*. Thus, the doctrine of the separation of powers is both preserved and observed.

The next tier in the hierarchy of legislative norms consists of the constitutions of the twenty regions that make up the territory of modern Italy. Five of these regions are designated special regions, while the remaining fifteen are ordinary. The constitutions of the fifteen ordinary regions are passed by means of ordinary national legislation, while the constitutions of the five special regions are enacted by constitutional legislation and brought into force and effect by delegated legislation. Beneath these, comes the legislation of the twenty regional parliaments themselves, which legislation, made under the provisions of article 117 of the Constitution, is only binding in the region for which it is made, while below this comes the provincial legislation of the two provinces of Trento and Bolzano, the two provinces which comprise the region of Trentino -

Alto Adige. These provinces enjoy special legislative powers because of the peculiar linguistic and social conditions that prevail there, German being the dominant culture and language of Bolzano. Again, the legislation made by these provinces is only binding within their respective borders.

Mention needs also to be made of legislation made by the regional parliaments under express powers granted to them by the national parliament, and also of powers to legislate given by specific enactments to various executive bodies. These forms of legislation occupy the bottom rungs of the legislative ladder.

4 Other Sources of Law

Inferior to legislation, and incapable of modifying or abrogating it, are administrative acts. These acts are normative measures taken by the executive to regulate certain activities. They may be made by the national administration or by the organs of local government at regional, provincial or even communal level. Minor public entities also have a similar norm-making capacity. Occasionally, such administrative acts by the executive take the form of ordinances, which are of temporary validity geared to a particular emergency or necessity. These can, within those closely defined limits, modify the operation of higher legislative norms.

Custom is to a limited extent also recognized as a living source of law in the Italian republic. Custom can be the source of law in areas where legislation has not provided any rules. These are most commonly encountered in the fields of international, constitutional and administrative law. It may also, however, be a source of interpretative rules in areas for which the legislature has provided. In this second manner, custom can be a method of interpreting legislative and other rules so as to fill gaps left by the enacted law, *praeter legem*, or it can be a method of making sense or greater sense of written rules where those rules specifically require that they be interpreted according to prevailing usage, *secundum legem*. Custom can never, however, abrogate an enacted law, that is be *contra legem*, as this would be offensive to the hierarchy of norms which places legislation above usage. It is also worth noting that as there can be no crime without an enacted law, *nullum crimen sine lege*, custom can only operate *secundum legem* in relation to the criminal law.

To the common lawyer, nothing perhaps is more striking in a civil law system than the lack of space accorded to case law in the hierarchy of legal sources. A strict modern civilian would hold that the doctrine of the separation of powers demands that the legislature alone make law and that the judiciary do no more than apply it. Judicial law-making to such a jurist is anathema.

It is worth pausing to reflect upon this in the context of Italian legal history. The modern civilian who holds this strict view is, in effect, saying that the law is what is contained in the written sources of legislation, crudely the book. His attitude is not far removed from that of the Glossators of the eleventh, twelfth and thirteenth centuries who held that the Corpus Iuris Civilis contained all the legal knowledge that man required. However, the Glossators had to concede that to discover the full reason of the Corpus Iuris the text stood in need of explanation to reveal certain solutions which were not apparent on its face. Thus was produced the *Glossa ordinaria*, and thus today do jurists seek to overcome apparent contradictions within the codes of civilian systems by harmonizing those apparent conflicts. Such juristic opinion in Italian law is termed *la dottrina* and is carried out by academics, as were the Glossators. The criterion which is employed, to ensure that each law fits among the other laws of the system, is also employed by the courts in interpreting legislative enactments, and is called the systematic criterion. The contribution of the courts to this process of interpretation through application is called *la giurisprudenza*.

To less strictly minded jurists, the activity of the courts does not stop at interpretation. Rather the courts are participating in the activity of law-making itself. When the judges recognize that the legislation does not provide a solution to the instant case, then the judges make law based on the principles or policies contained in the legislative sources so as to provide the necessary solution. The goal is still set by the legislature, but the rule itself, the means by which the goal is achieved, is made by the courts in the arena of action. Such creative interpretation is described as being according to the teleological criterion. This second approach, which still accords the legislature the goal-setting, principle- and policy-making role, but is prepared to allow the courts the freedom to look behind the legislative enactments for material with which to fashion a suitable rule, is not unlike the activities of the Commentators of the fourteenth and fifteenth centuries, who used the *Glossa ordinaria* as a quarry to supply the raw material from which to fashion legal norms fit for their own societies' needs.

It is important to an understanding of the Italian legal system to realise that this divergence of opinion, between the strict separation-of-powers supporters and the more liberal followers of a creative role for the judiciary, reflects a tension that has existed in the Italian legal tradition since the revival of civil law studies in the Middle Ages. To ignore this feature would be to endeavour to know the facts about case law in Italy without attempting to understand them. As well as the systematic and teleological criteria, the courts also employ what is termed the historical criterion to aid them in interpreting legislation. This criterion allows them to look at the parliamentary debates and reports which led up to the legislation in question so as to ascertain the problems with which it was meant to deal and thus elucidate how the rules are to be applied. This formed no part of the mediaeval Italian legal tradition, but it is not fanciful to recognize here the influence of the Humanist school of jurisprudence which flourished in France in the sixteenth century. The Humanists believed that the rules of classical Roman law could only be understood if they were interpreted so as to accord with what was known of the social circumstances in which they were to be applied and for which they were designed to serve. This is the belief which underlies the historical criterion. Until 1992, English law set its face entirely against the use of such historical materials in the interpretation of statutes, but even in England and Wales the use of Parliamentary debates is now allowed the courts in their task of legislative interpretation.[3]

The application of the historical, systematic and teleological criteria constitutes what Italian law terms the logical interpretation of legislation. Alongside the literal interpretation technique, which interprets according to the meaning of the words used, this constitutes the manner in which the judiciary seeks to apply the laws made by the legislative organs of the State in difficult cases. Although case law is not binding upon other courts according to a strict system of precedent as in England and Wales, there is no denying that the decisions in individual cases, particularly those of the higher courts, are of considerable persuasive authority. The principles 'identified' by the courts in such cases are collected and published as *massimari*, which are of great importance in unifying the interpretation of laws by the courts throughout the republic.

Finally, mention must be made of *equità* as a subsidiary source of Italian law. It is not a complementary system of rules as in common law countries, but rather a sense that justice and fairness must sometimes dictate the actual decision in a particular case. Specific enacted laws sometimes contemplate the intervention of equity; otherwise it means the application of the law with strict equality.

5 The Divisions of Modern Italian Law

One of the important distinctions which civil law systems generally have drawn fron Justinian's Corpus Iuris Civilis is that between public law and private law. Italian law conforms to the civilian norm in this, and the dichotomy is important to an understanding of the Italian legal system. Basically, private law is concerned with those rules which regulate the activities of individuals or groups of individuals one with another. Public law, on the other hand, has for its subject matter those legal relationships in which one of the parties at least is the State or some organ of the State or government. It is a hallmark of most civil law systems that a special body of law deals with legal relationships where the State is involved. It was this feature of French law which drew the fire of the British jurist, Albert Venn Dicey, when he attacked France's *droit administratif* so vehemently in his *Introduction to the Study of the Law of the Constitution.*[4]

In Italy, public law is divided into two broad areas: international and domestic. Public international law concerns those rules which govern the State's relations with other States, largely through treaty relations and through the working of organizations such as the United Nations. Also in the domain of international public law is that body of law which governs the relationship of those States which comprise the European Union. Neither of those areas falls for analysis in this work as they are not governed by laws made by the nation of Italy itself.

Public domestic law on the other hand does fall for consideration here. This is the body of law which concerns relations with the State and its organs within the Italian territory. Public domestic law is usually subdivided into the following areas: constitutional law; administrative law; criminal law; procedural law; ecclesiastical law; finance law, and various laws concerned with navigation, agriculture and the economy.

Constitutional law

Constitutional law is that part of the law which concerns the workings of the main organs of the State. It concerns the composition, function and working of Parliament and the Executive. It also deals with the fundamental rights which citizens enjoy, including political, ethical-social, civic and economic rights. The protection of these rights is guaranteed by the Constitution, and the mechanism by which this protection is afforded is through the Constitutional Court.

It is worth noting at this point that for every theoretical division of public domestic law that is made, there exists a discrete body of rules to regulate the area and usually a separate court or structure of courts to enforce those rules. Thus, constitutional law implies a constitution and a constitutional court.

Administrative law

Likewise, the existence of the division *administrative law* betokens the existence of a separate body of rules, *diritto amministrativo*, and administrative courts in which to enforce them. Somewhat contrary to what one would expect in a civil law system, Italy had no separate system of administrative courts prior to 1971. In that year, a body of administrative law was introduced on the French model, and special courts, the *Tribunali Amministrativi Regionali* or TARs as they are widely known, were created to operate the system.

Criminal law

Criminal law is that which is contained in the 1931 Penal Code. It is administered by a set of courts, some of which are devoted entirely to the administration of criminal justice, while others also have a civil jurisdiction. Criminal law thus satisfies the criterion outlined above by which a department of law indicates a set of rules and a set of courts dedicated to it.

Procedural law

Procedural law is that body of law which regulates the workings of the administration of justice. One can therefore speak of a law of administrative procedure, a law of criminal procedure and a law of civil procedure. The last two categories are the subject of special codes, namely the 1989 Code of Criminal Procedure and the 1942 Code of Civil Procedure. There are no special courts dealing with these codes as they are concerned with the workings of the courts which administer the Penal Code and the Civil Code respectively.

Ecclesiastical law

Ecclesiastical law is that part of the law of the Italian republic which regulates the relationship between the Italian State and the Roman Catholic Church. At the time of the unification of Italy in 1861, the Church was strongly opposed to the creation of a nation State in the Italian peninsula. This was mainly due to the fact that a large part of central Italy was governed directly by the Church, the so-called Papal States. When the Church lost temporal control of this patrimony, it for a long while refused to recognize the Italian government which it believed had usurped its powers in those areas. It was not until 1929 that Mussolini succeeded in negotiating with the Church a series of agreements, the Lateran Pacts, by which the Church recognized the Italian State and the Italian State in turn recognized the sovereignty of the Church within what became the Vatican City State, an independent State within the Italian territory. At that time also, the Church won major concessions with regard to both its spiritual and temporal rights in Italian life, becoming in effect the official religion of the Italian State.

The fall of the Italian monarchy after the Second World War and the introduction of a republican constitution saw the recognition of the concept of freedom of conscience in religious matters together with the equality of various religious beliefs before the law. In effect, this should have terminated the special position of the Roman Catholic Church in Italian life. However, the Lateran Pacts were not in fact renegotiated until 1984, and even after that date the Church continues to have special privileges under the law particularly with regard to marriages.

Insofar as the Vatican is an independent State in international law, that portion of Italian ecclesiastical law which deals with the relationship between Italy and the Vatican can properly be regarded as part of public international rather than public domestic law. However, the geographical situation of the Vatican within Italy militates against such a pedantic, theoretical approach. The rejection of such a technical attitude was apparent in the prosecution by the Italian State of Mehmet Ali Agca for the attempted murder of Pope John Paul II in 1979, even though the shooting took place within the Vatican City State and the victim was not an Italian citizen.

The Lateran Pacts constitute therefore the distinct body of rules which in Italy make ecclesiastical law. There are no distinct courts however dealing with this subject. Most questions concerning the Pacts have come before the Constitutional Court or sometimes the Supreme Court of

Cassation. Ecclesiastical law must not be confused with Canon law, which is the law that the Church itself makes to regulate its own internal affairs. The Canon law of the Roman Catholic Church is contained in its Code of Canon Law published in 1983, and that law is administered in the Church's own courts. Those courts are not answerable to the State, although certain decisions of those courts, particularly regarding matrimonial matters, were until the 1984 Pacts automatically recognized by the Italian State courts. Since the 1984 Pacts, however, judgements of the Church courts have to be formally recognized by the State courts in the same manner as the judgements of any other foreign legal system.

Finance law

Special sets of laws deal with financial matters involving the State. Thus, the laws relating to taxation are administered by the Taxation Commissions, while the Court of Accounts has a general supervisory role over State financial matters with a judicial jurisdiction in relation to disputes regarding the State's property and finances, pensions generally and the employment problems of its own staff.

Navigation law, Agrarian law and the Public Economy

Special sets of laws also regulate these areas, the most obvious being the Navigation Code itself. The administration of these laws is again entrusted to special courts, for instance the Tribunals for Public Waters in relation to navigation matters.

Private law on the other hand is concerned with legal relationships between individuals or groups of individuals. The State is not party to a private-law, legal relationship. Traditionally, in civil law countries, private law is divided into civil law and commercial law. However, in Italy since 1942, such a distinction is misleading. Following on the criterion mentioned earlier, there is no distinct body of commercial rules in Italy administered by a distinct set of tribunals. Since 1942, there has been only the Civil Code, which now encompasses the law relating to commercial matters. The civil courts administer the whole of the code, including once more its commercial aspects. Accordingly, if one seeks the divisions of private law in Italy, it is submitted that these can only be found today in the divisions of the Civil Code itself, Italian private law being synonymous today with its civil law. This is particularly true in that even the Supreme Court of Cassation, *Cassazione*, is no longer divided into specialist sections.

The Civil Code is divided into six books. These are concerned respectively with the law of persons, the law of succession, the law of property, the law of obligations, labour law and the protection of rights. The law of persons embraces what an English lawyer would describe primarily as family law. It contains for instance the laws concerned with marriage, filiation, parental authority and the like. In a sense, the law of succession follows naturally from this, in that it is concerned with the question of who succeeds to the control of a person's estate, or patrimony as it is termed in civil law, when that person dies. The law of property is concerned to regulate the ownership of things, how that ownership comes into being, how it is tranferred and the types of rights over things that are recognized by law.

The law of obligations covers what a common lawyer would understand by the subjects of contract and tort, together with quasi-contract or restitution. To a common lawyer, these are discrete topics with some interconnecting features, while to the civilian the law of obligations is definitely a unity of which the elements of contract, tort, etc., are subsidiary parts. The fifth book of the Civil Code is concerned with employment law, including the various forms of enterprise that are possible in contemporary Italy. Some aspects of this topic blur the line between public and private law, particularly as the State steps in to regulate terms of employment and protect against unfair treatment of workers. Finally, the sixth book of the Civil Code deals with the protection of rights, by means for instance of registration and the taking of security.

A substantial part of this book will be concerned with the law contained in the Civil Code. It has been worthwhile therefore to delineate its contents at this early stage. However, it should be remembered that the Civil Code is itself a unity and that the civil courts are responsible for the administration of all parts of it. It constitutes in itself the whole of Italian private law. Having emphasized that fact, attention must now be returned to public domestic law, to the structure and functions of the modern Italian State and to the form and substance of its constitution.

Notes

---

[1] Caesar Bonesana, Marquis de Beccaria (1735-94), published his essay on crimes and punishments, entitled *Dei delitti e delle pene* in 1764. It proved a tremendously influential work in the movement to abolish torture and the death penalty as parts of the criminal process.

[2] See Alan Watson, *Failures of the Legal Imagination* (Edinburgh, 1988), for a careful discussion of this idea.

[3] See *Pepper* v *Hart*, [1993] 1 All E.R. 42.

[4] See A.V. Dicey, *An Introduction to the Study of the Law of the Constitution* (London, 1885) chapter XII.

4 The Modern Italian State

1 Territorial Divisions

According to article I of the Constitution of the Italian republic, the modern State is a democratic republic in which sovereignty pertains to the people. As will be seen, the idea that sovereignty is the property of the people is one which is followed through into the political and legislative processes with considerable thoroughness in modern Italy.

The national territory is today divided into twenty regions, which regions are then subdivided into provinces and the provinces into communes. In fact, the division of the State into provinces is an older division than that into regions, the regionalization being the creation of the modern republic. There are two kinds of region in modern Italy: the special and the ordinary. The five special regions are Valle D'Aosta, Trentino-Alto Adige, Friuli-Venezia Giulia, Sardegna and Sicily. The geographical separation of the last two is reflected in their having special region status given their distinct cultures and needs, while the first three special regions are accorded this status for historical and linguistic reasons, although geographically they are also border areas. Valle D'Aosta occupies a tract of land in the North West of Italy which historically has had close ties with France and in which many of the inhabitants still speak French as their first language. The population of the region is small and for some purposes it is grouped with the larger, neighbouring region of Piedmont; for instance it is the only region which does not constitute an appeal court district in its own right, sending cases on appeal to the Piedmontese *corte d'appello* at Turin. Trentino-Alto Adige on the other hand has much stronger regional affinities with Austria. The language of the province of Bolzano is overwhelmingly German rather than Italian, and many natives do not accept that the area should remain part of Italy. There have been terrorist outrages in the region in recent years, committed by extremist elements in the separatist camp, and the distinct German culture of these parts is reflected in the special status given not only to the region but also in the legislative powers given to the provinces of Trento and Bolzano. Students from Bolzano prefer to study at Austrian universities rather than at Italian ones, and Italian Law is therefore taught at the Law Faculty of the University of Innsbruck in Austria's South Tyrol. The last of these special regions lies in the North east, being Friuli-Venezia Giulia. Again, this part of Italy borders on Slovenia, a part of what was the old Yugoslavia. After the Second World War, Italy was involved in a long-running dispute about sovereignty over this part of the national territory, in particular with regard to the city of Trieste. The dispute was not resolved until the early 1960s, and even now it is tempting providence to speak of the dispute as having been finally settled. The recent resurgence of nationalist concerns in the territories of the former Yugoslavia raises the spectre in many Italian minds that there might yet be a renewed claim by Slovenia to sovereignty over this part of Italy.

The remaining fifteen ordinary regions do not have the same marked degree of local autonomy and identity as that to which the special regions might lay claim. They are a product rather of the post-war bias toward decentralization in government, born of the distrust of centralized government bred by fascism. Although the ordinary regions are therefore a modern creation, they nevertheless reflect in some cases a continuation of the old loyalties which existed in Italy up to and beyond unification. Some of the modern regions are in effect old territorial divisions making a fresh appearance in a new and less powerful garb. Thus, for instance, Liguria has strong affinities with the old Republic of Genoa, Piedmont corresponds to the old northern Kingdom around which Italian unification developed, and Tuscany is based on the territory of the old Grand Duchy. Moreover, some of the new regions correspond to areas of contemporary economic strength and the social and political pride that goes along with it. Thus there is an ever-present danger that old loyalties and economic sufficiency could combine to undermine the unity of the Italian State in favour of greater or even complete regional autonomy. This fear has been very prevalent in recent years with the rise of separatist parties in northern Italy, particularly the Lega Nord. Likewise, regionalism in the South of Italy, the *Mezzogiorno*, has increased prejudices in other parts that the South is another country and that there is no real unity within the modern Italian State, thus posing a further threat to the unified nation. In full, the fifteen ordinary regions are: Piedmont, Liguria, Lombardia, Emilia-Romagna, Veneto, Tuscany, Umbria, Molise, Marche, Abruzzo, Lazio, Campagna, Basilicata, Puglia and Calabria.

At all levels of governmental activity in Italy, as in most modern civil law countries, considerable emphasis is placed upon the doctrine of the separation of powers. This basically means that the legislative, executive and judicial functions of government should not be confused. In particular, the importance of having a legal system and judiciary which is free of the influence of the executive is stressed, as is the impropriety of judicial law-making, seen as a trespass upon the preserve of the legislators. Although some overlapping of functions is unavoidable, it will be seen that much is done to respect this principle in Italian governmental arrangements and that in many ways it is carried into effect. For legislative and executive purposes, the division of the national territory into regions, provinces and communes holds good, but for judicial functions other territorial divisions prevail. These latter will be dealt with when the civil justice system is examined in chapter seven. In the present chapter, the focus of attention will be legislation and executive government.

2 The State : the Italian Parliament[1]

Remembering that the Constitution provides that sovereignty resides in the Italian people, the questions that have to be asked at each level of government pertain to how the sovereignty of the people finds its mode of expression at that level of the nation. At the level of the State, the main organs of legislative and executive government are the State legislature, the Italian parliament, the President - who is the head of State, and the council of ministers or cabinet, the prime minister being the head of government.

The Italian parliament is a bicameral legislature, that is to say it is composed of two chambers or *camere*. Unlike the British House of Lords and House of Commons, the two chambers of the Italian parliament are of equal status, despite being termed the upper and lower chambers. The upper chamber is the Senate, *senato*, a designation which in Italy recalls the Roman senate of ancient times which advised the magistrates on their legislative projects, while the lower chamber is called the Chamber of Deputies, following the French model.

The lower chamber consists of 630 members all of whom are elected, while the senate contains 315 elected members, but also has seats for life senators. All past presidents of the republic are life senators and there are also seats for up to five further life senators who are appointed by the president in office. The qualifications for being a member of the respective chambers also varies a little. While one has to be an Italian citizen and of unblemished public record to stand for either chamber, deputies must be at least 25 years old while senators have to be 40. Likewise, while virtually all citizens over the age of 18 have the right to vote in elections for the Chamber of Deputies, only those over 25 are eligible to vote for the Senate.

Not only do such citizens in Italy have the right to vote, they are also under a duty to do so. Those who do not fulfil their obligations to exercise the franchise have a black mark placed against their names in the electoral register, reminiscent of the *nota censoria* placed against the names of citizens who incurred infamy in ancient Rome. The effect of this notation in modern Italy is to render the citizen concerned ineligible to serve in certain public offices, including ineligibilty to stand for election to the legislature.

Until 1993, elections to both the Chamber of Deputies and the Senate were effected by proportional representation, although different systems were employed for the two chambers. For the purposes of elections to the lower chamber, the country was divided into 32 electoral districts, each district being in effect a group of provinces; Valle D'Aosta being the only district which comprised a whole region. Each of these districts was accorded a certain number of seats in the Chamber of Deputies according to its population. The largest district was that comprising the provinces of Rome, Viterbo, Latina and Frosinone, which had 53 seats. Valle D'Aosta was the smallest with only one. Each voter would vote in the election for the party of their choice. The total number of votes cast in the election would then be totalled and the total divided by the number of seats allocated to that district plus 2. The resulting number was the quota of votes that a party must have won in order to gain a seat within that district and each party would be given a seat for each such quota of votes it obtained. Any remaining votes were placed into a national pool which was used to allocate further seats on a national basis, mainly to allow parties which had not won many seats locally but which had polled reasonably nationally to have an enhanced representation.

At one time, the voters were also asked to place the particular candidates of the parties for which they had voted in an order of preference. The candidates with the highest number of preference votes were then allocated seats in turn on each party list. However, even before 1993, this system of preference voting had been abolished in favour of a party list drawn up by each party according to which seats for that party would be allocated on the basis of the election results in each district.

This system of proportional representation was a modified version of the *Imperiali* system. For elections to the Senate, a different system was used, known as the D'Hondt Highest Average Formula, which combines proportional representation with weighted majority voting. Prior to 1993, senatorial elections were conducted as follows. Each region was allocated a certain number of seats in the Senate according to population, and the region was then divided into electoral districts equal to the number of seats allocated. Valle D'Aosta once more was the only region which constituted a whole electoral district returning only one senator. Each party would field a candidate in each district and the voters voted for the party and the candidate. If in any district, a candidate obtained 65% or more of the votes cast, that candidate was elected. Such a share of the vote was but rarely obtained. In the absence of a candidate getting such a share, each party's votes in the districts were added together so as to produce regional totals for each party. The party with the highest total was then allotted the first seat and that party's total then divided by the number of seats it had won so far, viz., one, plus one, and this new figure, the average, was then treated as the party's regional vote. The party with the highest average in the region was then alloted the next seat and the same calculation made again, and so on until all the seats had been awarded. The seats given to each party were then distributed amongst their candidates in the different districts in accordance with the number of votes each candidate had polled.

Although both the systems employed were aimed at ensuring that the political mix in the nation was mirrored in the composition of the parliament, the result in Italy was that no party ever got sufficient seats to be able to control either, let alone both, chambers. Governments of necessity therefore required coalitions to be formed. The most popular party between the Second World War and 1990 was the *DC*, the Christian Democratic party. This party managed to form governments regularly throughout this period by forming coalitions, primarily with the Socialists, the *PSi*. One of the main objectives of these coalitions was to keep the communists, the *PCi*, out of power. With the collapse of Soviet communism in the late 1980s, the fear which the communist threat engendered abated, and support for the *DC* and *PSi* waned, particularly as leading figures in both parties became the object of corruption investigations. The result was a demand for reform of the electoral system which would in effect return power to the voters rather than let political power be bargained among the party bosses in the wake of inconclusive election results. There were demands for a reform of the electoral system which would enable strong party governments to be elected. Faith was placed in a first-past-the-post system, seen to be producing one party governments regularly in the UK. Accordingly, in 1993, following a referendum on the mode of electing to the senate, laws were passed introducing new methods of electing both deputies and senators. The basis of the reform in both chambers was that three-quarters of the seats in each should be filled by a first-past-the-post system, the remaining quarter being allocated by proportional representation.[2]

For elections to the Senate, the country is now divided into 232 electoral seats distributed amongst the twenty regions. The remaining 83 seats in the Senate are to be allocated by proportional representation on the D'Hondt system described above. The candidate with the most votes in the constituency in which he or she stands is elected. This accounts for 232 seats nationally. The remaining seats are allocated regionally. The total vote for each party in each region is calculated. However, where a party has already won seats in that region on the first-past-the-post system, the votes cast for winning candidates in the region are deducted from the regional total for the party, thus ensuring that only those votes which have not so far elected a candidate are carried forward into the PR stage. The D'Hondt highest average formula is then applied to the figures. The party with the highest number of votes gets the first seat, its total is halved and the process and calculation repeated until all the PR seats for the region have been allocated. The number of seats granted each region reflects its population. Roughly, 186,000 voters secure one senatorial seat.

The PR system for the Chamber of Deputies is more complicated. The country is divided into 26 electoral districts which return more than one deputy. Valle D'Aosta is an additional single-member constituency. All the other constituencies return at least 7 members, other than Molise which returns only 2. These multi-member constituencies are allocated seats in the Chamber according to population size. 474 seats are so distributed. The remaining 155 are to be allocated on a PR basis across the constituency as a whole. The constituencies are divided up into a number of electoral colleges, the number of which corresponds to the number of deputies to be elected on the first-past-the-post basis. The candidate with the highest number of votes in each college is elected. Thereafter, the remaining PR seats are allocated as follows. Within each constituency, each voter will have been able to cast two votes; one for a candidate standing in his own college, and one for a party standing in the constituency as a whole. For each party standing in the constituency, the electoral total or *cifra elettorale* is calculated. This is the total vote for the party in the constituency minus the number of votes polled by the runner-up in a college won outright by that party in the first-past-the-post poll. If in any college, a winning candidate polled more than 25% of the vote, then if the runner up polled less than 25% of the votes cast in that college, the winner's vote must be reduced by 25% of the votes cast. When the *cifra elettorale* has been calculated for each party in each constituency, the sum of all the *cifre* for each party throughout the country is calculated. This is the party's national electoral total. These are then added together (ignoring any party the national electoral total for which is less than 4% of all votes cast) and divided by 155, the number of seats to be allocated. The result of this calculation is called the national electoral quotient. This gives the number of votes which should result in the award of a seat. The national electoral quotient is then divided into the national electoral total of each party with 4% or more of the votes cast, and this gives the number of seats the party should obtain nationally.

The seats are then distributed amongst the parties on a constituency basis. To do this, the sum of all the *cifre ellettorali* of the qualifying parties in a constituency are added together to give the constituency electoral total. This is then divided by the total number of PR seats allocated to that constituency to produce the constituency electoral quotient. This is then divided into the *cifra elettorale* of each party to give the number of seats which that party wins by PR in that constituency. Any remaining seats are then allocated among the parties with the highest remainders in each constituency and thereafter the same is done nationally until all seats have been distributed.

Under both the senatorial and chamber of deputies systems, it can be seen that care has been taken to ensure that votes are not wasted. Wherever a vote is cast, then unless it is for a party with a very small share of the vote, there is a good chance that it will contribute at some stage towards the election of a senator or deputy of the elector's political persuasion. Thus, even though full PR has been abandoned in Italy since 1993, every effort is still being made to ensure that electors feel that their vote has counted and not merely been counted. This conscientious adherence to the principle that the views of every voter should if possible find expression exemplifies the manner in which the law seeks to uphold the constitutional principle that sovereignty does indeed reside in the people.

The parliament is elected for a period of five years, although it can be dissolved within a shorter space if it becomes clear to the President of the Republic that it is no longer representative of opinion in the nation, if it is impossible to form a government which commands the confidence of both chambers or if relationships between the chambers have become unworkable. It is also possible for the life of a parliament to be extended for a further five year term in time of war when it is not feasible to hold elections, although only one such extension is permitted. Otherwise, the only extension permitted is to allow the existing parliament to remain in place until a new one has been elected and then only for a period of ninety days in all.

The members once elected are required to swear an oath that they will serve the republic in their office and not be bound by any other mandate or instruction. In effect, this is clearly meant to place loyalty to the Constitution and the nation above party loyalties. Nevertheless, members are grouped in the chambers along party lines. The Senate meets at Montecitorio and the Chamber of Deputies at its seat in the Palazzo Madama, both in Rome.

The functions of the parliament are primarily legislative, and the legislative process is described in the next chapter. However, the parliament also has some other functions of importance in the effecting of which it represents the Italian people. For these functions only, the parliament meets in plenary session, that is there is a joint meeting of both chambers. The functions which the parliament discharges in this manner are: the election of the President of the Republic; the election of five of the fifteen judges of the Constitutional Court, and the election of one-third of the members of the *Consiglio Superiore della Magistratura*. These are regular functions which the parliament must discharge from time to time. However, it is also in plenary session that it would meet to impeach the President, the prime minister or any other member of the government for treason or breach of the Constitution, and also in plenary session that it would draw up the list of lay members of the Constitutional Court who would join the regular judges for the trial of such an accusation.

3 The State : The President and the Executive[3]

The President of the Republic is the head of State and represents the nation on formal occasions both at home and abroad. The president is elected not by the people but by their representatives in a plenary session of the parliament. He then holds office for a term of seven years but can be re-elected. The president must be an Italian citizen who has attained the age of 50 and who has an unblemished character both civilly and criminally. In addition, he must not be a member of the erstwhile royal family, the House of Savoy.

The president is not a member of the executive and in effect stands above the other organs of government as a neutral constitutional guardian. As he does not exercise legislative, executive or judicial power himself, this may explain why the people are not directly involved in choosing him. His functions include calling and dissolving parliament; calling for elections; choosing a person whom he believes will command the confidence of both parliamentary chambers to form a government, that is become prime minister; and, formally appointing the other ministers whom the prime minister nominates to be members of his government. It is he who also formally promulgates national legislation, which is always published in his name. In effect, he speaks for the people in this regard when their representatives have passed legislation in conformity with the Constitution. It is however his duty to ensure that such measures have been appropriately passed, and if he is unsure, he can exercise a suspensive veto so as to pass the matter back to parliament for reconsideration. It is he also who may grant pardons and amnesties, he who is the nominal chairman of the *Consiglio Superiore della Magistratura* - although the Council is chaired by its elected Vice-Chairman. He it is who chairs the Supreme Defence Council and who is Commander in Chief of the armed forces. He also appoints five of the fifteen judges who sit on the Constitutional Court, and he is the fount of honours within the republic.

His most important role is probably choosing a prime minister in the wake of an election or when a coalition government has broken up. He is not required to choose a prime minister solely from among the ranks of parliamentary members. In certain circumstances, for instance where the fall of a government is going to necessitate fresh elections, he is sometimes more likely to appoint a caretaker from outside the political fray. The prime minister is technically the President of the Council of Ministers. He it is who chooses the other members of this cabinet, although they are formally appointed by the President. They too do not have to be members of parliament. All government bills are introduced into parliament for consideration in the name of the President of the Republic.

After appointment, a prime minister must obtain a vote of confidence in both chambers of parliament. Failure to do this means his government cannot continue. Likewise, failure to win a vote of confidence in either chamber at any time forces the government to resign. When the prime minister resigns, all his ministers lose office with him. The president cannot of his own motion dismiss a prime minister.

4 Regional Government[4]

As stated earlier, Italy is divided into twenty regions, five of which are special regions, the remaining fifteen being classified as ordinary. Of the five special regions, four were given their regional constitutions in 1948 while the fifth, Friuli-Venezia Giulia received its in 1963 after the resolution of the problem of Trieste with Yugoslavia. The constitutions of these special regions were passed in the form of constitutional legislation by the national parliament and were therefore the creation of the State rather than of the regions themselves. To this extent therefore the special regions may be said to have had less autonomy with regard to the content of their constitutions than the ordinary regions, for the latter, which obtained their constitutions in the five years following 1970, were allowed to determine their own constitutions in their regional councils, which constitutions were then submitted to the national parliament for approval, that parliament having either to accept or reject the constitution agreed by the regional council, but with no power to amend it. Thus, it can be claimed that the ordinary regions have had greater control over their constitutions than the special regions.

Although there is some room for diversity as between region and region, each regional constitution provides for a roughly similar governmental structure. This structure is set out in Title V of the Italian constitution. Each region is to have a Council, elected by its own population, which Council has legislative and administrative authority within the region within the limits allowed by the State constitution and national laws. The Council is currently elected by proportional representation and the members of the Council then elect from among their own number the *Giunta* or executive arm of regional government. It is the Council also which elects from among its members the regional President. The Council has the authority to legislate on the matters which the State constitution remits to the regions for control. It is a unicameral legislature, and proposals passed by it are to be promulgated as laws by the regional President. However, the regional president does not have quite the same role as the State president in this regard. The State president can refer the proposal back to the State parliament for further consideration if he is unhappy with regard to its constitutionality. However, that vetting function in the regions is performed not by the regional president, who is also the chairman of the executive *Giunta* and unlikely to be neutral with regard to the content of regional legislation, but by the Government Commissioner, a

State appointee to be found in every region. It is he who actually approves a regional law prior to its promulgation by the President.

The Government Commissioner is sent every item of regional legislation for approval. He forwards it to the State government which can either clear it for his approval or send it back for reconsideration by the regional council. If the regional council amends it as required, the Government Commissioner will again forward it to the State government for clearance for his approval. If however the regional council, by an absolute majority of its members affirms its original decision, then the State government, if it persists in its opposition, must either refer the enactment to the Constitutional Court, if the irregularity is formal, or to the legislature, if the object of disapproval is a matter of substance. If either body rejects the enactment, it cannot become law; if the enactment is upheld, then the Government Commissioner must approve it and send it to the regional president for promulgation. The Commissioner therefore has a substantive role, the president's promulgation being formal. This not only protects the doctrine of the separation of powers, but also ensures the accountability of the region to the State, whose official the Government Commissioner is.

The matters over which the regional council is entitled to legislate are those listed in article 117 of the Constitution together with such other matters over which the State legislature gives the regions control from time to time. The regional council is also permitted to adapt the methods by which State legislation is implemented in the region. The areas covered by article 117 are: the control of officers and administrative bodies dependent on the region - basically the provinces and communes; communal boundaries; urban and rural police forces; fairs and markets; public works and health and hospital care; technical, professional and scholastic provision; local museums and libraries; town planning; tourism, hotels and catering; regional public transport; regional communications, acqueducts and public works; navigation and inland ports; mineral and thermal waters; quarries and turbaries; hunting; fishing in inland waters; agriculture and forestry; handicrafts and other matters set out in constitutional legislation.

The regional council not only has the power to legislate on these matters but also to provide for their administration within the region. This however it does through the agency of the provinces and communes, which are administrative but not legislative divisions of the State.[5] The region provides for the regulation of the matters within its purview by delegating their administration to the bureaucracies of the provinces and communes, but needs therefore to oversee their work in much the same manner as the

Government Commissioner oversees the region's efforts on behalf of the State. The work of the provinces is overseen by a *Comitato di Controllo sulle Province*, and the same body may well supervise the communes as well, but regions may if they wish set up a separate *Comitato di Controllo* to supervise the *comuni*. These bodies review administrative measures undertaken by the provinces and communes, and each is composed of three experts in administrative law nominated by the regional council, a nominee of the Government Commissioner and a judge of the regional adminstrative tribunal - TAR - nominated by that court's president.

Regions do not have powers of taxation but they do control the manner in which the budget allocated to them by the State is spent with regard to the matters within their control.

5 Provincial and Communal Government[6]

Unlike the regions, provinces and communes are not regulated by the State constitution. They are administrative not legislative districts. Each province has a provincial council, which is elected directly by the people by proportional representation. The council, like its regional counterpart, elects from among its own members a *Giunta*, which is the province's executive organ. Until 1994, the provincial council also elected the provincial president who headed the executive and represented the province on formal occasions. However, since 1994, the electorate itself now chooses its president by a first-past-the-post electoral system, in which the two candidates with the highest number of votes in the first ballot contest a straight fight at the second ballot if neither obtained more than 50% of the poll at the first ballot.

The basic duties of the province are to carry out those administrative functions allocated to them by the region in which they are situate. These usually include health and hygiene, public works and services, public transport and the regulation of hunting and fishing. Large provinces can be subdivided into *circondarii* for administrative efficiency.

Communes vary in size from small villages to large cities. Rome and Milan were once communes. Each commune has a council, directly elected by the citizens on the basis of proportional representation. The council then elects the *Giunta* from amongst its members. Like the province, until 1994 the commune council also elected the mayor or *sindaco*, but since 1994 the *sindaco* is now elected directly by the local population on a first-past-the-post system, a candidate being elected if he gets more than 50% of the vote on the first ballot or otherwise the two candidates with the highest votes on the first ballot going to a straight fight on the second. Large communes are, like provinces, sometimes subdivided into districts, each with its own council and president. These only have significance within the commune however and are set up purely to protect local interests within the commune. Very small communes may not have a *Giunta* but only a council and a *sindaco*, the council being small enough to perform the work of an executive committee.

The *sindaco* is a State as well as a communal functionary, carrying out duties on behalf of the State government as well as the commune. The mayors of large communes such as the great Italian cities occupy positions of considerable political power as well as national prestige. They resemble their opposite numbers in the USA and the civil law countries of Europe more than they do the mayors of towns and cities in England and Wales. The commune's functions include local police, health, public works, social services and town planning. It is also responsible for the maintenance of the civil registry and organizing military service by conscription. The town hall or *comune* is of considerable significance in the life of the Italian citizen in private as well public law matters.

Since 1990, the largest Italian cities - Rome, Milan, Turin, Genoa, Venice, Bari, Naples, Florence and Bologna - have been designated *aree metropolitane*. Each now has its own metropolitan council and *sindaco*. Encouragement has also been given to other *comuni* to integrate where this would produce a more efficient management of local resources. The new metropolitan arrangements are still in their infancy but have ended the difficult and somewhat unrealistic division of provincial and communal responsibilities in the largest urban areas.[7]

5 Conclusions

As can be seen from the preceding discussion, the structure of government from the most local to the national level in Italy conforms to a certain pattern. Leaving aside the judicial power for the moment, this pattern provides for a deliberative body - the parliament or council, an executive organ - the cabinet or *Giunta*, and a titular head, the president or *sindaco*. It is a pattern which can be repeated so as to extend the hierarchy upwards or downwards. Thus, large communes have their district councils.

It is worth however noting that the structure is capable of upward extension beyond the level of the nation State. The European Union, with its deliberative but not legislative parliament, its Commission and president reflects the pattern which is readily familiar to the Italian sense of governmental structure. It is a pattern which is equally familiar to the citizens of other European countries who share Italy's legal heritage. It is not familiar, indeed it is foreign, to those raised in the common law tradition of England and Wales. Herein lies part of the problem of British integration into Europe - the lack of a common governmental structure and heritage. Italians can feel at home with the institutions of the new Europe by reason of their structural familiarity, while their structural unfamiliarity leads to them being perceived as a threat by some in the United Kingdom.

Notes

---

[1] *Costituzione*, art. 55-69.
[2] L. 4 August 1993, nos. 276 & 277.
[3] *Cost.*, art. 83-100.
[4] *Cost.*, art. 114-132.
[5] With the exception of the provinces of Trento and Bolzano which are accorded legislative powers.
[6] *Cost.*, art. 114, 133.
[7] L. 8 June 1990, no. 142.

5 The Legislature and the Legislative Process

1 Introduction : The Phases of the Legislative Process

In the ancient Roman republic, legislation was enacted by the assembly of the people, the *comitia*. The *comitia* would be convened for this purpose by one of the magistrates, usually one of the consuls, who held office for one year only. Prior to putting the proposal before the *comitia*, the consul would have taken the proposal to the Senate, a body composed of the representatives of the leading patrician families of the Roman republic. The Senate had the right to discuss the proposed legislation and to advise the magistrate with regard to its content. The Senate was in other words a body which debated the proposal but which did not decide whether it was to be enacted. The *comitia* on the other hand, which had the power to enact the proposal as a law, had no right to discuss its content. The function of the *comitia* was solely to vote upon it, to pass or reject the proposed statute. In some ways therefore it is misleading to think of the *comitia* as a parliament, given that the word parliament is derived from the French *parler* meaning 'to speak'. A parliament is a place for discussion and that the *comitia* was not. However, as a parliament today is thought of as being a legislative assembly, it is difficult to describe the Senate as a parliament, despite it being a body which met to discuss legislative proposals, for it had no power to enact them. Thus, it might be said that the functions that tend to be associated with modern parliaments were divided in the ancient Roman republic between the Senate and the *comitia*. Moreover, if it is borne in mind that in the modern British parliament only members may introduce bills, it might be more accurate to say that the functions were distributed amongst the magistrate, the Senate and the *comitia*, one having the power to introduce legislative proposals, the second having the right to debate them and the last having the right to decide upon them. Thus, one can distinguish three phases in the legislative process of the Roman republic - the introductory phase which belonged to the magistrate; the deliberative phase, which appertained to the Senate, and the decision-making phase, which was the role of the *comitia*. Perhaps the most important thing to note about these three phases at this stage is that ancient Rome illustrates something which may seem surprising to those who are used to seeing the British parliamentary process as the norm, namely that these three phases do not have to be the preserve of one institution, but can be divided among several persons or bodies.

Once one has identified these three distinct phases in the legislative process, one can proceed to ask of the actual legislative process of any State how each of these phases is performed and by whom. Thus, one must ask who may introduce bills, or who has the legislative initiative. Secondly, one may ask who may deliberate upon and discuss their content or who performs the deliberative phase, and thirdly, who decides whether the bill will pass into law - who has the decision-making power. As will be seen, in modern Italy, unlike the United Kingdom and perhaps not surprisingly with some affinity to ancient Rome, not all of the phases are necessarily the preserve of the Italian parliament. Indeed, it pays to remember in this regard that the Italian constitution states that sovereignty belongs to the people, and much of what follows illustrates the manner in which that principle is worked out in the practice of legislation.

2 The Introductory Phase

The introductory phase is that by which a legislative proposal, in the form of a draft law, is placed before both chambers of the parliament for consideration. The Constitution grants the legislative initiative to the government and to members of the parliament. In the United Kingdom, only members of one of the houses of parliament may introduce bills. Even government bills have to be sponsored by members of parliament so that ministers must of necessity be members of one or other House. In Italy, this is not the case. A government minister may introduce a bill into the chambers of the Italian parliament for consideration even though the minister himself is not a member of either chamber. He is allowed to speak to the bill in the chamber and answer questions on it and its policy, but he is not allowed to vote on it unless he is also an elected representative of the people. Italy does not require that the introductory and decision-making roles should rest in the same hands.

Likewise, the Constitution also provided that other bodies or entities may introduce bills into the Italian parliament. Currently, the only body which has this power is the *Consiglio Nazionale di Economia e Lavoro*, the National Economic and Labour Council. Again, the recognition that non-parliamentary bodies may enjoy the legislative initiative is an indicator of the Italian Constitution's view that although only those who represent the sovereign people may decide upon the worth of legislative projects, the right to have proposals considered by parliament does not have to be confined to the decision makers.

Regional parliaments also enjoy the legislative initiative within the national parliament, thus ensuring that the nation must respond to the needs of each region at least to the extent of considering the proposals put forward by the region's representatives in the regional parliament. Most significantly, however, the Constitution grants the legislative initiative to electors themselves. In Italy it is the right of electors in groups of 50,000 or more to present draft bills to the national parliament which the parliament is then bound to consider. This is a very significant implementation of the principle that sovereignty resides in the people themselves and not with their representatives in parliament. In the United Kingdom, an elector can vote for a party with a particular manifesto, but can do nothing if when in power that party fails to implement a part of its programme. Likewise, the United Kingdom electorate cannot force parliament to consider any matter other than through the ballot box. Italians have a greater say in what goes on during the lifetime of their parliaments. Their exercise of sovereignty does not end at election time. It can be exercized during the lifetime of the parliament elected. 50,000 is not a large number. It is less than 0.1% of the population. The only restriction is that such proposals must not pertain to the budget, taxation, amnesties, pardons, or international treaties.

Italians also have the right to petition parliament individually or in groups on matters of interest to them. Such petitions may come from individual citizens who do not have to be qualified electors. Moreover, petitions do not have to be couched in the form of a draft legislative bill. United Kingdom citizens also have the right to petition, but there is a great deal of difference between petitioning for a favour and having the right to have parliament consider a legislative proposal provided only that it has the support of less than one in every thousand of the population who is an elector for the lower chamber.[1]

3 The Deliberative Phase

Once a bill has been introduced into the Italian parliament, the deliberative phase begins. It is important at the outset to note that what begins is described as deliberation and not debate. Debate conjures up a confrontational scenario, with one side proposing and another opposing a particular point of view. The procedure of the United Kingdom parliament is confrontational; everything proceeds by means of debate. Indeed, in the House of Commons, government and opposition benches are lined up confronting one another and, along the floor, before the front benches, there run two parallel lines the length of the chamber, one in front of the opposition benches and one in front of the government members. These lines are drawn at a distance of two swords' lengths apart from each other so as to ensure that if honourable members became so heated in the course of argument as to draw a sword, the swords could not meet. Honourable members are not allowed to step beyond these lines while debating.

The lines may be a quaint memorial of more troubled times in British parliamentary history. Nevertheless, the very architecture of the United Kingdom parliament speaks of confrontation as a model. Most continental legislatures on the other hand are circular or semi-circular in shape, with speakers addressing the chamber from a central rostrum. The architecture of these buildings speaks less of confrontation than of discussion. Members may occupy seats in party groupings from left to right. but they do not confront one another. Instead, they are arranged in a sort of spectrum of political opinion. Despite the fact that television pictures of blows being exchanged in the Italian parliament are more common than any form of physical violence in the British House of Commons let alone the House of Lords, it is the underlying ethos that is of significance. The emphasis in civil law countries is less upon confrontation than upon consensus, and the procedure of the legislature as well as its architecture bears this out.

When a legislative proposal has been received by the Italian parliament, it is referred to the appropriate parliamentary commission in each chamber. This commission then reports to the chamber on the proposal and proposes a sub-committee of its members to consider and report on amendments that may be suggested during the course of the deliberative stage. The President of the chamber then decides which of four methods of deliberation shall be employed. In the Senate, the President's decision is final, while the Chamber of Deputies has the right to oppose its President's recommendation.

The standard form of deliberation involves the whole chamber considering the bill article by article, with a vote being taken on each. Strict time limits are set down for the consideration of each article so as to ensure that adequate time is given for members to assess the merits of the proposals and to suggest amendments. When all of the articles have been considered and voted upon, the chamber is then required to vote on the bill as a whole, which is the decision-making phase.

In cases where the legislation is required to be passed as a matter of urgency, an abbreviated form of this procedure may be used. This involves the halving of all the time limits which are utilised for the full deliberation, thus allowing the bill to proceed with greater expedition.

The consideration of the bill article by article by the whole chamber suggests that every part of it requires consideration by all of the nation's representatives. Clearly, this is an expression of the idea that every elector has a right to be represented when legislation is being made. Equally clearly, however, experience shows that not all matters which are the subject of legislation are controversial. It may be apparent from the moment that the bill is introduced that all of or large parts of it are completely non-controversial. In order not to reduce the deliberative phase to a farcically formal rubber-stamping of non-controversial proposals, it is open for the President to choose a decentralized form of deliberation. Under this method, the whole of the deliberative phase is undertaken by the relevant parliamentary commission. The bill only returns to the full chamber for the decision-making phase, that is for the final vote upon it as a whole. It is also open for the President to opt for a mixed procedure, with some matters being remitted to the parliamentary commission but some being reserved for the full chamber. It is even possible for the bill as a whole, article by article, to be dealt with by commission but a deliberation on it as a whole to take place in the chamber.

The full deliberative phase has to be employed if the bill relates to the Constitution, the electoral process, the budget, the delegation of legislative powers or to the ratification of international treaties.[2]

4 The Decision-Making Phase

Once the deliberative phase has been completed, each chamber of the Italian parliament has to vote on the proposal. For the bill to pass into legislation, it must be passed by a simple majority of members present and voting in each chamber. If it is passed in one chamber but not the other, it cannot be re-introduced into that chamber for further consideration until six months have elapsed.

Once the bill has been passed by both chambers, it passes to the President of the Republic for promulgation. Before he promulgates the law by publishing it, it is his duty to vet it both with regard to its form and its substance. If he feels that it is offensive to the Constitution, he can remit it to the parliament for ratification, but if parliament does so ratify it he must then promulgate it. The law must also be countersigned by the Minister of Grace and Justice who certifies that it has passed through the necessary legislative procedures. Thereafter the law is published in the Official Gazette and comes into force and effect fifteen days after its publication at the earliest, unless there is special urgency requiring its earlier enforceability or unless by its own terms it is to be brought into force and effect at a later date.

At this point, it might be asked what has happened to the all important sovereignty of the people, the deliberative and decision-making phases having been completely dominated by their elected representatives. However, the role of the people in relation to such ordinary, that is non-constitutional, laws does not end with their having a possible role in the legislative initiative. At any stage after a law has been passed, it is open for its desirability to be challenged by the electorate. Any 500,000 electors - a larger number than is needed to initiate legislation but still less than 1% of the population - to call for a referendum on the law. If 500,000 qualified electors call for a referendum, one must take place. There is no time limit after the passing of a law within which this request must be made. Thus every legislative enactment, with the exception of those concerning the budget, taxation, international treaties, amnesties and pardons, remains vulnerable while it continues in force. Every law is constantly open to review by the electorate if 500,000 electors so require.

Such a referendum is known as an abrogative referendum because by it existing laws may be repealed. There can be no doubting the force or significance of this institution of direct democracy. It was an abrogative referendum which challenged the pre-1994 electoral system by calling for a plebiscite on the law requiring all the seats in the Senate to be filled by proportional representation. The abrogation of that electoral law meant that a different, non-proportional system had to be introduced for some seats and, as it would have been very difficult for government and legislation to continue if the two parliamentary chambers were to be elected on radically different bases, it was this referendum which led to the reform of the electoral system for the Chamber of Deputies as well.

When an abrogative referendum is called, every qualified elector for the Chamber of Deputies has both the right and the duty to vote. Provided that more than half of those entitled to vote do so, whichever side gets a simple majority of the votes cast wins the referendum. Thus if a simple majority of those voting favours the legislation's abrogation, it is repealed, while a simple majority against its abrogation secures its retention.

Such referenda have become a regular feature of Italian political life. Since the 1970s, issues such as the introduction of divorce, the availability of abortion, the hunting of wild birds, the development of nuclear energy and the electoral system itself have all fallen for review by the sovereign population.[3]

5 Legislative Decrees

As stated above, it is possible for a law to delegate legislative power to a person or body other than the parliament. Such proposals have to be deliberated upon article by article by each chamber of the parliament. Delegated legislation can however be authorized in this manner. Also, as stated above, in an emergency, parliament can provide that a law is to come into force and effect immediately and not fifteen days after its publication by the President. However, this nevertheless means that the law has to go through all the phases of the legislative process before it comes into force, and this can take time of an order which is not commensurate with the needs of a moment of emergency.

Accordingly, it is open for the government to legislate by means of *decreti-leggi*, that is legislative decrees. Such a decree can be made by the government, that is the executive authority, thus contravening, in an emergency situation, the strict doctrine of the separation of powers. However, adherence to the requirements of that doctrine is nevertheless observed, for the government must lay the decree before parliament the very day that it is issued. Parliament must then meet within five days to consider the decree. Even if it is in recess, it must meet within this time.

If parliament ratifies the decree it is treated as having come into force and effect from the day on which it was issued. If parliament rejects the decree, it is treated as having been void *ab initio*. If the decree is not ratified within sixty days of its issue, it automatically becomes void *ab initio*.[4]

6 Constitutional Legislation

Laws which seek to amend the Constitution itself are subject to a more stringent legislative process. The legislative initiative is restricted to the government, members of parliament, regional parliaments and 50,000 electors. Others bodies, such as the CNEL, cannot be empowered to introduce constitutional legislation. This in reality illustrates the fact that their powers are granted solely to enable them to introduce legislation on matters within their purview of which the Constitution is not one.

Secondly, having been introduced, constitutional legislation must proceed by a full deliberative procedure, each article of the bill being considered and voted upon in turn. The role of the parliamentary commission, in this case the Constitutional Affairs Commission, is thus limited to reporting to the chamber on the contents of the bill. The bill must be passed on two occasions by each house, and these occasions must be at least three months apart. Any amendment at the second deliberation necessitates a further consideration of the bill at least three months later. In other words, it must be the selfsame text that is passed on both occasions. On its first passage through each chamber, the bill must secure a simple majority of members present and voting, but on its second passage, it must secure an absolute majority of the members of the house, that is more than 50% of the membership and not just of those who are there and casting their votes.

If the bill receives a two-thirds majority in both of the chambers at its second reading, it passes immediately to the President who, if satisfied with its propriety, publishes it as law, thus amending the Constitution. However, if the bill does not gain a two-thirds majority in each chamber at its second reading, the President, even if satisfied with its propriety, may not publish it as a law for three months. This period is allowed for the exercize of popular sovereignty on the issue.

If the bill has not received a two-thirds majority in each chamber, it is treated as though it has not been passed by a consensus of the elected representatives of the people. The people are therefore allowed to reclaim their sovereignty on the matter. 500,000 electors or any five regional parliaments or one-fifth of the membership of either chamber may require that the matter be put to a referendum. If such a request is made, the promulgation of the law is suspended until such time as the result of the referendum is known. All voters for the Chamber of Deputies are entitled, indeed obligated, to participate. If a majority of those voting favour the change, the President must proceed to promulgate it, but if a majority of those voting is against, the whole project fails. Thus, on constitutional matters, unless the elected representatives are overwhelmimgly in favour, the mechanism is in place for the will of the people to be ascertained and its voice heard and obeyed.

It may be asked why the President retains a power of veto in these circumstances. Firstly, he has this power even if the amendment obtains a two-thirds majority at its second deliberation in each house, so that it can be exercized even when a referendum is not possible. Secondly, the President is not concerned with the desirability of the amendment but rather its propriety. This involves questions as to whether the amendment is permissible under the Constitution, in that it is not open even to parliament to amend the Constitution in certain ways. Thus, a Constitutional amendment may not alter the republican form of the State, particularly by reinstating a monarchy, nor may such an amendment seek to violate those rights recognized by the Constitution as being inviolable. This brings us to a discussion of the contents of the Constitution and its protection by the Constitutional Court, which topics will be considered in the next chapter. For the moment, the role of the President in protecting the Constitution merits note, for it reflects the clear recognition by the State that mechanisms are needed to protect the people's Constitution even from the people's elected representatives in the legislature.[5]

Notes

[1] *Costituzione*, art. 71.
[2] *Cost.*, art. 72.
[3] *Cost.*, art. 73-75.
[4] *Cost.*, art. 77.
[5] *Cost.*, art. 138-139.

6 The Italian Constitution

1 Introduction

A constitution is the fundamental law of a State. It is the set of legal rules upon which all other legal rules are ultimately based and from which they draw their validity. It is part of public law in that all the rights and duties which a Constitution contains involve the State as one of the parties in each legal relationship described thereby. The Constitution is not however just the law which describes the manner in which other laws are made or which describes the manner in which legal power is distributed between the organs of the State. An English lawyer might well begin from that perspective because that is what an English lawyer probably means when he speaks of the British Constitution or of British constitutional law. However, to a civil lawyer, the Constitution of his country is much more than that, which is why he may perplex an English lawyer by saying not just that the United Kingdom has no written Constitution, but also by claiming that it has no Constitution at all.

There is a sense however in which the civil lawyer who made that latter claim would be justified. To understand the nature of a Constitution in a civil law country, one must begin by asking what is the purpose of a State of which the Constitution is a fundamental law. One Latin American country actually begins its Constitution by answering that question in terms. The first two articles of the Constitution of the Republic of Guatemala are very educative of the whole constitutional ethos of civil law countries. Leaving aside the specific application of the provisions to Guatemala, article one states that "the State is organized in order to protect the individual person and the family; its supreme goal is the realization of the common good". Article two then sets out the duties of the State as being "to guarantee to its subjects life, liberty, justice, security, peace and the full development of the individual person".[1]

From this, it can readily be seen that the function of the State is clearly defined both in terms of its basic duties and its basic aspirations. The State is there to protect its subjects as individuals and in family groups and has as its goal the realization of the common good. It is in return for pursuing these fundamental duties and goals that subjects owe the State loyalty and obedience to those laws which it makes in pursuance of those ends. It must be realized that everything therefore contained in a Constitution about the granting of powers to State organs and about the manner in which laws may be made and enforced within the State are about how those fundamental duties are carried out and how the fundamental goal is to be achieved. The Constitution is not a compromise agreement about how power is to be shared between a monarch and his people; it is a statement of fundamental duties and aspirations under which all are to live their common social life within the community of the State. The Head of State's role is a role under the Constitution; he or she has duties under the Constitutional law in the same way as any other citizen. The Head of State has duties to the State which are not owed as a matter of grace and favour or convention but as of obligation. The Head of State is not the person in whom the State is personified, although he or she may represent the State in certain circumstances and situations. The Constitution is not a document like the English Magna Carta under which a sovereign lord concedes certain powers to his subjects. Rather it is a recognition of certain basic rights and duties which are antecedent to the making of any human law or the formation of any human society. Social life presupposes some of the rights which a Constitution guarantees.

The underlying theme therefore of the constitutions of civil law countries such as Guatemala and of Italy is that certain human rights are basic in the sense that they exist regardless of whether there are laws in existence to protect or guarantee them. In other words, these rights exist independently of law and do not owe their existence to the law. They are recognized by law but are not created by law. The question of where they have their origins would take the discussion away into the realms of jurisprudence, general philosophy and theology, but it should be noted that any hard line between the sphere of operation of these disciplines and that of law is not so clearly drawn in the civil world as in that of the common law. The civil lawyer knows of two words for law: *ius* and *lex*, in Italian *diritto* and *legge*. The former connects law with what is right and just, while the latter refers to law which has been enacted, that is, is formally correct. The former sense makes a connection between law and justice of which the common lawyer has become over the centuries shy and suspicious. The connection is born of the Roman jurists' view of law as being of three sorts: the law of an individual State; the law which was common to all men, and the law which was common to all living things, the law of nature. Each of these is a form of *ius*: *ius civile*, *ius gentium* and *ius naturale* respectively. For human law to be truly proper, it has to conform with law of a higher order. Thus, the Romans defined jurisprudence not as legal philosophy or the science of law, but the knowledge of things human and divine, the science of the just and the unjust.[2] Justice, an immutable order to which human society attempted to conform, was the context for human law-making, and the latter could not really be independent of it.

Thus, when the constitution of a civil law country speaks of recognizing certain human rights, this is not just a statement about what the inhabitants of a particular State value; it is a statement of the context within which they believe their community exists. A Constitution is almost a secular creed. It is not just a list of agreed rights; it is suffused with the notion that these rights exist independently of human agreement. No power within a human community can deprive a human being of these fundamental rights. The State may be permitted by its inhabitants to interfere with these rights for good reason, where the State is justified - an important word - in so doing, but such permissions relate only to specific individuals in situations predetermined by law. The rights themselves remain generally inviolate. Human beings enjoy the right to life, the right of liberty, personal integrity etc., not because they are citizens of a particular country which has agreed through its legislative processes to protect such rights; they enjoy those rights because they are human beings. The State guarantees the protection of those rights because it is an association of persons who enjoy those rights in a world where not everyone will respect them. The State is a means of achieving the basic ends enshrined in the Constitution. Loyalty to the State is not an end in itself; it is predicated upon the State's delivering the protection which the Constitution binds it to supply.

Returning for a moment to the Constitution of Guatemala, it may have been noticed that the protection and guarantees afforded by the Constitution were not just given to individuals but also to families. The family is an association of individuals, and by recognizing the rights of the family as requiring State protection, the Guatemalan Constitution also recognizes that the family, as an association of human beings, antecedes the State. This again harks back to the Roman jurists' concept of the family as a natural law institution. That one human association is singled out in this way opens the door to constitutions recognizing that human beings generally may wish to associate in different ways for different purposes. In other words, as the family does not owe its existence to law but pre-exists the protection which the law may afford it, so also the human wish to associate with others, to form communities of various sorts, also may be taken to predate the existence of States, or at least a particular State, and such associations may also therefore merit the protection of law. Indeed, some associations or groupings may merit protection as being basic to the human condition. Thus, various groupings - cultural, linguistic, religious and so on - may be protected under a country's Constitution, as may trade associations and trade unions and other such groups. The right to associate freely for purposes which do not undermine the basic rights of others may also therefore be a right which finds itself given constitutional protection.

When one turns, therefore, to examine the Constitution of a particular country such as Italy, one should ask what it is that the Constitution sets out to achieve, and what does it identify as the basic human rights which require guaranteeing and protection. One must also ask how the State is enabled under the Constitution to guarantee and protect those rights, that is how it is empowered to make laws. One must ask how it distributes the power at its disposal among the State organs to achieve the goals set by the Constitution and how it seeks to ensure that those organs - legislative, executive and judicial - do not in exercising their powers undermine the basic rights which they are meant to safeguard and promote. These questions will now be put regarding the Constitution of the Italian republic.

2 The Structure of the Italian Constitution

The Italian Constitution of 1948 consists of two parts, preceded by a section on fundamental principles. The two parts are concerned with the rights and duties of citizens and the structure of the republic respectively. In sum, the first part is concerned with the civil, political, economic and social rights of citizens, while the second part concerns the mechanisms by which the State creates laws, governs the country, provides for resolution of disputes and polices the Constitution itself. The fundamental principles with which the Constitution begins are concerned to enunciate certain basic principles about the manner in which the rights and duties which follow in Part One are distributed amongst the citizens and indeed others.

The Constitution begins by defining the form of the Italian State and its form of government. The State is a republic, following the decision to abolish the monarchy after the Second World War, while its form of government is democracy. The foundation of the republic is said to be work or labour. At the outset, therefore, a work ethic is espoused, expressing the belief that a main concern of the individuals and groups of individuals who make up the republic is that they are to work together. Their association as a State is based upon work. Sovereignty is said to reside in the people, and is to be exercized according to the forms and limitiations of the Constitution. The Constitution in other words addresses how popular sovereignty is to be exercised. Article one makes it clear that the organs which exercize legislative, executive and other State powers are not sovereign; they act in the name of the people.

Article two recognizes and guarantees what it describes as the inviolable rights of man, either as an individual or in the associations within which each may develop his personality. This emphasizes the point made earlier that these inviolable rights are not the creation of Italian law or of any other legal order. They exist as part of the human condition. The republic merely recognizes their existence as a fact and guarantees respect for them. Notably, once more, such rights are seen to extend not just to individual persons but to groups which individuals need to belong to to develop their personalities. The republic requires that political, economic and social solidarity be achieved as inderogable duties.

Moreover, these rights which are part of the human condition and which the State recognizes are the property of every human being. All citizens have equal social dignity and are to be equal before the law. Discrimination on grounds of sex, race, language, religion, political opinion, or social and personal condition is not admitted. This means that the rights and duties which will be described in Part I of the Constitution, cannot be limited to any one or more classes within the community, nor can any class be excluded from their enjoyment. The republic is obligated as an ongoing matter of aspiration to remove social and economic obstacles which limit the freedom and equality of the citizens, impede their full development as human beings and their effective participation in political, economic and social organizations within the country.

It has been asked whether the list of possible forms of discrimination given in this third article is a closed list or whether it is capable of extension by analogy. Different jurists and different times answer this question differently. Some say that the Constitution is definitive and must not be added to by judicial interpretation, not even by the Constitutional Court. Others believe that it is proper for the judges to recognize new forms of discrimination and extend to them the principle contained in article three of the Constitution on the basis that the fathers of the republic would have outlawed such forms of discrimination had they addressed the issue when the Constitution was being drafted. The important thing for the student of the Italian legal tradition to realise is that these two approaches are deeply rooted in the history of Italian law. The literal approach is nothing more than the belief that the law is the law of the text, a view as old as the Glossators, while the logical approach is redolent of the attitude of their successors the Commentators, who sought the principles underlying the rules in order to develop the rules to meet new situations. That this divide continues to haunt the precincts of Italian jurisprudence is as fascinating as it is likely to prove unresolvable.

The republic also recognizes the right of every citizen to work and its duty to promote the conditions which make this right effective. Moreover, given the fact that the republic is founded upon work, every citizen has a duty to develop according to his or her own potential, an activity or role which contributes to the material or spiritual well-being of society.[3]

While the republic is one and indivisible - a form of words reminiscent of the doctrine of the Holy Trinity - it nevertheless recognizes and promotes local autonomy and decentralization. This article is a distinct departure from the centralizing tendencies of the fascist years and marks a clear acceptance of the divergence of loyalties which continues to exist over a century after unification. Moreover, it marks an early recognition of the merits of subsidiarity, the recognition that decisions should be taken at the level at which they are most pertinent, a concept which has, more recently, had a profound influence within the structures of the European Union and which also had an important role within the Second Vatican Council which addressed the problems of over-centralization within the Roman Catholic Church.[4] Likewise, the Constitution, recognizing that membership of a linguistic group is of basic importance to human beings, commits the republic to guard with appropriate norms the rights of linguistic minorities within the State, such as the French speakers of the Piedmont and Valle D'Aosta and the German speakers of the Alto Adige.[5]

Membership of religious groups is also recognized as a basic human right, with the State refusing to discriminate amongst differing religious faiths and denominations, although the independence of the Roman Catholic Church from the State is specifically recognized as is its sovereignty within its proper sphere of operation, which sphere is defined within the Lateran Pacts, made between the Italian State and the Vatican as a sovereign State in its own right.[6] As well as religion, the republic is bound to promote the development of culture and scientific and technical research, each seen as ways in which the human quest for truth may be pursued. The republic is also bound to safeguard the countryside and the historical and artistic heritage of the nation.[7]

The Constitution also binds Italy to observe international law, and foreigners within Italy are to be treated in accordance with international treaty obligations. Political asylum is to be available to those whose basic rights according to the Italian Constitution are not respected in their own lands and extradition is not permitted for political crimes.[8] Again, this witnesses the clear belief that basic rights antecede political and national orders and that human rights deserve greater recognition than the claims of other nation states. Commitment to human values is placed above international comity. The nation exists for the people and not the other way round.

Italy repudiates war as a method of international dispute resolution and is committed to the development of international organizations which promote peace and justice among nations.[9] This can be legitimately viewed as an extension of the recognition of groups of human beings which help develop the human personality.

Somewhat incongrously, but typical of the Constitutions of civil law countries, the fundamental principles section ends with a prescripitive description of the Italian flag - the green, white and red tricolor.[10]

3 The Rights and Duties of the Citizens

Part I of the Constitution deals with the rights and duties of citizens and is itself divided into four titles, dealing respectively with civil relations, ethical-social relations, economic relations and political relations. In each case, the relations in question are those between the citizen and the State, thus illustrating the public law nature of these relationships.

Civil Relations[11]

Personal liberty and the home are both said to be inviolable. Again, this is not a grant of the Constitution but a recognition by it. This means that the State is bound to protect and indeed guarantee personal liberty and the homes of its citizens. Any interference with the same by the State is therefore prima facie unlawful, as is any interference by another citizen. If another citizen interferes with a subject's personal liberty or invades the home of another, not only is this an offence against that other but it is also a failure by the State to provide the protection that it has bound itself to supply. The State therefore has an interest in such wrongful interference.

The State however does reserve to itself the right to interfere with these rights, for instance by restricting personal liberty in certain circumstances, such as by detaining those convicted or even suspected of having committed crimes, but a reasoned order of a judicial authority is required for such acts and they must be referrable to situations which have been previously identified as meriting such treatment by law. *Ex post facto* ratification of such situations is not admissible, but in cases of urgency and in the interests of public security, personal liberty may be interfered with provided a reasoned judicial order is subsequently obtained ratifying what has been done within forty-eight hours of the action. Preventitive detention is only allowed within the limits set by the law. With regard to respect for the home, similar restrictions apply to powers of entry and search, and inspections for health, public order, economic or financial reasons must be regulated by legislation.

The Constitution also demands respect for the liberty and secrecy of correspondence and other forms of communication, interference again requiring reasoned judicial acts, and citizens have the right to move around and rest freely within the national territory, subject to the requirements of public health and order. Interference for political reasons is specifically outlawed. Entry and exit from the national territory is also a constitutionally protected right of the citizenry.

Provided they are not armed, citizens have the right to hold peaceful gatherings even in places open to the public, although gatherings in public places - as opposed to places open to the public - should be notified to the authorities in advance, who may forbid them on grounds of security or public order, but reasons must be given. Likewise, citizens are allowed to associate freely with one another for any purpose which is not forbidden by the criminal law. Secret associations are however prohibited as are those which either directly or indirectly pursue political goals by means of military or para-military means.

Freedom of religious expression, individually and in groups, is protected as are the rights to evangelize and to worship in private or in public subject to demands of public decency. Religious organizations are not to be subjected to legal limitations nor to fiscal demands by reason of their religious character.

Freedom of thought and of expression is accorded to all, including the freedom to publish opinions in writing or by any other means. The press is not to be subjected to licensing nor to censorship. Provision is however made to ensure that the press does not invade the rights of others and that the press does not offend against public morals.

No one is to be deprived of their legal capacity, their citizenship nor of their name for political purposes. It is interesting that the three matters mentioned here relate to freedom, citizenship and family, the three matters which the Roman jurist Paul said were of prime importance to Roman citizens in the ancient world.[12]

No personal or property demands are to be enforced other than in accordance with the law. Everyone has the right to bring legal actions to protect their rights and legitimate interests, while the right to defence in legal matters is recognized as inviolable at every stage of judicial proceedings. Persons who lack the means are to be assisted in bringing and defending legal actions and judicial errors are to be correctable in the manner provided by law. No one is to be tried other than by the judge preconstituted by the law and no one is to be punished under a law which was not in force at the time that the act called into question was committed. Retrospective laws are not therefore allowed in criminal matters. The courts could not discover the existence of a crime in the course of legal proceedings, as for instance occurred in England and Wales in 1962 in *Shaw* v *D.P.P.*,[13] when the crime of conspiracy to corrupt public morals was identified during the course of an accused person's trial. Criminal responsibility is personal to the wrongdoer and no one is to be considered guilty of a crime until finally convicted. Punishments must not be inhumane and ought to be aimed at the reform of the convict. Thus, the death penalty, which gives up on the convict, is not allowed other than in military law during wartime.[14] State and public functionaries are responsible for illegal acts committed in the course of their employment. Civil liability in such cases extends to the State and public bodies. Thus, it is not open to State officials who break the law to plead their State employment or any reason of State as a defence. Their prime responsibility is to the law. Although the Italian Constitution does not mention the concept in terms, the rule of law clearly permeates its provisions.

The title on civil relations gives the basic principles upon which criminal law and criminal justice within the Italian republic must by law be based. Interferences with the rights protected by this part of the Constitution have to be taken seriously by the State, investigated by it and where appropriate prosecuted as a matter of public duty. Likewise, those suspected of having committed crimes are persons with the same rights as those who have suffered them. Accordingly, the criminal justice system must be organized in such a way that the rights of the suspect and of the accused are respected until conviction. As seen, even after conviction, the convict is not without rights. The Constitution enforces the rule of law within the law codes and enactments of a subsidiary nature made under it. It is important to see this relationship between the Constitution as the fundamental law of the State and lesser forms of legal regulation. These latter carry the duties and aspirations of the Constitution into effect, but must never do so in a manner which compromises or offends the Constitution's principles.

Ethical-Social Relations[15]

The republic recognizes the family as a natural society based upon marriage. This article at once bears witness to the State's commitment to the family as a basic social unit, one of those associations of individuals which do not depend upon the legal order of the State for their existence. The family is recognized by the law; it is not the law's creature. Moreover, it is described as natural, that is existing in a state of nature not a civil society, and is based upon marriage, thus emphasizing again that although the State may regulate the institution of marriage, the institution is prior to and independent of the State's regulation. The State does however now insist that marriage is based upon the moral and legal equality of the spouses, within the limits established by law to guarantee the unity of the family. This notion of moral and legal equality between the spouses is new. Originally, Italian law regarded the husband as the head of the family, the *padre di famiglia*, and it can be questioned whether in all parts of the republic the notion contained in the Constitution is actually accepted in practice. This provision is an example of the Constitution leading the way, setting an aspiration which the law will then follow in order to lead society rather than follow social trends. It bears comparison with the way in which legislation, such as the Race Relations Acts in England and Wales, moved ahead of public opinion to shape a more racially tolerant society.

Within the family, the Constitution provides that parents have the duty as well as the right to maintain, educate and bring up their children, regardless of whether the children are born in or out of wedlock. The law is obligated to provide for what is to be done in the case of parental incapacity. Illegitimate children are assured the same social and legal rights as those born within marriage, and the law has to furnish means for ascertaining paternity.

The republic is to facilitate, by means of economic and other provisions, the formation of the family and the fulfilment of its aims, particularly with regard to large families. It is to offer protection during maternity, infancy and growing up.

Within the ambit of ethical-social relations, health is safeguarded as an individual right and as a public interest. Free health care is to be provided for those unable to afford it. The arts and science are free to all, as is education. The republic must provide the legal structures for education and establish institutions of learning at every level. Private educational institutions may however be established free of State burdens, within which education is to be regarded as in every sense equal to that provided by the State. Schools are to be open to all, and primary education for at least eight years is obligatory and free. Those who are qualified to proceed further are to be permitted to do so. The republic is bound to provide scholarships to help those who wish to pursue this right, which may however be awarded competitively.

All of these Constitutional rights bear witness to the State's aim to assist in the full development of the human personality, whether in relation to the individual or in groups which further that aim.

Economic Relations[16]

It will be recalled that article one of the Constitution stated that Italy was a democratic republic founded upon work. As work is seen as a foundation of social life, it is not surprising therefore that labour is a constitutionally protected right in all its forms and applications. Those who work are given special protection as is their professional development. Agreements and organizations which uphold and regulate the rights of labour are promoted and favoured, as is the right to emigrate to find work and the rights of Italian workers abroad. Recent events have shown, however, a less than reciprocal enthusiasm to protect the rights of immigrant workers within Italy.

The labourer has the right to remuneration proportionate to the quality and quantity of his work and in every case it must be sufficient to assure a free and dignified life for himself and for his family. This relation between work, the individual and family life is also affirmed by the Italian Constitution's requirement that the law should fix the maximum length of the working day and the requirement that every worker should have a weekly day of rest and paid annual holidays, neither of which rights may be bargained away. Market forces are not allowed to overcome the development of the human personality nor the fulfilment of its potential. Work is made for man, not man for work.

Female workers are to have the same rights as male workers and the same rights to remuneration, but the needs of the family must be borne in mind and specific and adequate protection afforded to mothers and their children. A minimum working age must be set by law and special laws are required to protect minors in the working environment to prevent their exploitation. Those unable to work are to be provided with the necessary means of maintaining their existence, and security of adequate means of subsistence is to be given to workers against the possibilty of accident, illness, disability and old age, as well as involuntary unemployment.

Trade unions are free to organize themselves without restriction, other than the need for local or central registration in accordance with the law. They must however to be registered be organized on a democratic basis. Once organized they have legal personality. The right to strike exists but must be exercized in accordance with the law regulating it.

Enterprise is free and private. It must not however be developed in a manner which is contrary to human security, liberty or dignity. The law is entitled to provide the means whereby economic activity in the private and public domains may be made to conform with the goals of society.

The ownership of property, both public and private, is permitted as a constitutional right. Private property is recognized and guaranteed by the law, which determines the methods by which it may be acquired, enjoyed and the limits which assure that its social purpose is not undermined for the benefit of all. Expropriation of private property for the general interest is permitted in situations provided for in advance by the law, and the law also establishes the rules and limits within which testamentary and intestate succession shall operate and the rights of the State in inheritance. It is worth noting that these Constitutional provisions relating to private property and succession underly the provisions of the Civil Code which govern its acquisition, enjoyment and disposal, including transfer on death. This again illustrates the manner in which the Constitution supplies the fundamental law, and the lesser sources of law, including the legal codes, carry the fundamental law into effect. The Civil Code determines how property is to be acquired, enjoyed, transferred, etc., but that it may be acquired, enjoyed, transferred, etc., is a constitutional right.

In the same manner as the Civil Code carries the above constitutional requirements into effect, so certain other constitutional requirements are carried into effect by administrative norms. Thus, the Constitution permits the law to expropriate private property so as to ensure that certain resources and public services are properly managed for the public benefit, even if that requires a monopoly situation to arise. Likewise, to ensure the proper enjoyment of private property in a manner which is not detrimental to society, the law is able to impose obligations and restrictions upon private owners so that land is properly managed rather than exploited in accordance with the needs of regions and other localities. Mountain regions can also be protected by law. Institutions which favour co-operative and mutual activity in the prosecution of work can also be protected as can trade guilds and the like. The formation of firms and companies to promote enterprise is also specifically permitted. Finally, investment in all its forms, together with credit control, is encouraged and safeguarded by the republic, with particular reference to the needs of buying homes, cultivating the land and investing in the major production industries of the country.

Political Relations[17]

The title relating to political relations deals with the right to vote, join political parties, submit petitions to the chambers of parliament and stand for public office. These rights and duties have been more fully considered in Chapter Five, dealing with the legislative process.

However, also in this section, the defence of the Fatherland is described and prescribed as a sacred duty of the citizen. Military service is enjoined, and the armed forces are required to be informed by the democratic spirit of the republic. Everyone is required to contribute to the public purse according to their ability - a provision which allows for the development of tax laws, and the tax laws are required to be informed by criteria of progressivity.

Finally, all citizens have the duty to be faithful to the republic and to observe, not merely obey, the Constitution and the laws. Those who hold public office in particular are required to fulfil them with discipline and honour, taking oaths when required to do so by the law. Loyalty to the republic or the State is what the citizen must give in return for the protection which the State through the Constitution and the laws provides. It is the other half of the bargain.

Part II of the Constitution deals with the structure of the State. In successive titles, it deals with the Italian Parliament, the President of the Republic, the Government, the Magistracy and the Regions, Provinces and Communes. These have been dealt with in Chapters Four and Five of the present work, while the Magistracy is examined in Chapter Eight. The last title of Part II consists of two sections. The second section relates to the legislative procedure for amending the Constitution and has also been dealt with in Chapter Five. The remaining section, which deals with the Constitutional Court alone remains to be dealt with in this chapter.

4 The Constitutional Court[18]

The Constitution contains therefore the basic legal norms of the State. It states the basic rights of the citizen and the mechanisms for making, administering and adjudicating upon laws to uphold those rights. As has already been said, in civil law countries, each type of law, each department of the law, has its norms set out in a particular code and has a court or set of courts with jurisdiction to adjudicate upon that particular body of law. The Constitutional law of the State is contained in its Constitution, and the court in Italy which has jurisdiction over the norms contained therein is the Constitutional Court.

The Constitutional Court is separate from the jurisdiction of the other courts of law within the Italian republic. This is because it is meant to be above the various State powers concerning which it must adjudicate. If the courts of ordinary jurisdiction were, for instance, charged with the functions of the Constitutional Court, this would leave them open to the charge of being judges in their own cause or at least to the opinion that the judicial power of the State was to that extent superior to the legislative and executive arms of government in that it had the power to judge the activities of the others. Accordingly, the Constitution provides for the existence of a separate Constitutional Court which alone has jurisdiction to settle questions relating to Constitutional law.

The Constitutional Court consists of fifteen judges, each of whom must either be at the time of his appointment a senior judge within the Italian judiciary, an advocate of at least twenty years standing or a full professor of law at an Italian university. Each judge serves on the Constitutional Court for a period of nine years from the time of his appointment and is not eligible for immediate re-election to the Court at the expiry of that term. While the judge is in office, he is not permitted to practise a range of other professional activities, for instance he must not practise as an advocate nor sit as a judge in the courts of ordinary jurisdiction. Moreover, judges of the Constitutional Court are barred from holding any office in the legislative or executive areas of government, as this would compromise their neutrality as between the three powers of the State.

The judges are chosen by three methods, five being chosen by each route. Five are appointed by the President of the Republic; five are elected by a joint sitting of both chambers of the Italian parliament, and five are elected by the senior judiciary. Again, this balance reflects the need to ensure equal representation from amongst those chosen by the executive, legislative and judicial powers of the State respectively. The judges of the Constitutional Court elect a President of the Court from amongst their membership, who holds office for a period of three years. The Court sits as a collegiate body, the quorum for which is eleven, thus ensuring that the Court can never decide an issue without at least one member being present who has been elected by each of the three elective bodies. Moreover, it ensures that even a majority decision requires the consensus of judges from at least two of the elective sources. The balance reflecting the separation of powers within the court can therefore be seen to be taken very seriously.

The jurisdiction of the court is concerned solely, as one would expect, with questions of Constitutional law. It does however have a criminal as well as a civil side. On the criminal side, the court is charged with trying accusations against the President of the Republic relating to his State functions. For trials of this sort, the professional judges of the Constitutional Court are supplemented by sixteen other lay judges, that is judges who are not legally qualified, in the same manner that in the criminal courts which try serious criminal cases both at first instance and on appeal, the *corte d'assise* and the *corte d'assise d'appello* respectively, the career judges are supplemented by lay judges to make up the *giuria*. The sixteen lay judges who join the panel of judges in the Constitutional Court for trials on its criminal side are chosen from a list of persons all of whom must be qualified to stand for the Senate of the Italian parliament. Thus, they must all be over forty years of age.

On the civil side of its jurisdiction, the Constitutional Court is charged with dealing with disputes of a Constitutional nature between the various organs of the State, the State and the regions, or between the regions themselves. The work with which it is most popularly associated is however its jurisdiction to consider the legality of laws made by bodies including the

Italian parliament. It has in other words the power to adjudicate upon the propriety of laws made by parliament and other lesser legislative bodies at State, regional and other levels, in order to ensure that they conform both to the requirements of the Constitution with regard to the methods of law-making - that is that they are formally valid, but also that they conform to the requirements of the Constitution in respecting the rights which the Constitution as the fundamental law gives Italian citizens. In other words, it is possible for the Constitutional Court to declare invalid laws which contravene the constitutional guarantees with regard to their substantive content. What the court cannot do is consider laws on their merits if they do not offend against the constitutional guarantees.

Such cases come before the Constitutional Court by reference from other courts within the Italian legal system, most typically from the courts of ordinary civil jurisdiction, courts of criminal jurisdiction or administrative courts. It is not open to Italian citizens, as for instance is the case in Spain, to impeach a law before the Constitutional Court even if not a party to litigation in which the law in question is vital to the decision of the case. If, before a court hearing a particular case, the constitutionality of a rule which is necessary to the decision of the case is raised, the court must adjourn and refer the matter to the Constitutional Court for adjudication. If that court is satisfied that the issue has to be resolved for the case in the ordinary court to be settled, the Constitutional Court will then accept the reference. One of the judges will be asked to consider the complaint against the rule in question and report to the full court with his findings. In other words, the inquisitorial model of proceeding is followed, the investigating judge not so much taking evidence as he would in a civil or criminal trial, but nevertheless investigating the question which the court has to determine which is, of course, in this context always a question of law. The full court then sits to receive the report of the judge and to hear the submissions of the parties. The State always has the right to be represented in these hearings as a State power obviously has an interest on every occasion in the outcome of the case.

The Constitutional Court can reach one of three decisions in relation to a reference of this sort, and its decisions are never open to appeal or review. Firstly, it may find that on this particular occasion, and it is important to emphasize that such a finding is limited in its applicability to the occasion in question, the rule has not been shown to be unconstitutional for the reasons advanced. The case will then be remitted to the court from which the reference came to be determined according to the rule which was challenged, such rule not having been shown to be invalid. It is important to emphasize that this type of decision does not hold a rule to be valid; the court never decides this. It is merely a decision that on this occasion for the reasons advanced, the rule has not been shown to be invalid. This leaves it open to others, or even the same parties on a different occasion, to challenge the rule afresh.

The second decision open to the court is to allow the reference and to rule that the norm in question is unconstitutional. This renders the law in question completely invalid, and the case will then be remitted to the court from which it came for adjudication accordingly. This may for instance mean that a criminal trial will collapse. This passes the issue in a sense back to parliament or whatever other body made the rule, either to re-enact it in a manner which is formally valid, if the defect is one of form or procedure, or to reconsider what steps if any are necessary to be taken if the defect was substantive.

The third decision which the court can take is to uphold the law but to rule that a particular interpretation of it is invalid. This limits in effect the range of the norm in order to prevent its transgressing the requirements of the Constitution. Both the second and third type of decisions are obviously binding, although the third type does not preclude the court from holding on a later occasion that the rule is more generally offensive or even totally invalid.

An example may serve to illustrate what has been described above. Article 559 of the Penal Code criminalized adultery. However, adultery was only a crime when committed by the wife. It was not a crime for the husband to commit adultery although it was obviously a breach of the matrimonial duty of fidelity as set out in the Civil Code. In 1961, the Constitutional Court was invited to consider whether this provision of the Penal Code offended against two articles of the Constitution, namely article 3 - which says that all citizens are to have equal social dignity and be equal before the law, regardless of, among others things, their sex, and also article 29 which states that marriage is to be based on the moral and legal equality of the spouses. The Constitutional Court held that article 3 was concerned with avoiding the distribution of rights and duties among citizens on the basis of privilege for certain classes of persons, and did not prevent the legislature passing laws which, in order to preserve the unity of the family, distinguished between the different roles of the spouses. It would not for instance prevent special provision for maternity leave or benefits being granted to women merely because men would not qualify. Accordingly, article 3 was not thought to be relevant. The court also held that article 29 was not contravened in that article 559 of the Penal Code was concerned with upholding the unity of the family, and the adultery of the wife was of a different order to the adultery of the husband in this regard as it could lead to confusion with regard to the paternity of children born during the marriage. Accordingly, the reference was rejected.[19]

As stated above, although the reference was rejected in this case, this did not prevent the same issue being raised again. This indeed happened seven years later in 1968.[20] On that occasion, a differently constituted Constitutional Court upheld the reference and decided that article 559 of the Penal Code did offend against the principle of equality of the spouses within marriage as set out in the Constitution, article 29. Accordingly, the court struck down comma 1 and comma 2 of article 559, which respectively criminalized the conduct of the adulterous wife and her partner in the act. The following year, comma 3 was also struck down as unconstitutional, in that it also discriminated between the husband and wife, in this case in relation to pursuing an adulterous relationship rather than just one act of adultery.[21] The penalty for an on-going relationship had been more severe - up to two years, rather than up to one year's, imprisonment. A glance at the current editions of the Penal Code will find either the omission of this section with a note describing its fate, or its inclusion in italics or parentheses with an explanation as to why it is no longer law. It is a very vivid illustration of the workings of the Constitutional Court.

Although the Constitution from its inception in 1948 provided for the setting up of the Constitutional Court, it was not until 1956 that it was established. The Constitution, as has been said, is meant to chart the aspirations of the State as much as prescribe for what must occur at the present moment. Despite this, the delay is difficult to justify. Eventually, the court was established, but for some years it was but little used as the older, more senior members of the magistracy were reluctant to refer cases to it. Their younger brethren, many of whom had qualified since the inception of the 1948 Constitution, were less nervous about using the court, and many of them had in fact agitated for its being set up in accordance with the Constitution. Its early years, as the above example suggests, found it acting rather timidly and perhaps conservatively, but by the end of the 1960s it had found its feet and its place in the Italian legal order. Today, it is generally accepted as a necessary part of the legal scene in Italy, bringing that country even more close to the paradigm of civilian legal systems.

Notes

[1] *Constitucion Politica de la Republica de Guatemala* (1985) articulos 1 and 2:

> **Articulo 1o. Protección a la persona**. El Estado de Guatemala se organiza para proteger a la persona y a la familia: su fin supremo es la realización del bien común.
>
> **Articulo 2o. Deberes del Estado.** Es deber del Estado garantizarle a los habitantes de la República la vida, la libertad, la justicia, la seguridad, la paz y el desarrollo integral de la persona.

[2] Justinian, *Institutes*, I.1.1.
[3] *Cost.*, art. 4.
[4] The merits of subsidiarity were advocated by Pope Pius XI in *Quadragesimo Anno* (1931), and developed by Pope John XXIII in *Mater et Magistra* (1961).
[5] *Cost*, art. 6.
[6] *Cost*, art. 7-8.
[7] *Cost*, art. 9.
[8] *Cost*, art. 10.
[9] *Cost*, art. 11.
[10] *Cost*, art. 12.
[11] *Cost*, art. 13-28.
[12] See Justinian, Digest IV.5.11.
[13] *Shaw* v *D.P.P.* [1962] AC 220
[14] Although the Constitution still permits this, military law itself has recently been amended so as to prohibit the death penalty; see L. 13 October 1994, n. 589. I am grateful to my colleague Dr. S. Manolkidis for drawing this to my attention.
[15] *Cost*, art. 29-34.
[16] *Cost*, art. 35-47.
[17] *Cost*, art. 48-54.
[18] *Cost*, art. 134-137.
[19] Corte Costituzionale, sentenza 28 November 1961, n. 64.
[20] Corte Costituzionale, sentenza 19 December 1968, n. 126.
[21] Corte Costituzionale, sentenza 3 December 1969, n. 147.

7 Civil Justice

1 The Courts of Civil Jurisdiction

When the various divisions of Italian law were enumerated in Chapter Two, it was stated that in Italy, as in most civil law countries, for each type of law listed - for instance, criminal law, administrative law, constitutional law - there also existed a legal text setting forth the norms of that system and a set of courts to administer those norms. Thus, criminal law is contained in the Penal Code and administered by the criminal courts; administrative law is contained in *Il codice repertorio amministrativo* and enforced through the *Tribunali amministrativi regionali*, while constitutional law is contained in the Constitution and implemented by the Constitutional Court.

In each of these instances, the courts in question have jurisdiction over the type of law in question. This is what is meant by jurisdiction, *giurisdizione*, in Italian law. With regard to the norms contained in the Civil Code, jurisdiction is enjoyed by the civil courts, or the ordinary courts as they are sometimes called. As in most civil law countries, these courts are markedly decentralized in comparison to their counterparts in England and Wales. Justice is administered as locally as is consistent with the efficient exercize of the judicial function concerned.

For the purposes of administering civil justice, Italy is again divided into units. Whereas politically, legislatively and administratively, the units were the State, its twenty regions, the provinces and the communes, for the purposes of civil justice the state is divided into twenty-seven judicial districts, which are in turn divided into *circondarii*. Each *circondario* is then divided into *mandamenti*, and each *mandamento* is composed of *comuni*. Thus, the political and judicial divisions coalesce only at national and the most local level - the State and the communes.

Only one court operates at the level of the State in the civil system. That court is the Supreme Court of Cassation, *la Corte Suprema di Cassazione*, which sits at Rome and, as will be shown, is a court which reviews decisions taken by lesser courts to ascertain whether points of law have been correctly decided by them. Its role is to ensure that the law is interpreted and applied consistently throughout the national territory. It is logically necessary therefore that there be only one such court in existence operating at State level.

In each of the twenty-seven *distretti* into which the state is divided, there is a court of appeal for civil causes, the *corte d'appello*. This court also has no first instance jurisdiction with regard to causes arising within the Italian republic, although it does have a kind of first instance jurisdiction in that it is before this court that foreign judgements must be approved before being enforceable in Italy. The procedure by which such judgements are registered is termed *delibazione*, and it should be remembered that this process now applies to the judgements of the courts of the Roman Catholic Church with regard to such issues as nullity of marriage. The appeals which come before these courts may be either on points of law or on the merits of a decision by a lower court. It is from these courts that review on points of law only is available to *Cassazione* in Rome.

The twenty-seven appeal court *distretti* are by and large coterminous with the regions of Italy. However, one region, Valle D'Aosta, does not constitute a *distretto*, appeals from its *circondario* lying to the *corte d'appello* at Turin in Piemonte. Several regions contain two appeal court *distretti* owing to their physical size or configuration or their concentration of population. Thus, Lombardy has two *distretti*, centred on the appeal courts at Milan and Brescia; Lazio likewise has two, both in Rome but one dealing with the capital's disputes exclusively, and Campagna has two, one based in Naples and the other in Salerno. Farther south, Puglia has appeal court districts centred on Bari and Lecce respectively, as has Calabria, where the appeal courts are at Reggio and Catanzano. Sicily alone has more than two *distretti*, with four appeal court centres at Palermo, Messina, Catania and Caltanisseta.

Each *distretto*, as has been said, is divided into *circondarii*. Each *circondario* is based upon a local centre of population so that each provincial capital tends to be the centre of a *circondario* with its own court of *Tribunale*. The *Tribunale* is the equivalent in Italy to the High Court in England and Wales. Although the High Court has sat since the 1970s at venues other than London, it does not function in every county town. The local nature of the *Tribunale* in Italy exemplifies excellently the decentralized nature of the administration of justice in Italy mentioned earlier.

The *circondarii* are divided into *mandamenti* which are the units served by the courts called by the ancient name of *pretura*. These are roughly equivalent to the modern County Courts of England and Wales.

The *pretura* take its name from the judge who presides in them, the *pretore*. This title derives from the ancient Roman magistracy of the Praetor; the Praetor was the magistrate in republican Rome who was responsible for the administration of justice and who made an enormous contribution to the development of Roman law during the later republic through his Edict. Virtually every Italian town is the centre of a *mandamento* and has a *pretura*. These *mandamenti* are composed of the various *comuni* situated in them, and every *comune* has the services of what might be termed a small claims court, which court is now that of the *giudice di pace*. Until 1993, the *comuni* were served by the predecessors of the *giudici di pace*, the *conciliatori*.

2 The Competence of the Civil Courts[1]

Whereas all of the courts mentioned above, from that of the humblest *giudice di pace* right up to the Supreme Court of Cassation, share jurisdiction over civil causes, they are differentiated by their competence. The competence of the various courts is delineated by three factors: subject-matter, value and territory. Subject-matter and value distinguish the level of court at which litigation must begin - that is at the level of the *giudice di pace*, the *pretura* or the *Tribunale*. Territorial competence on the other hand distinguishes the competence of courts at the same level within Italy - that is whether the case is to be heard before the *giudice di pace* in one commune or another, before the *pretura* in one *mandamento* or the next, or before the *Tribunale* in this or that city. These factors determining competence must now be examined.

Competence over subject-matter and value[2]

Prior to the reforms of 1993, the competence of the *conciliatori* was very limited. Basically, they were limited to hearing disputes concerning moveable property only, where the value of the dispute did not exceed one million lire, roughly £500. Even this was much greater than their competence only ten years earlier, when the value of the disputes they could hear was limited to 50,000 lire, roughly £25. They were also competent to hear disputes relating to the use of shared facilities in blocks of flats. The *conciliatori* were replaced by the *giudici di pace* in 1993.

The *giudice di pace* have a much greater competence. They are permitted to hear cases relating to moveable property, the value of which does not exceed 5 million lire, as well as claims for compensation relating to traffic accidents up to a limit of 30 million lire. Further, there is no monetary limit set upon their competence to deal with disputes relating to the planting of trees and hedges, services in flats, nuisances caused by emissions of smoke and other such elements from properties and opposition to certain administrative sanctions.

The *pretura* has competence over moveable and immoveable property, the value of which does not exceed 20 million lire. It also has competence with no monetary limit set over possessory actions and to denounce new works and feared damage, unless the latter two matters arise in the course of other litigation when the Code of Civil Procedure makes special provision for their determination. New works relate to building, mining or some other activity to which a neighbour objects, while feared damage corresponds to the subject matter which in English law could form the basis for the issue of a *quia timet* injunction, the petitioner fearing that something to be done by the respondent will result in his suffering damage. The *pretura* is also competent to deal with causes relating to the leasing or lending of urban immoveables and the renting of estates other than those dealt with by special agricultural tribunals.

The *Tribunale* has competence over all matters which do not fall within the competence of either the *giudice di pace* or the *pretura*. It is the main court of first instance. It alone has competence to deal with causes concerning taxes and duties, personal status and capacity, honorary rights, and *querela di falso* - that is a claim that a duly authenticated deed is a forgery.

Territorial Competence[3]

Territorial competence is generally decided according to where the defendant, *il convenuto*, has his residence, domicile or abode. If these are unknown, or the defendant does not live in Italy, then the appropriate judge of the locality in which the plaintiff, *l'attore*, lives has competence. If the defendant is not an actual person but a juridical one, such as a company, then the place of the company's address, or that of any branch or authorized representative of the company gives competence to the appropriate court in that locality.

Cases involving immoveables can be heard where they are situate, while possessory actions and actions for the denunciation of new works and feared damage may be brought where the deeds complained of are being committed.

3 Procedure in Civil Actions[4]

The civil process is set in motion as a result of a *domanda*, a petition, lodged by the plaintiff to the action, the *attore*. This immediately indicates that the process is a party process, one set in motion and sustained by the parties as opposed to a process which is set in motion by the State or the magistracy as a matter of duty on their part, so-called *ex officio* procedure, as occurs in criminal prosecutions. The civil process is also a party process in that only matters raised by the parties can be adjudicated in the dispute before the courts, and the courts are generally only permitted to decide these issues on the evidence produced by the parties. Some argue from this that the civil process is therefore adversarial or accusatorial in style rather than inquisitorial. This conclusion can however be disputed on the basis that this distinction has more to do with how the process is conducted than how it is initiated and its ambit circumscribed. Many of these latter features point to the process being inquisitorial.

The process is divided into three phases, called respectively the introductory phase, the instruction phase and the decision-making phase. The introductory phase in concerned with the court checking that the *domanda* is in order and that the particulars of the parties etc., have been properly notified. The defendant to the action, the *convenuto*, is then summoned to appear. The action will normally be heard in the competent court according to subject-matter and according to the territory in which the *convenuto* is resident. If he has no established residence, is a foreigner or has no discoverable address, the action will commence in the competent court where the *attore* resides. In the case of a company or some other such business entity, the action will be heard in the competent court of a place where the firm has its established address.

Once the action has been accepted as valid, the instruction phase begins. This consists of two parts, the *trattazione* and the *istruzione probatoria*. For both parts, a *giudice istruttore* is appointed who will conduct the instruction phase of the proceedings. In the case of an action before the *Tribunale*, the *giudice istruttore* will be one of the three judges who will eventually decide the case. This has generally been the case under Italian civil procedure, although when the current Code of Civil Procedure was promulgated in 1942, it was provided that the *giudice istruttore* should not be one of the trial judges but another magistrate who would report on the instruction phase to the Bench. However, in 1950, when the current Code underwent substantial modifications, this provision was dropped and the previous practice of appointing one of the trial judges to act as the *giudice istruttore* returned. The 1950 reforms also ended the experiment, begun in 1942, of attempting to make the trial predominantly an oral rather than a written process. This was to enable the three judges who had not been present when the evidence was taken during the instruction phase to hear the testimony of witnesses and have every opportunity of assessing their credibilty and reliabilty. However, with the return of the practice of using one of the trial judges as the *giudice istruttore*, there was thought to be no further need of repeating the evidence before the other judges in this way, and accordingly proceedings have reverted to being more written than oral, the other judges relying on the reports of their colleague who conducted the instruction, to give them his impressions of the worth of the witnesses and their testimony. Indeed, since 1995, when reforms made to civil procedure in 1990 were finally implemented, it has been possible for the *giudice istruttore* alone to decide a first-instance case before the *Tribunale* without remitting it to the usual college of three judges.[5] This has considerable advantages from the perspective of accelerating the administration of justice. It is too early however to assess the impact which this reform will have upon civil justice in Italy, although it does mean that the deciding judge has immediate experience of the evidence as it was taken.

When the trial is before the *pretura*, the *pretore* who is to hear the case acts as his own *giudice istruttore*. This increases quite significantly the inquisitorial nature of the proceedings, and it is quite in order for the *pretore* to conduct the instruction according to his wishes, choosing the witnesses and the questions he wishes to ask, and then in effect foregoing a formal trial and just accepting the verdict of the *pretore* on the evidence he has collected during the instruction, with very little intervention by the parties or their counsel. In proceedings before the *conciliatori* or the new *guidice di pace*, the same applies but proceedings are even less formal and the parties are allowed to proceed without legal representaiton or even to appear for themselves.

The first part of the instruction phase is the *trattazione* during which the pleadings are settled by the judge. If the *convenuto* wishes to make a straightforward denial he may do so, or he may demur, raising a point of law, or confess some of the *attore*'s claims while denying others. He may even put in a counterclaim of his own. Once the *giudice istruttore* has discovered what issues are in dispute and which are not contested, the *trattazione* is at an end, and his next task is to gather the evidence which will allow him or, in the case of trials before a collegiate *Tribunale*, the full court to decide the matters which are in dispute. It is for the parties to prove the matters which they assert and for them to adduce the evidence upon which they wish to rely. The judge does not generally have the right to take evidence on his own motion, although this is not uncommon before the *preture* and the *giudici di pace*. The parties therefore submit a list of the evidence and witnesses upon which they wish to rely to prove their respective cases.

If some of the matters raised require the opinion of a professional or technical expert, then the court will usually choose its own expert to report to it on the facts in question. Such a need may arise for instance in cases concerned with medical negligence or mechanical failure. That the expert is of the court's choice and responds to questions put to him or her by the court, again underlines the inquisitorial element in this form of proceeding. It is open to the parties to employ their own technical consultants if they wish and they can suggest that they be called to give evidence if they feel that the court expert has not presented all of the issues which they would wish to see taken into account. The *giudice istruttore* may also receive documentary evidence in relation to the matters in dispute, which will be either public documents of the sort drawn up by notaries proving conclusively the facts to which they attest unless challenged by *querela di falso* as forgeries, or private documents which are not conclusive evidence in the way that notarial documents are. The judge may also receive tangible items, what common lawyers call exhibits, in evidence and visit locations which are relevant to the action. There is very little enthusiasm in Italian law however for witness testimony as a reliable source of evidence. Witness testimony will however be taken. It is for the parties to suggest the names of witnesses to the judge, but it is he who chooses whom to call. The parties have to submit questions which they wish the witness to be asked, but it is the judge who chooses which questions to put and indeed he who carries out the witness examination. All this is again very inquisitorial in style. The parties are not competent witnesses, nor were their immediate families originally, but the Constitutional Court has ruled this restriction invalid and spouses and lineal relatives of the parties are now competent witnesses although they remain uncompellable. The same is true of those professional persons, such as priests, doctors and others who may have confidential information, who are connected in that capacity to the parties.

Although the parties are not competent witnesses, it is open for them to be questioned by the judge and to make admissions at any stage of the proceedings. Such admissions when made are conclusive evidence of matters unfavourable to the party or favourable to the opposition. It is indeed open for the parties to place formal interrogatories to their opponents through the court. Such questions are framed by one party to be put formally to the other by the judge. Such formal interrogatories seek admissions, and the refusal to submit to them or answer them allows the *giudice istruttore* to draw a conclusion unfavourable to the party. Informal interrogatories are those which the judges themselves at any stage of the process choose to put to the parties, possibly in a situation of formal confrontation in an attempt to clear up a disputed fact or facts usually for the interrogatee's benefit. Informal interrogatories differ from formal ones therefore in that the answers to them are not conclusive evidence of any issue but can be weighed against other items of evidence, and whereas formal interrogatories are aimed at provoking admissions unfavourable to the party making them, informal ones are not.

Given the nature of formal interrogatories, it is but a short step to the party oath, that is a challenge thrown down by one party to the other to swear on oath as to the truth of some fact which is usually crucial to the outcome of the action. When a decisory party oath is demanded on such an issue, if the party takes the oath, he wins the suit, but if he refuses he loses. Alternatively, and this is the sting in the tail for the challenger, the party challenged is allowed to turn the tables on his challenger and demand that the other party swear an oath to the contrary. If he then does so, he wins, but if he refuses, he loses. It is unwise therefore to lay down such a challenge unless one is prepared to pick up the gauntlet oneself if it is returned. One may wonder why parties do not constantly resort to such a device to win their suits. The answer is that although the oath is decisive in the instant case, if the winning party at any time thereafter can be shown to have sworn to facts which were untrue or incorrect, they will be punishable for perjury and be liable in damages to the unsuccessful party for any loss caused through their winning the earlier action by oath. The decisory oath is therefore only for those who are absolutely sure of their facts.

The decisory oath can be put at any stage of the instruction phase by either party, the object clearly being to save the time and trouble of continuing litigation on a matter of which the party making the challenge feels sure. At any stage of the proceedings, the court may demand that either party take what is called a supplemental oath if that is the only way in which a matter in dispute can be resolved. The party must then take the oath to win but is not allowed to turn it on the other party. Only the full trial court can demand that a supplemental oath be taken, and it is a sort of last resort when the court is not able to adjudicate the dispute with confidence on the evidence but feels that one of the parties knows the answer to a crucial question. The supplemental oath has shades of the ordeal about it, but without the ordeal's element of torture. Likewise, the decisory oath has a distinguished history behind it, having been part of the law of evidence in civil proceedings in ancient Rome.

When all the evidence has been gathered by the *giudice istruttore*, the *istruzione probatoria* and the instruction phase is at an end. It remains only for the parties, through their respective counsels, to make their final submissions to the judge. The action then moves to the decision-making phase, which in the case of trials before the *Tribunale* traditionally brings it before a full court of three judges. Before this court, the *giudice istruttore*, acting as *rapporteur* presents his report of the instruction phase to the court, and the parties' counsel are invited to speak to their submissions. Despite the pretence of this being a full trial in open court, usually both of these stages are taken for granted, the judges relying on the documentation which has emerged from the instruction phase. The judges then retire to consider their verdict, before returning to the open court where in turn - the *giudice istruttore* first, the other puisne judge second and the court President last - they pronounce their verdict. Thereafter they will produce a reasoned, written judgement which will be deposited in the court registry. This should be done - but rarely is - within thirty days of the verdict being given. It is from that date that time begins to run with regard to the bringing of an appeal.

Where the process is one before the *pretura*, one can see that the decision-making phase is even more of a formality. In that case, the *pretore* is both *giudice istruttore* and trial judge. In effect, therefore, the instruction phase leads inexorably to the giving of the verdict. This makes the procedure very inquisitorial. It is however also open to the parties to request before any court that the decision should be made according to *equità* and not strict law. All decisions before the *conciliatori* were of this type. In effect. the parties are asking for the judges to decide according to their consciences and not according to the rules laid down in the law codes. The parties cannot therefore in such cases complain of the judges' decision. Accordingly, there is no appeal from a decision according to *equità*.

4 Appeals and Review[6]

Appeals lie from each of the courts of first instance to the court which has the functional competence to hear an appeal from it. The *pretore* had the functional competence to hear appeals from the *conciliatori*, but today it is the *Tribunale* which has the functional competence to act as an appeal court from both the *pretore*, a competence it has always enjoyed, but also from the *giudice di pace*. Decisons taken at first instance by the *Tribunale* may be appealed to the *corte d'appello* of the *distretto* in which the *Tribunale* lies. The *corte d'appello*, like the *Tribunale*, is a collegiate court, consisting of three judges, the presiding judge being of the status of a judge of *Cassazione*, the other two being of the status of appeal court judges.

An appeal from the relevant court of first instance to the appropriate court of appeal has to be made within 30 days of the judgement being handed down. The appeal is an opportunity for the case to be retried in effect upon its merits. The appeal is therefore composed of an instruction and a decision-making phase. It is open to the parties to require the court to consider the matters afresh on their merits without adducing new evidence, in which the judge in charge of the instruction phase will probably confine himself to examining those bits of evidence which he feels require reassessment or which the party lodging the appeal has asked should be reassessed. It is possible however for the appeal to be based on the availability of fresh evidence in which case this will be taken by the examining magistrate. At the end of such examination, the full court repeats the decision-making phase as conducted during the trial at first instance.

The appeal can also be grounded upon a point of law. If a point of law is still contested at the end of the appeal, or if a point of law is contested after a first instance trial for which no appeal is allowed, that can be reviewed at the request of a party by the Supreme Court in Rome, *Cassazione*. This is also a collegiate court with competence to deal with final reviews on points of law arising from trials anywhere within the national territory. Normally, *Cassazione* sits with a bench of five judges, but in cases of exceptional difficulty or sensitivity it can sit as a full court of nine judges. The point of law will be argued before it by appropriately qualified counsel, and the decision of the court on a point of law is final. If it upholds the decision of the appeal court, or the court of first instance if there was no appeal allowed, the matter is at an end. If however it believes the decision of the lower court was wrong on a point of law, it can quash the verdict of that court in whole or in part and remit the case to be retried there on that issue in accordance with its own interpretation of the legal issue involved. The lower court which retries the case is always of the level from which the case came to *Cassazione*, but differently composed with regard to personnel, and is bound to apply the law in that case in accordance with the decision of the Supreme Court. The decision does not however, as would a decision of the House of Lords in Britain, make law and become binding upon lower courts in future cases, although such decisions are usually treated as being of considerable persuasive authority as sources of *giurisprudenza*.

As well as appeal on the merits and review on a point of law, two other mechanisms need to be mentioned, revocation and third-party opposition. Revocation, which can be ordinary or extraordinary, can be requested by a party if it becomes apparent that the decision in a case was arrived at on account of errors of fact on the face of the court record which affected the decision of the court - this is ordinary revocation. Extraordinary revocation is available when it is discovered that the decision was the result of fraud on behalf of the other party or of a judge, or when the evidence relied on is found to be false, or when decisive documentary evidence has been discovered since the trial which was not available to the court through duress or deceit. Ordinary revocation has to be requested within thirty days of the judgement; extraordinary revocation within thirty days of the ground for revocation being discovered.

Third-party opposition exists to allow someone who was not a party to the proceedings, but believes himself to be prejudiced by them, to seek protection of his rights from the courts.

5 Enforcement of Civil Judgements[7]

The process which has been described above is aimed at establishing that one person has a right to a thing or against another person, and the extent of such a right or rights. It is not aimed at enforcing any obligations which are recognized. This appears strange to a common lawyer, used as he or she will be to a system, the civil process of which acts both to establish and enforce rights. The common law aims at providing a remedy. The civilian civil process however aims to establish what is due. It is then for the parties to act justly and render to each other what is due. The Roman lawyers said that there were three precepts of the law: one was to give to each his due; another was to harm no-one; the third was to live virtuously or honourably.[8]

Living honourably would entail fulfilling the terms of any judgement given. The courts do not therefore automatically enforce a civil judgement.

In a sense, as the civil process is a party process, the courts have been acting at the request of the parties to solve their dispute. This reflects the Roman origins of the process, for under both the ancient *legis actio* procedure and the later classical formulary procedure, the parties approached the magistrate, the praetor who sorted out the matters which were in dispute, and then the case was referred to a judge to decide according to the principles set out by the praetor. The division between proceedings *in iure* and *apud iudicem* correspond very closely to the distinction between *trattazione* and *istruzione probatoria* today, the judge deciding the issue as would a modern *pretore*. The parties had sworn to abide by the judge's verdict, and only if one broke this undertaking would enforcement proceedings be taken. Although the modern courts derive their authority from the State, nevertheless in civil cases they act as a result of party initiative, but if one party proves recalcitrant in obeying the judgement, the other party can go back to the courts to complain of the former's failure to honour the judicial decree. In effect, this is a form of contempt of the command of a State organ, the judicial apparatus of a State which through its laws protects the rights of all those subject to those laws. The State is therefore entitled to interfere with the rights or property of the person who has not obeyed the judgement, that is acted unjustly, so far as is necessary to restore the correct balance between the parties.

The civil courts will grant enforcement proceedings not only following a judgement which is *res iudicata* in a civil action but also on the basis of some forms of legally enforceable document, for instance negotiable instruments. Applications for enforcement are overseen by a single judge, who acts with the assistance of a court bailiff and where necessary the judicial police. The judge normally involved is the *pretore*, but where execution is to be levied against immoveable property, the *giudice d'esecuzione* is a judge of the *Tribunale*.

Enforcement is dealt with in Book Three of the Code of Civil Procedure, and can be of one of three kinds: liquidation of assets, an order for the transfer or release of certain property, or an order requiring the doing or not doing of a particular act. The latter two kinds do not necessarily require a court hearing, only the precept of the judge requiring the bailiff to oversee the transfer, release or performance. Enforced liquidation of assets however demands greater formalities and safeguards. Accordingly, the judge himself supervises the three stages of attaching the property, giving other creditors of the defaulting debtor an opportunity to declare their interests, and, if necessary, the sale of the assets to satisfy the judgement debt. Such enforced liquidation is resorted to only if the judgement debtor has failed to observe a precept requiring the debt to be paid.

It is open for a debtor to contest the proceedings, but not by so doing to challenge any matter determined in the judgement giving rise to the obligation. That would after all allow him to reopen the issues decided at the original trial and which are now *res iudicata*. He may however challenge the right to bring the proceedings, the *locus standi* of the plaintiffs to them and the formal exactitude with which the proceedings have been taken. It is also open for third parties affected by the proceedings or their outcome, such as those with an interest in the property which is being attached or sequestered, to oppose the proceedings on such grounds.

The idea of taking a portion of the debtor's property sufficient to satisfy the judgement debt and so to satisfy it by its sale is derived from the later Roman law procedure of *sequestratio bonorum*. Any surplus moneys after the debt has been satisfied must be returned to the judgement debtor.

Notes

[1] *Codice di Procedura Civile*, art. 7-50.
[2] Ibid., art. 7-17.
[3] Ibid., art. 18-30.
[4] Ibid., art. 163-322.
[5] The reforms were commenced by L. 26 November 1990, n. 353, and came into force and effect at the end of April and the start of May 1995..
[6] *Cod. Proc. Civ.*, art. 323-408.
[7] Ibid., art. 474-632.
[8] Justinian, Institutes, I.1.3.

8 The Italian Legal Profession

1 Introduction

If one approaches the Italian legal profession from the direction of its counterpart in England and Wales, what one encounters will probably appear very unfamiliar. The lawyer or law student who is acquainted with the structure of the profession in England and Wales is used to the dominant professional division being between barristers and solicitors. The solicitor is the lawyer whom a client approaches to make a will, execute a conveyance of a house or advise in relation to matrimonial difficulties. He is also the lawyer whom one employs to defend one in the magistrates' courts and possibly to bring or defend an action in the County Court. However, to be defended in the Crown Court on a more serious criminal charge, or to be represented in the higher civil courts, a barrister will be instructed. The barrister will receive his instructions through a solicitor, and likewise if specialist advice is required outside of the context of litigation, the services of a barrister may be called upon. The barrister is seen as a specialist or consultant, as well as being a professional advocate. The solicitor is more in the mode of a general practitioner. It is only in the last quarter of a century that solicitors have begun to win the right to appear before the higher courts and to be considered as candidates for judicial office. Although they have acquired such rights, it is still rare for a solicitor to be appointed directly to the High Court bench. High Court judges are still almost exclusively appointed from among the ranks of practising barristers. Judges are usually approaching fifty years of age when appointed; senior judges in the Court of Appeal and the House of Lords are almost invariably in their sixties.

In Italy as in other civil law countries, the situation is markedly different. To begin with, the great professional divide is not between barristers and solicitors, but between practising lawyers and magistrates. Those who choose to practise law by advising clients and appearing for them in court eschew for ever the possibility of a career on the bench. A judicial vocation must be recognized early; all judges must be under forty at the time of their initial appointment. The magistrates form a distinct professional class employed by the State, in effect a branch of the civil service. Practising lawyers are in business on their own account. The magistrates comprise the judicial magistrates who hear and determine cases before the courts, but also include those who work in the *pubblico ministero*, the investigating magistrates who inquire into crimes and initiate and prosecute all criminal proceedings. The practising profession is divided into procurators and advocates, which two occupations are not mutually exclusive. The temptation to equate procurators with solicitors and advocates with barristers should be resisted. Most advocates are also procurators, and most procurators proceed in a short while to become advocates.

Among the class of practising lawyers should also be included the notaries. They have very important functions in civil law systems where they form a distinct professional caste. Although there are notaries public in England and Wales, their role is nowhere as extensive nor their position so important as that of their counterparts in the Italian republic.[1] While most notaries in England and Wales are also practising solicitors, in Italy a notary may not be a procurator or advocate.

Having made these initial points concerning the structure of the Italian legal profession, one can proceed to consider the work of these various branches of it. First, however, it is as well to recognize certain common qualifications for entry into the legal professions. Thus, in all cases, the prospective lawyer must be an Italian citizen, must have attained the age of 21 and be in possession of all civil rights, must have an unblemished character and must not follow a range of other professional activities from journalism to the priesthood. Nor must a prospective notary, magistrate or practitioner belong to any other branch of the legal profession. In all cases, the prospective lawyer must have obtained a law degree from a recognized Italian university.

2 The *Laurea in Giurisprudenza*

To acquire an Italian law degree, the *laurea in giurisprudenza*, a student must study for at least four years at the law faculty of an Italian university. Most students take advantage of the flexible nature of university study in Italy, and take longer than this minimum period to complete their degrees. In Italy, the university year begins in November and continues until May, with short breaks for Christmas and Easter. Examinations are held at the end of the academic year in May and June, with a further sitting of examinations in September. The September examinations are not resits for candidates who failed earlier in the year. Rather students are permitted to defer examination in one or more subjects studied until later in the year if they believe this is in their best interests. Students may even defer examination in a subject studied in one year until a later year of their course.[2]

The system of tuition is also markedly less structured than that given in a British university. Teaching is by means of large lecture classes, which all students reading a course may, but need not, attend. The lecturer will probably be responsible for that course and that course alone. He will usually give three hour-length lectures in that course every week. While he will usually be prepared to see students with problems in the immediate aftermath of his lectures, he will not usually be available to see students at other times. Indeed, he is unlikely to be at the university at other times. Many professors do not reside in the university city in which they hold their chairs. Many are leading practitioners of the law, as university teaching does not preclude practice as an advocate, procurator or notary. There are no tutorial or seminar classes as a rule in Italian law faculties.

To obtain a degree, students must study a total of twenty-seven subjects. The last of these is the preparation of a thesis on a legal subject. The other twenty-six may be divided into compulsory subjects and options. The compulsory subjects are Roman law, Roman Legal History, Italian Legal History, Constitutional law, Administrative law, Criminal law, Criminal Procedure, Civil law, Civil Procedure, Commercial law, Labour law, political economy, public finance and taxation, international law, ecclesiastical law, the philosophy of law and private law. Options are then chosen from lists including subjects such as Canon law, Comparative law, Regional law, and the like. The content of the degree is much less prescriptive in terms of subjects to be studied than it was prior to the reforms of 1970. These reforms were the result of the student unrest which disrupted university life in much of Europe in the spring and summer of 1968. The provision of optional subjects, in particular, is the result of these reforms.

After a student has studied each of these subjects, an examination must be taken in it. The examination is conducted orally by three examiners, although it is not uncommon for only two to be present. Each student is questioned on the subject for ten to fifteen minutes. There is no choice of questions. At the end of the examination, the examiner proposes a mark on a scale from 0 to 30. The pass mark is 18. Marks in the upper 20s are deemed good. An outstanding student may be awarded 30 *e lode*, 30 and praise. A student who is unhappy with the result may choose not to have it recorded, preferring to sit the examination again at a later date in order to improve his performance. This practice is nowadays being discouraged.

Upon graduation, the aspiring lawyer has a choice regarding which branch of the profession to enter. The choice lies between becoming a notary, following the path of qualification that leads from procurator to advocate, or deciding to become a magistrate. All three courses involve further examinations, but the remaining steps are not as extensive as those which face the English law graduate who wishes to become a barrister or a solicitor. Nor can a non-law graduate proceed to take those remaining steps by any other route than acquiring a law degree.

3 Notaries

One choice that is open to the Italian law graduate is to become a notary. If this is his wish, then the law graduate, provided he is over twenty-one but under fifty, has an unblemished character and is eligible for service as a juror, must register with the Notarial Council of a *circondario* and undertake a period of apprenticeship in a notary's office, at the end of which the admission examinations will be taken. In each year, there will only be a certain number of vacancies for notaries, as the profession is controlled by the State through the Ministry of Grace and Justice. Each *circondario* is allocated a fixed number of notaries. The number of successful candidates cannot exceed the vacancies which exist in any given year among that fixed number.

Three of the examinations consist of written papers. These focus on very important aspects of a notary's work, namely, transactions *inter vivos* - such as the transfer of land or a car or a ship, the making of a will and a non-contentious legal process. In addition, the candidate must take three oral examinations: one in civil and commercial law; one in notarial records and organization, and the last in the taxation of notarial transactions. Those who pass the examinations are placed in order of merit, and the highest-placed candidates succeed in obtaining employment. Those who pass but are not successful in gaining a place in the profession are allowed to take the examinations in subsequent years, when for their perseverence they are granted two extra marks in token of their previous merit. The successful candidates are able to commence practice in an assigned locality. upon their taking an oath of office and surrendering a bond to protect against any malpractice on their part. They receive the official seal which is central to their work from the Notarial Council, to whom they give a specimen of their signature.

In practice, the notary is responsible for two basic forms of work. Firstly, he acts as a public official, responsible for authenticating documents which constitute absolute proof that certain transactions have taken place. Thus, the transfer of immoveable property in the Italian republic must be executed by means of a notarially authenticated deed. Such a deed is the only permissible evidence that the transfer has taken place and is conclusive evidence of the fact. A notary authenticates the transfer by drawing up a deed according to a standard from, which deed he authenticates by sealing it with the official seal consigned to his custody and witnessing the sealing with his signature. Thereafter, the transfer can only be challenged by *querela di falso*, the action which claims that the deed is a forgery. If the deed is accepted as genuine, then nothing that it authenticates is open to query.

The notary also authenticates in this manner other transactions concerning immoveables, for instance documents witnessing the granting of immoveable property as security for a loan - a hypothec, or documents bearing conclusive witness to the granting of interests over land such as rights of way. Standard forms are again used for these purposes. Notarial authentication is also required for the transfer of what Italian law terms registrable moveables, namely, cars, boats and planes.

4 Legal Practitioners : Advocates and Procurators[3]

Another choice which is open to the Italian law graduate who wishes to pursue a legal career is to enter legal practice as a practising procurator and/or advocate. Unlike certain civil law countries, such as Spain, it is possible to practise in Italy both as a procurator and as an advocate; indeed, becoming a procurator is for most practitioners but a step on the road to eventual qualification as an advocate as well. The normal progression in this branch of the legal profession is to qualify first as a procurator and then to proceed in a few years to qualify as an advocate.

To embark upon this career progression, a law degree from an Italian university is an essential qualification. The graduate must also be an Italian citizen, have an unblemished civic record and be resident in the judicial district within which he or she wishes to practise. These branches of the profession are not open to men of commerce, ministers of any religion, professional journalists nor employees in the public sector, excepting university professors and schoolteachers. Notaries and magistrates are also barred from this kind of legal practice.

The aspiring legal practitiioner must first of all join the law office, the *studio legale,* of a qualified procurator, where he becomes what is called a *praticanto.* He will usually remain such for a period of at least two years and possibly longer until he is ready to take the examinations for admission to the profession of *procuratore.* During his second and any subsequent years as a *praticanto,* he will however be allowed to appear before the *pretura* of the *mandamento* where he is training. At this stage, he is known as a *praticanto abilitato.*

The examinations for admission to the profession of *procuratore* consist of written papers on civil, criminal and administrative procedure. If successful, the entrant takes an oath swearing loyalty, honour and diligence in the performance of his duties and his name is entered in the register of procurators kept by the guild, the *ordine dei avvocati e procuratori,* of the *circondario* in which he is resident and within which he is now permitted to practise his chosen profession. A procurator is limited to practising within the *circondario* of the *Tribunale* where he is registered.

A procurator is only allowed to transact certain kinds of legal business. In essence, he is allowed to perform certain functions or tasks in place of his client, but not to interpose his judgement for that of the client. Thus, if the client has to make an appearance in court, the procurator can register that appearance on his behalf. If authorized by the client so to do, he may sign a document in the client's place. He is not however allowed to substitute his idea of what is in the client's best interests for that of the client, nor to exercize any discretion on the client's behalf. He cannot argue a case in court for his client nor decide tactics with regard to the conduct of litigation in which the client is involved. All such functions which involve the exercize of a professional judgement on the client's behalf are the preserve of the advocate and are barred to the mere procurator.

Mere procurator is literally what is meant, for the vast majority of procurators are also qualified as advocates, making the technical distinction set out above somewhat unimportant in practice other than for the young legal practitioner who is making his way from qualification as a procurator along the road to 'full' qualification as an advocate. A procurator may become an advocate either through practice as a procurator for a period of six years, or by taking further examinations in civil, criminal and administrative procedure after a minimum of two years practice. Upon qualification as an advocate, the entrant again has his name entered in the register, *albo*, that is the white book, of the *ordine* in his local *circondario* but this time as an advocate as well as as a procurator. As an advocate, he will now be allowed to perform advisory functions on behalf of his client, exercizing discretion and interposing his professional judgement for the client. He will be allowed to develop his client's case tactically and develop arguments in favour of his client as he thinks best before the courts. The courts before which he is now allowed to appear extend beyond the *circondario* of the *Tribunale* where he is registered. He is now allowed to practise before any court, up to and including the level of the appeal courts, the *corti d'appello* and the *corti d'assise d'appello*, throughout the national territory. His territorial competence is therefore greatly enhanced.

There are however still limits upon his functional competence. He is not allowed to appear before the chief courts of the State, that is *cassazione*, the *Consiglio di Stato*, the Court of Accounts, and the Constitutional Court. To be qualified to appear before these courts, a further career progression is required, which will accord the advocate the status of an *avvocato cassazionisto*. This step may be taken either upon the completion of eight year's practice as an advocate or following a minimum of one year's practice, in which case examinations relating to the work of the courts in question must be passed.

Praticanti, procuratori, avvocati, and *avvocati cassazionisti* are readily identifiable in court by their garb. When appearing in court, a practitioner will always address the court wearing the *toga*, a black gown. The gown of the *praticanto* is unadorned by any tassles, while that of the *procuratore* has a black tassle, that of the *avvocato* a silver tassle and that of the *avvocato cassazionisto* a gold tassle. Gowns with gold tassles are by far the commonest seen in Italian courts. They are also worn by magistrates, of both judicial and prosecuting varieties.

Studii legali are businesses as well as the offices of legal professionals. Fees are charged in accordance with minima set by law for specific tasks. Italian law firms are generally much smaller and more local in character than their counterparts in England and Wales.

5 The Magistracy[4]

A choice which seems remarkable to those who approach the Italian legal profession from the standpoint of that in England and Wales is that of becoming a magistrate. Professional judges in England and Wales are almost always in middle age. The idea of a newly-qualified law graduate choosing to become a judge seems presumptuous in the extreme.

Yet that choice is there for the Italian law graduate. Italy has a career magistracy, so that to become a magistrate, that must be one's choice of career. Such a choice rules out working as a notary, procurator or advocate, and it must be made relatively quickly, for to be accepted into the magistracy one must be under forty years of age. The other requirements are that one must be over twenty-one, in good health, have no black marks against one's character - such as a criminal conviction or a bankruptcy, have an Italian law degree and have passed the State examinations for admission to the magistracy.

The examinations for admission as a magistrate are regarded as the most difficult of all those set for aspiring public servants. Each year, the *Consiglio Superiore della Magistratura* informs the Ministry of Grace and Justice of the number of vacancies that will need to be filled in the ranks of the magistrates. This number will determine how many candidates will be successful in that year's examinations. The candidates will sit written examinations in Roman law, civil law, criminal law and administrative law, as well as taking oral examinations in those subjects and constitutional law, international law, ecclesiastical law, civil and criminal procedure, labour law, social welfare law and statistics. Preparation for these examinations is now provided in some Italian university law faculties. Those who are successful in these examinations are appointed *uditori giudiziari*, and are allocated to a *distretto*, that is the area of territorial competence of a *corte d'appello*. There, they serve an apprenticeship of roughly six months before actually starting to try cases at the level of a *pretura*. They remain as *uditori* for two years.

At the end of this two-year period, the *uditore* is eligible for promotion to the status and salary of a judge of *Tribunale*. The young *uditore* will be granted this promotion for the asking provided that there is no reason for refusing it. This means that the promotion is in effect automatic; it is not dependent upon merit nor is it attained in competition. Rather, to fail to achieve promotion is dependent upon demerit, the existence of proven incompetence or the presence of some negative factor with regard to the candidate. Moreover, this approach to magisterial promotion is the one adopted in relation to progress from each rank of the profession to the next. Thus, after eleven years as a magistrate of the standing of a judge of *Tribunale*, promotion again follows automatically subject to the absence of negative factors, this time leading to the acquisition of the status and salary of a judge of the *corte d'appello*.

It should be emphasized at this point that promotion to the status of a judge of *Tribunale* or to the status of a judge of the *corte d'appello* does not mean that the magistrate actually serves as a judge in either of those courts. He is qualified to do so and may, if he wishes, be considered for a post at that level, but he is by no means obliged to do so. Thus, a particular magistrate may be quite content to stay deciding cases at his local *pretura* or *Tribunale*. He may have no desire to disturb his or his family's life with a move to the city in which the local *corte d'appello* is situate nor wish to commute to that place on a regular basis. Instead, he may choose to stay where he is, but he will still enjoy the fruits of his promotion. He will have the status of an appeal court judge, and the salary.

Having noted this important distinction between rank and function, one can follow the magistrate's judicial career even higher. After seven years at the status of a judge of *appello*, promotion, subject to demerits, follows automatically to the status of a judge of *Cassazione*, without again any suggestion that the magistrate in question need move to Rome and sit in that court. After eight years at that level, a further automatic promotion follows, this time to the highest echelon, namely that of a judge who is qualified to be an office superior, that is one who is in charge of a particular court - *pretura*, *Tribunale*, *corte d'appello* or even *Cassazione*. Again, this promotion does not entail that the judge in question will actually function at that level, but he is qualified to do so and will be accorded the status and salary appropriate to such seniority. There are in all some eight thousand magistrates in Italy and, given a retiring age of seventy, hundreds have the status of office superior while a couple of thousand enjoy the status of judges of *Cassazione*.

The magistracy, however, is not composed solely of the judicial magistrates, that is those who sit and decide cases in the courts. There are also investigating magistrates, known as the *pubblico ministero*. At every court at every level, there is an office of the *pubblico ministero*. At the level of the *preture* and the *tribunali*, the offices of the *pubblico ministero* are known as the *procure della repubblica*, while at the level of the *corte d'appello* and *Cassazione*, they are known as the *procure generali della repubblica*. The magistrates who work in these offices are responsible for the investigation and prosecution of crimes in Italy. The manner in which they perform this task will be examined closely in the next chapter on criminal justice, but their existence must be noted now. They qualify in the same manner as their judicial brethren, and their promotion and career progress occurs in exactly the same way. Theoretically, it is perfectly possible for a magistrate to move from judicial duties to the *pubblico ministero* or vice versa, indeed to move regularly between them, during his career. In reality, it is unusual for a magistrate, once he has settled to either judicial or investigative work, to change functions and move to the other branch of the magistracy. The *pubblico ministero* has some functions also in civil litigation.[5]

Since 1946, the *pubblico ministero* has worked under the supervision, rather than the direction, of the Ministry of Grace and Justice. This has meant that the *pubblico ministero* has come to enjoy much the same independence from executive intervention as the judicial magistracy. Whereas previously, the *pubblico ministero* had been thought of as a virtually separate body from the judicial magistracy with a distinct hierarchical structure, today it is more generally regarded as being at every level a department of the magistracy generally. Thus, in the past, the *pretori*, who performed both judicial and investigative functions at the level of the *mandamenti* were regarded as being answerable in their investigative role to the *procure della repubblica* at the *Tribunale* of the *circondario* in which their *mandamenti* were situated. Similarly, the *procure della repubblica* at the *tribunali* were treated as accountable to the *procure generali della repubblica* at the *corte d'appello* of the *distretto* in which they were to be found, while the *procure generali* of each *distretto* were thought answerable to the *procure generali della repubblica* of the court of *Cassazione*. This has now changed. Today, the *pubblico ministero* at each level is regarded as answerable not to those who have the same functions at the next highest tier, but rather to the office superior of the court at which they work. Thus, at each level and in each territorial court at that level, the *pubblico ministero* is answerable to that court's office superior in the same manner as are his judicial brethren. This has greatly increased the independence of the *pubblico ministero* from executive interference.

Office superiors are responsible for running the court of which they are head. Thus, they are in charge of drawing up the lists of cases to be heard at their court, allocating such hearings among the judges who work at that court and supervising the work of the *pubblico ministero* attached to that court. The office superiors are the presidents of the court of *Cassazione*, the various *corti d'appello* and *tribunali*, and the *pretore* in each *pretura*, together with the procurator general at *Cassazione* and each *corte d'appello* and the procurator of each *Tribunale*, these latter being the office superiors of the *pubblico ministero* at each court.

Within each *distretto*, there is a judicial committee. This committee is composed of the President of the *corte d'appello* and the Procurator General of the *distretto*, together with eight elected representatives of the magistrates serving in that area. The committee is responsible for supervising the development of probationary magistrates within its territory and for the submission of reports regarding the suitability of magistrates within the *distretto* for promotion. The appointment of office superiors, however, is not made by the judicial committees but is reserved to the *Consiglio Superiore della Magistratura*.

The *Consiglio Superiore della Magistratura* is a national body set up under the provisions of the Italian Constitution of 1948, but which was not actually brought into existence until 1958. It is composed of the President of the Republic, the President of *Cassazione* and the Procurator General of that court, together with thirty other members, twenty of whom are magistrates, elected from among their own ranks to serve on the *Consiglio Superiore*, while the remaining ten are either advocates of at least fifteen years practising experience or full university law professors, *cattedrattici*, all of whom are elected by a joint session of the two houses of the legislature. The President of Italy is *ex officio* president of the *Consiglio Superiore*, but the chair is usually taken by the vice-president of the *Consiglio* who is elected by the members. The fact that the *Consiglio Superiore* has complete charge of the appointment of magistrates, their discipline and administration, ensures the independence of the magistracy from outside pressures. The *Consiglio Superiore della Magistratura* is a bulwark of the doctrine of the separation of powers in Italy.

This goes some way to explaining the extraordinary events which have taken place in Italy during the 1990s. Few can be unaware that investigating magistrates in both the south and the north of Italy have become the new heroes of the republic. In the south, particularly in Sicily, investigating magistrates have led the onslaught against the mafia. The names of the two murdered magistrates, Giovanni Falcone and Paolo Borsellino, are already the stuff of popular legend, their killing at the hands of the mafia being seen as martyrdom in the cause of cleansing the republic from the evils of organized crime. In the north, political corruption has been the focus of magisterial attack. The Milanese magistrate, Antonio Di Pietro, likewise became a folk hero as he strove to reverse the reputation of the commercial capital as *tangentopoli*, 'bribe city', with his *mani pulite*, 'clean hands', inquiry removing from the scene ever increasing numbers of politicians and businessmen.

That employees of the State, for magistrates are in the last analysis a type of civil servant, are able to attack leading figures in the world of government and commerce is remarkable. In effect, the magistracy has undermined the political establishment of the first Italian republic. To do this, they have required immunity from interference from both the executive and the legislature, the two most powerful institutions in the State, but in doing so have demonstrated that the magistracy also is a State power to be reckoned with. This immunity is almost entirely due to the development of the structures discussed above in the years since the end of the Second World War.

In the immediate aftermath of the War, although the monarchical constitution gave way to that of the republic and the principle of the separation of powers was enshrined in the 1948 constitution, progress in achieving an independent magistracy was slow. Many of the magistrates who held office in the decade after the War had been appointed under fascism and were slow to embrace the philosophy of the new order. Thus, it was not until 1956 that the Constitutional Court was actually set up. When it was, the older generation of magistrates were loth to forward cases to this new court for adjudication of the constitutionality of certain laws. The younger magistrates were however not so timid, and it was from amongst their ranks that the bulk of cases went to the Constitutional Court in the early days of that institution. Critical resistance to their activities from their seniors and the Ministry of Grace and Justice meant that their promotion prospects looked decidedly bleak if they were dependent upon the favour of their superiors and the government. Hence, pressure was brought to bear to ensure that the *Consiglio Superiore della Magistratura*, required to be set up under the Constitution, was actually established. The *Consiglio Superiore* was brought into being in 1958.

While the *Consiglio Superiore* guaranteed the independence of the magistracy from interference by politicians, it still left the younger magistrates at the mercy of their senior colleagues. A movement therefore began to introduce the system of automatic promotion according to seniority rather than competitive promotion according to merit, it being strongly argued that only if magistrates could exercise their responsibilities without fear or favour regarding their career prospects could they really be expected to fulfil their judicial and investigative functions without bias or undue influence. As the number of pre-republican magistrates decreased through retirement and death, this argument won through, and in 1966 it was accepted that promotion from the status of a judge of *Tribunale* to the status of a judge of the *corte d'appello* should follow upon eleven years service, while in 1973 promotion from the status of a judge of *appello* to that of *Cassazione* was rendered automatic upon seven years service. The independence of the magistracy was won.

An independent magistracy, however, is also a powerful magistracy. Freedom from interference has meant that magistrates, particularly investigating magistrates, could feel free to pursue their own ideals of justice through the exercize of their magisterial office. The spectre of left-wing magistrates investigating the deals of right-wing politicians and of right-wing magistrates inquiring into the affairs of trade unionists and socialists has often been realized. Thus it is that a magistrate like Antonio Di Pietro can single-mindedly pursue some of the leading political and financial figures of the day, without having to worry that his activities will in any way damage his career, his salary or his status. Only the unsubtle weapons of the bullet and the bomb can be used to get at the magistrates of the Italian republic, and it is to these devices of terror that the Mafia and the Camorra have resorted to intimidate and eliminate their opponents in Sicily and the South.[6]

Notes

[1] See C.W. Brooks, R.H.Helmholz and P.G.Stein, *Notaries Public in England since the Reformation* (London, 1991) for an account of the history of notaries public in this country.

[2] Some Italian universities have however recently converted to a system of two annual semesters, the first of which commences in September and has examinations at its end in January.

[3] R.D.L. 27 November 1933, n. 1578; L. 22 January 1934, n. 36; R.D. 22 January 1934, n. 37; D.M. 5 October 1994, n. 585.

[4] *Costituzione*, art. 101-110.

[5] See, for instance, chapter 11 for the *pubblico ministero*'s role in relation to the marriage of minors and adoptions.

[6] See also the author's "Seeds of Revolution", (1994) 144 *New Law Journal* 431.

9 Criminal Justice

1 The Concept of a Crime

The Italian Constitution, as has been seen, guarantees certain fundamental rights, such as the right to life, the right to physical integrity, the right to own and enjoy property, the right to enjoy family life, to work, and so on. Each one of these constitutional rights has as its object something which is to be protected, namely life, physical integrity, property, family relationship, livelihood, which can for want of a better term be called a good, a benefit or an asset. In Italian, the phrase used in the legal doctrine for these things is *bene giuridico*. If the State is serious about protecting such rights, it is not enough that it ensures, through the mechanism of the Constitutional Court, that the legislature and other State or public organs do not interfere with them, but also that they are not interfered with by other legal subjects. In other words, it is not enough that through the Constitutional Court, the legislature is prevented from interfering with life or liberty, it is also necessary to ensure that other individuals do not infringe upon these basic rights. This is the role of the criminal law.

The criminal law is classified as part of the public law of the State, even though its primary concern is with wrongs, interferences with rights, committed by private individuals against one another. It is classed as part of public law because the right interfered with is one which the State has guaranteed and for which, as a result, only the State can bring a prosecution. Although the victim of such an infringement can proceed in the civil courts for breach of an obligation owed him by the wrongdoer, such proceedings are aimed at ascertaining that a just compensation is due; they are not intended to lead to the punishment of the wrongdoer, and, as has been seen, even if just compensation is due, further proceedings are necessary if the wrongdoer proves reluctant to pay the compensation. Only the State is permitted to proceed against a wrongdoer in order to have him punished. The reason for this is not difficult to understand. Punishment, as opposed to the provision of a just compensation, inevitably entails an interference with certain of the rights of the person being punished, rights which the State has undertaken to protect: imprisonment entails an interference with liberty; a fine an interference with the right to enjoy one's own property. These rights are as fundamental to the wrongdoer as to the victim.

The criminal law is therefore concerned with defining the situations in which it is justifiable for the State to interfere with such rights in order to punish a wrongdoer. The Penal Code, as its name suggests, is about punishment. It sets out when and to what extent the State is justified in depriving a person of legal assets - life, liberty, property, work, social or family position - even though generally it is bound to protect such rights for its citizens and indeed for others within its territory who owe the State local allegiance. The basis of this approach is again the civilian concept of justice as defined by the Roman jurist Ulpian in the third century A.D. Justice is the constant and perpetual wish to render unto each his due. The criminal law defines in what circumstances the protection normally afforded a citizen may be withdrawn, and to what extent, or, in other words, when and to what extent punishment rather than protection is due to a person.

The way that crimes are defined in the Penal Code exemplifies this approach. Article 575 dealing with homicide is a good example:

Chiunque cagiona la morte di un uomo è punito con la *reclusione* non inferiore ad anni ventuno.

Whoever causes the death of a person shall be punished with not less than twenty-one years imprisonment.

The provision sets out the circumstances in and the extent to which the State will withdraw its protection of an individual's liberty. Indeed, it sets out the circumstances in which the State is obligated to withdraw such protection and substitute punishment therefor out of its duty to protect and uphold the rights of the victim. In that the victim's right to life as protected by the State has not been respected by the wrongdoer, the State is justified in withdrawing its protection from the wrongdoer.

Viewed from this angle, one can quickly appreciate why it is that in civil law systems generally, it is held that the State can only punish in those circumstances and to the extent which the penal laws allow. It is not open to the State, through its judicial organs, to hold that an act amounts to a crime after an individual has committed it, or to attempt to deprive an individual of his liberty or property as a punishment for conduct which was not defined as having penal consequences when the act in question was done. To do so would be to interfere unjustifiably with the rights of the person concerned. Thus, the State is only allowed to punish those acts which were defined as having penal consequences in legislation and only when they were so defined as having such consequences at the time when the acts in question occurred.

A crime therefore is an interference with the legally protected right of a citizen or person owing allegiance to the State which requires that the State punish the perpetrator. This means that it is the duty of the State to discover when crimes have been committed, to ascertain who committed them and to punish the criminal. This perspective is very important to an understanding of the manner in which the criminal justice system operates in civil law jurisdictions. It also entails that the State should have in place mechanisms with which to perform these tasks, that is the personnel to discover when crimes are committed, to search out and identify the criminal and to establish that punishment is indeed due to the person in question and that it is administered. It also follows that it would not be proper to allow private individuals the right to prosecute criminals, in that it is the obligation of the State to do so and only the State has the legal right to deprive a person of the rights it has given or guaranteed.

The circumstances which demand that the State punish an individual are the circumstances which constitute a crime. As has been said, this involves the interference with some right which it is the duty of the State to protect. This right may be a right of the State itself or one which it guarantees those who owe it allegiance. For a crime to have been committed, that is for the State to have the right to punish the perpetrator, it is necessary that a legal asset, a *bene giuridico*, has been harmed as the result of the activity of a particular individual and that that individual is responsible for the acts the outcome of which is the harm suffered. Moreover, some would argue that it is also necessary that the individual's acts should not have been justifiable in any way.

Italian law approaches this concept of a crime in two related ways. Firstly, it identifies the elements which a crime must necessarily entail according to the grammatical and logical examination of statements about crimes. This is called the synthetic approach, involving as it does the synthesis or bringing together of certain elements. It also adopts an analytic approach, which breaks down the composite elements of the crime in a manner which will allow a judgement to be made as to whether a crime has actually been committed. The synthetic approach establishes that a particular event in the abstract contains the ingredients which allow that event to qualify as a crime, that is which merit the State punishing it as such. The analytic approach on the other hand establishes that a particular event, a concrete case, conforms with the requirements of the law relating to a particular crime so that a particular individual can be punished for it. An example should make this clearer.

According to what has been said above, for the State to be justified in visiting a punishment upon an individual, that individual must have harmed a right or asset, a *bene giuridico*, which the State has guaranteed will be protected. The harm to the *bene giuridico* is termed the *danno penale*, the penal harm, the harm meriting punishment. That harm in turn must be the outcome of conduct committed by the supposed wrongdoer, which conduct caused that harmful outcome. The outcome is called the *evento giuridico*, a phrase which is best not translated as legal event but rather given its literal meaning - *evenire*, to come out; *eventum*, something which has come out, an outcome. In the case of homicide, the *bene giuridico* which the State has deemed worthy of protection is life. If a citizen has been killed, that asset has been harmed, his being killed is the *danno penale*. If his being killed was the outcome, the *evento giuridico* of conduct committed by another which caused that outcome, then that other may be guilty of a crime. For that conduct to be a crime, however, it is necessary that there be an asset which the law protects, the *bene giuridico*, in this case life; that it should have suffered a harm, a *danno penale*; that that harm should have been the outcome, the *evento giuridico*, of conduct which caused that outcome. The person whose conduct is called in question is called the active subject of the crime; the person whose asset was harmed is called the passive subject of the crime, the *persona offesa dal reato*.. This corresponds to how the crime might be described in two sentences according to whether one is concerned with the perpetrator, the active subject, or the victim, the passive subject.

A killed B. B was killed by A.

If all these elements are in place, then the transaction is capable of being classified as a crime. It has been established that homicide contains all the necessary ingredients for it to be a crime in law.

This leads to the question of whether A's killing B did in fact amount to a crime. So far, it has only been established that it could amount to a crime. The analytic approach sets out do determine whether A's killing B not only could amount to a crime, but whether it did amount to a crime.

There are two schools of thought about the elements which must be established to prove that A's killing B was actually a crime. One school, which can be called the bipartite school, holds that there are only objective and subjective elements. The tripartite school, however, holds that there is another element in addition to these two, namely the unjustifiability of the harm, its *antigiuridicità*. All of these elements must be proved to establish that A's killing B was a crime and therefore merits punishment.

The objective element is a combination of the three factors already mentioned, namely A's conduct, its outcome for B and the causal connection between the two. For instance, if A fired a gun which was pointed at B, this is the conduct in question; B's being wounded and dying of the wound is the outcome, and the fact that it was a bullet fired from A's gun which wounded B and led to his death supplies the causal link. There is still however the subjective element to be considered. The subjective element concerns whether there is any blame attached to A for the outcome, or whether the outcome can be said to be A's fault. According to Italian law, for the outcome to be A's fault, he must have either intended the outcome or performed the conduct with so little care that the outcome had to be attributed to his lack of care. If he intended the outcome, he is said to have acted with *dolo*; if he was negligent, with *colpa*. If he was aware of the risk that his conduct might produce the outcome but continued in it although not intending to produce that outcome, such *colpa grave*, grave negligence, is accounted equivalent to *dolo*, in the same manner that recklessness is treated as equivalent to intention in English law. In the absence of any fault, A will not usually be treated as guilty of a serious crime in Italian law, although strict liability is visited upon those who commit lesser crimes. Premeditation is not necessary to show intention, although it can be an aggravating factor, and Italian law also recognizes what is termed *preterintenzione*, which is a form of constructive intention whereby a person who intends to produce one outcome is deemed to have intended a worse outcome even if he cannot be proved to have realized the risk of that worse outcome. Thus, for instance, a person who intentionally commits a serious assault upon another of which that other dies is deemed to have committed *omicidio preterintenzionale*. It is also possible for a deliberately committed criminal act to lead to outcomes which aggravate the original wrong, *delitti aggravati dall'evento*. Thus, for instance, a person who performs an illegal abortion as a result of which the mother dies is guilty of an aggravated offence by reason of the outcome which he in no way intended or which was perhaps in no way attributable to his fault or lack of care.

Thus far, the objective and subjective elements of crimes in Italian law will appear familiar to the English lawyer, being reminiscent of the distinction between the *actus reus* and *mens rea* of English criminal law. However, according to the tripartite approach to the analysis of criminal liability, a third factor is necessary, namely the lack of justification for the conduct or outcome, the *antigiuridicità*. Thus, suppose that A has indeed killed B; that A pointed a gun at B, pulled the trigger and a bullet from the gun mortally wounded B. Suppose that when he pointed the gun at B and pulled the trigger, A fully intended that the outcome should be B's death. Is this of itself a crime? The supporters of the tripartite theory would answer not, in so far as it must also be established that A had no just cause for his conduct and intention to produce the outcome. If for instance A was a public executioner, carrying out a lawful sentence of death, his otherwise manifestly unlawful killing of B would be lawful and therefore no crime. The upholders of the bipartite view, on the other hand, would reply that the question of whether A has a lawful cause for his conduct goes to the question of whether any blame or fault attaches to him for his conduct. Lawful excuse for them negates fault, they treating the subjective element as consisting not just of intentional conduct but of blameworthy conduct, where the intention must be wrongful to be blameworthy. The adherents to the tripartite view on the other hand would argue that in so far as the criminal law exists to protect and to punish harms to legal assets, *beni giuridici*, if the law has already removed its protection from an individual in relation to a particular legal asset, as for instance with regard to the life of a condemned man, then for that reason visiting a harm upon that asset by his lawful execution is not a crime.

2 Classification of Crimes

While virtually all serious crimes have a subjective element, lesser crimes do not necessarily require fault in order for them to be punishable. Italian law distinguishes between two sorts of crimes, called respectively delicts and contraventions, *delitti* and *contravenzioni*. The Penal Code is divided into three books, the First Book containing the general rules relating to criminal responsibilty while the second and third deal with delicts and contraventions in turn.

The distinction between delicts and contraventions in many ways harks back to one developed by the canon lawyers of the mediaeval period, who in dealing with wrongs, *mala*, distinguished between those wrongs which outlawed conduct which was wrong in itself as a breach of the moral or natural law and which human law recognized as wrongs, *mala in se*, and those wrongs which outlawed conduct which was by no means wrong in itself but only became wrong by virtue of the fact that a particular legal system criminalized the conduct, *mala prohibita*. Thus, for instance, killing was regarded as being wrong in itself, every legal system recognizing this and making it a crime, while parking on a double yellow line, for instance, is a morally neutral act until a particular legal system declares that parking on such lines is an offence and indeed such lines only exist to indicate where people are not allowed to park their vehicles.

One consequence of this distinction is that *mala prohibita* have no moral content other than that which attaches to breaking a rule which the law has imposed. It is therefore not necessary for intention or fault to be proved in relation to such wrongs. Thus, parking on a double yellow line is wrong whether one intends to or not, although it can probably be said that one ought to take care not to do so and to park on such lines probably indicates a lack of diligence on the part of the wrongdoer.

Likewise, it is not criminal to attempt to commit a contravention as opposed to a delict. If one attempts to park on a double yellow line and fails - a most unlikely scenario in any event - no crime has been committed.

The second book of the Penal Code divides delicts into thirteen categories according to the legal asset that is harmed or put at risk,[1] while the third book divides contraventions into two broad categories.[2] Within each of these categories, the individual delicts and contraventions are defined in the articles thereof, and at the end of each definition there is set out a procedural note stating what powers of arrest exist in relation to each crime, what precautionary measures are available against an accused person, the court in which the crime is to be prosecuted at first instance and whether the crime is to be prosecuted *ex officio* by the magistracy or whether upon a complaint, *querela,* from the victim or other person prejudiced by the wrong.

3 The Criminal Courts

Just as there is a special court to deal with disputes relating to the Constitution and the ordinary civil courts deal with disputes relating to the Civil Code, so as there is a special Penal Code there is a set of courts with jurisdiction to administer the law contained therein. These courts are the criminal courts of the Italian republic and their workings are governed by the Code of Criminal Procedure, the current version of which was promulgated in 1988 and came into force and effect in October 1989.

These courts have in common the fact that they have authority to administer the criminal law; that is their jurisdiction. Within the criminal jurisdiction, the competence of the various courts is determined as with the civil courts according to three factors: territory, subject-matter and function. For the purposes of criminal justice, the republic is again divided into the same *distretti*, Court of Appeal districts, as was the case with civil justice, but for the purposes of criminal justice these *distretti* are divided into *circoli* as well as into the *circondarii* which are the territorial divisions within which the *Tribunali* have their respective competence. The *circoli* are territorial divisions which are served by courts having an exclusively criminal jurisdiction. These are the *corte d'assise* and the *corte d'assise d'appello*. The *circondarii* are then again divided, as for civil justice matters, into *mandamenti*, the areas of territorial competence of the *pretore*, which are the only other courts having general criminal jurisdiction in Italy.

As well as territorial competence, attention must be paid to subject-matter competence in selecting the appropriate court of first instance. The trial will usually be held in the court of the territory in which the crime was committed. However, according to the gravity or nature of the crime, its prosecution will take place in either the *pretura*, the *corte d'assise* or the *Tribunale*. The more serious sorts of crime are dealt with by the *corte d'assise* of each *circolo*. These are courts staffed by judicial magistrates, but which make use of the services of lay judges as well. These lay judges are ordinary citizens of at least a basic secondary education between the ages of thirty and sixty-five, and who do not have any blemish on their civic record. In a trial at first instance, the bench, or the *giuria* as it is called somewhat confusingly for the English lawyer, consists of eight judges, two of whom are judicial magistrates and the remaining six of whom are lay judges. The court is always presided over by a judicial magistrate of the status of a judge of the *corte d'appello*, while the remaining judicial magistrate is of the status of a judge of the *Tribunale*. In their deliberations, however, no distinction is drawn between the lay and professional judges as far as deciding issues of law and fact are concerned. It is not the case that issues of law are left for the judicial magistrates or that questions of fact are reserved for the lay judges. Both types of judge consider both types of issue. It is always however one of the judicial magistrates who draws up the judgement of the court which must, in accordance with the Constitution, be reasoned, *motivato*. The participation of the lay judges is another striking example of the manner in which the ordinary citizen is involved in the government, this time the judicial administration, of the State.

Lesser crimes are dealt with by the *pretura*. Unlike the *corte d'assise*, the *pretura* is a monocratic court in which the *pretore* sits as the sole judge, as indeed he does in civil cases. The *pretura* deals with contraventions and certain delicts committed within the *mandamento* which it serves. This leaves only the competence of the *Tribunale* to be discussed. This court has a residual competence over crimes which are neither allocated to the *pretura* nor to the *corte d'assise*. These crimes are those which involve difficult issues of financial accounting, such as fraud, or cases which involve complaints of defamation against the press. They are cases in which it is thought unwise because of the sensitivity or complicated nature of the charges, to submit the issues to lay judges, but are too serious to be left in the hands of the *pretura*. Kidnapping and organized crime cases are also referred to the *Tribunale*. The *Tribunale*, as when sitting on civil matters, is a collegiate court of three judges, all of the status of judges of *Tribunale*, the president being of the status of a judge of the *corte d'appello*.

All of these courts have first instance competence in relation to their respective subject-matters in each of their respective territories. This leaves the question of the functional competence of these and other criminal courts. As well as first instance courts, there are those of appeal and review. As with civil matters, generally an appeal on the merits is allowed to a court of second instance before a review on issues of law to *Cassazione* takes place. From the *pretura*, when an appeal is permitted by law, the appeal lies to the *Tribunale* of the *circondario* within which the *mandamento* served by the *pretura* is situated. If the case was originally heard in the *Tribunale*, an appeal lies to the *corte d'appello* of the *distretto* in which the *Tribunale* is situated. Both the *Tribunale* and the *corte d'appello* are constituted for criminal appeals in the same way as they are staffed for civil appeals, all having three judicial magistrates, in the *Tribunale* a president of *corte d'appello* status and two judges of *Tribunale* status, while the *corte d'appello* is staffed by a president of the status of a judge of *Cassazione* and his two judicial brethren are of appeal court status.

Appeals from the *corte d'assise* however go to a special criminal court called the *corte d'assise d'appello*, one of which sits in every *circolo* served by a *corte d'assise*. This court is like the *corte d'assise* served by two judicial magistrates, the president who must be of the status of a judge of *Cassazione* and another professional judge of the status of a judge of appeal. To hear appeals from the *corte d'assise*, they are joined on the bench by six lay judges, each of whom must be qualified in the same manner as those who sit on the *giuria* in the *corte d'assise*, but who must this time have had a full and not just a basic secondary education. All of these appeal courts deal with appeals on the merits against decisions made at first instance, whether the appeal concerns issues of law or fact.

After any appeal has taken place, it is possible for any question of law which is still in dispute to be referred for review to the Supreme Court of *Cassazione* in Rome, the only court which has competence in criminal matters throughout the whole of the national territory. All the judges are of the status of that court, the presiding judge being of the status of an office superior. The bench consists of a minimum of five judges and in difficult cases or cases of considerable importance the bench can be increased to a full court of nine. As in civil matters, *Cassazione* deals solely with the point of law that has been raised. If it agrees with the decision of the court from which the request for review has come, it confirms that decision and the matter is at an end. If it disagrees with the lower court's ruling, it quashes its decision or that part of its decision with which it disagrees and remits the case if necessary to the court from which the appeal came to be determined in accordance with the ruling of *Cassazione* on the issue.

4 The Civilian Model of Criminal Procedure

If a crime is an interference with the State protected right of an individual and the State has determined that only it shall have the right to deprive the wrongdoer of some or all of his rights as a just punishment, because his rights are also guaranteed by the State and therefore only the State should have the right to interfere with such rights, it follows that it is for the State to discover when rights it protects are interfered with, to investigate the breach to discover who perpetrated the wrong, to establish that the perpetrator is responsible in such a way that he ought to be punished, and to punish him. From this, the basis of the traditional model of criminal procedure in civil law countries should be apparent. The State has an interest in discovering when crimes have been committed; the State has an interest in discovering the identity of criminals, establishing their responsibility and having them punished.

If the State has an interest in discovering when crimes are committed, it follows that the State needs to have some mechanism by which it can discover that crimes have taken place. The obvious method is for the State authorities to receive complaints from those who have suffered or to receive information from those who are aware that some wrong has been done. There is however always the danger that the victim, because he is injured or afraid, will not be able to inform the State authorities or will be coerced from doing so. It may even be the case that the power of the wrongdoer is such that persons other than the victim will be in fear of bringing the delict to the attention of the authorities. In a country which has suffered much as a result of organized crime, and where the code of silence of organizations such as the mafia is well-known and well understood, there might well be difficulty in relying exclusively on complaints and informations. Accordingly, the State authorities, acting to ensure that no right guaranteed by the State is breached by anyone with impunity, have a duty to investigate any crime of which they have knowledge regardless of whether a formal complaint or information has been laid. When the police become aware by any means - complaint, information, notoriety or suspicion - that a crime has been committed, they must look into the situation, and if they believe that the allegation or suspicion is well-founded, they must formally notify the investigating authorities, the *pubblico ministero*, by serving on the magistrate a *notitia criminis*, formal notice of a crime having been committed. It is then the duty of the magistrate to investigate the circumstances to establish whether there has indeed been a breach of the criminal law and, if possible, who is responsible for the breach.

The *pubblico ministero* has this duty as a magistrate, that is a public official, trained in the same manner as the judiciary, but with the duty of impartially discovering the truth about whether there has been a breach of the criminal law. Again, it is a State official who has this role, emphasizing that it is the State which has the main interest in seeing that wrongs are punished as opposed to victims of wrongs being compensated. It is up to the victim or the victim's family to decide whether to pursue the wrongdoer for compensation, because it is the victim's private law right that has been violated in that regard. However, if the wrong is also a crime, this means that the wrong has interfered with a right which the State guaranteed would be protected and therefore a just punishment must be visited upon the wrongdoer, and only the State can interfere with the wrongdoer's rights so as to punish him. Accordingly, it is a State official who sets out to ascertain the truth.

The *pubblico ministero* is a magistrate, whose duty it is to investigate crimes notified to him, to establish that there has indeed been a breach of the criminal law and if possible to ascertain who is responsible. In performing this task, he is assisted by the police, who in the task of helping him are called the judicial police as they are at the service of the magistracy. The police in Italy, unlike England and Wales, are not necessarily organized on a local basis. In Italy, as well as local police forces, the *polizia*, there are nationally organized forces such as the *carabinieri*, who answer to the Defence Ministry, and the *Polizia Finanzaria*, the so-called *fiamme gialle*, after the yellow torches on their caps, who work for the Treasury and are responsible for excise and fiscal investigations. No one branch of the police constitutes the judicial police, rather officers from any branch can be called upon to serve the *pubblico ministero* and are then the judicial police for that investigation.

Under the pre-1989 Code of Criminal Procedure, the criminal process could be divided into three phases: the pre-instruction phase, consisting of the events leading up to the serving of the *notitia criminis* upon the *pubblico ministero*; the instruction phase, during which the crime was investigated and the evidence against the accused gathered, and the trial phase, when the evidence against the accused was considered by the appropriate criminal court to determine whether the accused was guilty or not guilty of the crime with which he was charged.

If the accused had been caught in the act, had committed the offence while in custody or had confessed to the crime, then regardless of the seriousness of the crime, a formal instruction phase would not be required. Instead, there would be what was termed a summary instruction. This would be conducted entirely by the *pubblico ministero*. The same was always so in the case of crimes within the competence of the *pretore*, who acted as *pubblico ministero* and as judge in the *pretura*. In the cases of non-manifest crimes within the first-instance competence of the *corte d'assise* or the *Tribunale*, however, there would have been a formal instruction. This involved the appointment of a judicial magistrate to assemble the evidence of the crime and its commission by the accused in a dossier or *atti*. Until the Constitutional Court ruled it unconstitutional, the judicial magistrate who conducted the formal instruction, the *giudice istruttore*, was one of the judicial magistrates who would then determine the guilt or innocence of the accused in the trial.

Offensive as this may appear to the common lawyer raised on the concept of judicial impartiality, it must be seen in the light of what has been said about the purpose of the criminal process. It is, in civil law countries, traditionally viewed as an investigation by the State for the State of the question whether the State has cause to deprive one of its subjects of his or her rights because that subject has interfered with the rights of another subject deserving of the State's protection. Accordingly, it is for the State to discover whether a subject has suffered and another has transgressed in this manner, and thus for the State to investigate these questions and decide them. Provided the State's interest in the question is kept in mind, it should be apparent that the criminal process is not a prosecution service called into action by a victim, and that the judiciary are not therefore referees in a contest between the prosecution and defence but part of an investigative process aimed at revealing the truth about what has occurred. This is what the inquisitorial procedure stands for, and what differentiates it from the accusatorial model of judicial proceeding familiar to common lawyers.

Whether the instruction is summary or formal, its function is the same. It is aimed at gathering evidence which will be used to determine whether the suspect should be accused of the crime and put on trial, evidence which will subsequently be used to determine whether the accused is guilty or not. The *pubblico ministero* or the *giudice istruttore*, acting through the judicial police, assembles this evidence in the *atti*. The instruction phase will involve perhaps the appointment of an expert by the judge to answer technical questions impartially, the visiting of locations and viewing of evidence. It will involve the collection of documentary evidence, where relevant, and the taking of the testimony of witnesses. The witness testimony will be in response to questions put by the *pubblico ministero* or the *giudice istruttore*, and the testimony will be recorded in written depositions which will be placed in the *atti*. Where witness evidence conflicts, it is open for the magistrate to call upon the witnesses to confront one another so that he can better inform himself of whose version of the facts is the more reliable. The magistrate could also interrogate the accused, but the accused was not on oath and was not obliged to tell the truth. It was up to the magistrate to decide whether to believe the accused as part of his duty to discover the truth. Only the magistrate had the right to ask questions in such interrogations of witnesses and the accused. The accused was allowed legal representation, but his counsel could only suggest questions that should be asked by the magistrate. Nor could the accused's defence demand that the evidence of certain witnesses be taken, only suggest that they be examined.

At the end of the instruction phase, the *pubblico ministero* or the *giudice istruttore*, depending on whether the instruction had been summary or formal, decided upon whether there was a case for the accused to answer. If there was, the accused would be committed to trial before the appropriate court. At that trial, the evidence collected in the *atti* by the investigating magistrate would be handed to the Bench and the judges would then consider the evidence, this time in the light of argument regarding its worth put forward by the defence and certain other parties to the process. The *pubblico ministero* would be there, sitting on the daïs with the judicial magistrates as part of the State team, but it was also open for the victim to be represented so as to have the accused's civil liability for the wrong determined in the same trial, and if another person was vicariously liable to the victim or if another person was civilly liable for any monetary penalty awarded against the accused, then those persons were also entitled to be represented and to speak to the evidence through their advocates.

Although the trial was meant to be a fresh assessment of the evidence, this time not to determine whether there was a case to answer but rather the guilt or innocence of the accused, in Italy before 1989 the trial had become basically a formal reception of the evidence already collected during the instruction phase. The *atti* would be examined by the court, the depositions of the witnesses read out and acknowledged by the witnesses rather than their being re-examined by the court, and the advocates being allowed in turn to argue their clients' case in relation to the evidence received and to argue on the reliability of the evidence. The *pubblico ministero* was of course meant to be an impartial State officer, arguing his interpretation of the evidence in order that the truth be ascertained by the court. The court would then retire and consider its verdict, which verdict would have to be accompanied by reasons, either immediately given, or more usually in a reserved judgement at a later date.

Clearly, in the *pretura*, where the *pretore* was both investigating magistrate and judge in a summary process, it would be very difficult for him to distinguish between his role as *pubblico ministero* and judicial magistrate. When he considered the evidence he had collected in order to determine whether the accused should stand trial, it would be very difficult for him not to have some opinion on the guilt or innocence of the accused at that stage. Therefore, although it was open for the *pretore* to decide that he wanted to hear counsel argue to the evidence in open court, if he felt that the accused was guilty, he could dispense with a trial and issue an immediate decree, stating the accused's guilt. The accused then had five days to challenge the decree. This was the inquisitorial process *par excellence*. The magistrate had investigated; the magistrate had decided. A trial was a luxury which the accused could call for, but was only necessary if he really wanted to challenge the verdict of the impartial truth-seeker acting on behalf of the State. This process by decree could not be used to deprive anyone of liberty as opposed to imposing a monetary penalty, and the accused could always claim a full trial. Where the *pretore* conducted a trial in open court, the role of the *pubblico ministero* would be taken by a *vice-pretore*, who would nonetheless be presenting the evidence collected by the *pretore* who was now judging the case.

Where the accused had been caught in the act or had committed the crime while in custody, but not where he had confessed his guilt, a full instruction would not be required. It was open for the case to go to trial immediately as the circumstances made the collection of proof unnecessary. This was the *procedimento direttissimo*. In such cases, the trial became virtually accusatorial, because there were almost no *atti* to present. Instead, the arrest in flagrance constituted the case against the accused, and it was for the court to hear what his advocate and those of the other parties had to say before reaching a verdict.

There were many criticisms of the procedure used in Italy prior to 1989. It was part of a Code of Criminal Procedure introduced in 1931 under the fascists, and some inevitably saw it as being representative of a political regime which subjugated the rights of individuals to those of the State. There was particular criticism that the accused was not allowed to dispute evidence as it was collected, to challenge State witnesses by cross-examination in open court, and of the fact that the magistrates were prosecution and judges in the same cause - a criticism particularly levelled against proceedings in the *pretura* where the vast majority of crimes were tried, albeit they were the least serious variety. All of these factors led to a growing call for the reform of the criminal justice system of the Italian republic, a reform which it was hoped would restore a parity between prosecution and defence, place the judiciary in a position of greater and more manifest impartiality, and safeguard the liberties and rights of individual citizens against the State.

While it is difficult for a common lawyer not to sympathize with these aspirations which blend so neatly with his own ideas of the fundamentals of criminal justice, it must be recognized that they mark a major departure from the traditional inquisitorial approach of civil law countries. They lose sight of the basic idea of the State's interest in the criminal process, and appear to accept that the State is not impartial. They mark a loss of confidence in the State as the protector of its subjects rights, and an acceptance that the subject sometimes needs protection against the State. Herein can be seen an unfortunate legacy of the fascist experience, but moreover a recognition that even the post-fascist republic, with its political scandals and organized crime, has not been able to guard and guarantee the rights of its subjects as the framers of the 1948 Constitution had intended and hoped.

5 The 1989 Code of Criminal Procedure[3]

Dissatisfaction with what was seen by many as being a system of criminal justice which favoured the State at the expense of its subjects led to many calls for reform. These came to a head with a proposal for a new draft Code of Criminal Procedure which was placed before the Italian parliament in 1978. The terrorism which affected the years 1974-82, the *anni di piombo* (years of lead), delayed the passage of these proposals. Accordingly, it was not until 1987 that Parliament agreed to a new code being drafted according to principles which it laid down. These included respect for the constitutional rights of subjects during the criminal process, respect for international treaties and declarations on human rights, abandoning the inquisitorial model for an accusatorial one, ensuring swiftness and simplicity in the criminal process and placing the prosecution and the defence on an equal footing before impartial judges. These principles guided the production of the new Code of Criminal Procedure which was promulgated during 1988 and came into force and effect in October 1989.

The new Code preserves the basic structure of the criminal courts and of the criminal process. Crimes may still be prosecuted *ex officio*, that is the State has a duty to discover and investigate crimes on its own account. However, there are some crimes which may only be prosecuted if the victim or his family have complained to the authorities, the complaint being made in the form of a *querela*. The Penal Code distinguishes between crimes which may be prosecuted *ex officio* and those which require a *querela*. The new Code however goes further than the old in recognizing the claims of the victim, the *persona offesa dal reato*, in that he is now treated as a party to the criminal process and can be represented before the court at all stages of the proceedings, thus recognizing his interest in the outcome as being separate from that of the State, and without the need of necessarily being constituted as a civil party to the proceedings seeking damages for a civil wrong. The victim can for instance object to the prosecution seeking to have the case dismissed for lack of evidence, so-called archivation.

In either event, a reported or discovered crime must be notified to the investigating authorities by the police as previously. The *pubblico ministero* is now much more the investigating prosecutor than previously, although he is still expected to behave as an impartial magistrate. His task is still to investigate the charge that a crime has been committed and, if one has, to gather evidence with which to prosecute the accused person. However, under the new Code the evidence is evidence with which to prosecute not evidence from which to try the accused, for it is now open as a matter of right for the defence and other parties to the process - the victim, the civil party, the person responsible for the civil wrong and the persons civilly responsible for the fine - to require that evidence be taken and that witnesses be called to testify at the trial. The dossier, the *atti*, compiled by the *pubblico ministero* is therefore no longer the sole source of evidence at the trial.

The *pubblico ministero* gathers the same sort of evidence as previously, but his task is to identify the sorts of evidence that are available and not actually to take the evidence. Under the new Code, the evidence is to be taken whenever possible in open court at the trial, when witness testimony, for example, can be challenged through cross-examination by counsel for the other parties. The new Code aims at a process which is open, oral and impartial, replacing the previous workings of the instruction phase, which were predominantly written, secret and dominated by the State officials.

There is of course the possibility that some evidence will not remain available until the trial takes place. The new Code therefore makes provision for the taking of such evidence. The instruction phase has been replaced by a phase called the preliminary investigation, the *indagini preliminari*. For this phase, a judge, a member of the judicial magistracy, is appointed, but not to act as an investigating magistrate but as a judge for the preliminary proceedings, the *giudice per le indagini preliminari*, popularly referred to as the *gip*. It is the function of the *gip* basically to do two things. Firstly, during the course of the *indagini preliminari*, he has the duty of taking evidence which will or may not be available at the trial. This he does in court, with an opportunity for the other parties to cross-examine or comment on the evidence. Proceedings are not open to the public at this stage, thus protecting the identity of the accused. Such taking of evidence is called the *incidente probatorio*. The *pubblico ministero* presents the evidence he wishes to be taken in advance of the trial, and the *gip* acts as an impartial judge in taking that evidence and referring it to the trial court. Secondly, at the end of the *indagini preliminari*, the *pubblico ministero* must apply to the *gip* either for the case to be archived, if there is no crime to be investigated or insufficient evidence to bring the suspect to trial, or to have the accused remitted to the appropriate court for trial. It is the duty of the *gip* to consider the evidence and to come to a conclusion on these issues alone. In doing so, he must again act as an impartial judge of the evidence put before him by the *pubblico ministero* and allow the other parties through their counsel to argue to the contrary. He is not investigating as did the *giudice istruttore* in the instruction phase, but judging as an impartial third party. Only if he feels that there is enough evidence to put the accused on trial will the accused be sent to the appropriate court for the next phase of the proceedings, namely the trial phase.

Under the new Code, the trial takes place in open court and the judges will not have had, as previously was the case, the *atti* available to them. In other words, it is at the trial that the evidence will first be put before them. Every piece of evidence must be presented to the court, and, in particular, witnesses are called to give their testimony and not just to confirm the written depositions made by them as previously. The *pubblico ministero* examines the witnesses in open court and counsel for the other parties have the opportunity of cross-examining them. Accordingly, all of the judges have the opportunity of hearing the testimony at first hand and making up their own minds with regard to its credibility, reliabilty and worth. Under the old system, they were presented in effect with the investigating magistrate's estimation of the evidence, and he of course had not in recent years been allowed to sit as a judge in the case. Although there are circumstances in which the judges can ask questions of the witnesses, by and large they are now questioned by the parties' counsel, who have the right to call whatever witnesses they wish and to ask them whatever questions they require. They are not controlled in these matters by the judges, who are now there to arbitrate and decide, not to investigate and therefore to control.

At the end of the *dibattimento*, as the trial phase is called, the respective counsel address the court in turn, arguing their point of view and estimation of the evidence. The court hears in turn the civil party, if damages for the civil wrong are being claimed as part of the same process, the *pubblico ministero*, the civilly responsible party if there is one apart from the accused, the party civilly liable for the fine if there is one, and finally counsel for the accused himself. If the victim has not been constituted the civil party, he too has various rights to be heard. At the end of these addresses by the advocates, the judges, *togati* and *populari*, retire together to consider their verdict and their reasons for it. They will then return to court to give their verdict openly, but the reasoning can be reserved to a written judgement. Only when the reasons have been given in writing does time begin to run for the purposes of initiating an appeal.

An appeal is available on the merits of the case, in which case the evidence is still handed on to the appeal court where only fresh evidence is heard in open court. Fresh evidence may be introduced in limited circumstances. The parties have again the right to address the court and cross-examine any new witnesses. The appeal judgement must again be reasoned. Finally, after the possibilty of any appeal has been exhausted it is open for any question of law to be reviewed by *Cassazione* in Rome, which may again either confirm the final judgement or quash it in whole or in part, in which case it may remit the incorrect item to the appropriate appeal court for a decision which accords with its ruling.

This at least in theory is how the new Code is to operate. Its reception has been mixed. Its critics in particular have been swift to point out that its accusatorial elements sit uneasily in a system in which the State has an acknowledged responsibility to discover and prosecute crimes. They argue that the new system is an uncomfortable mix of inquisitorial and accusatorial styles. Moreover, there has undoubtedly been a mixed reaction to the new system from established advocates. Many of these had for years practised in a system which required them to address the court but not to cross-examine witnesses. In so far as the techniques of cross-examination have to be acquired, it has been difficult for the older generation of advocates to adapt to the requirements of the new style.

It is however questionable how far the new Code has changed the nature of the vast majority of trials in the Italian republic. Most crimes are tried by the *pretore*, and at this level the inquisitorial model can be argued to be still prevalent. The new Code allows various exceptions to the ordinary procedure described above with its distinction between the *indagini preliminari* and the *dibattimento*. As with the old system, it is possible for the process to move straight to the *dibattimento* if the accused was caught red-handed or has confessed his guilt. In such circumstances, the *indagini preliminari* is not required and the case moves immediately to trial. This is the *giudizio direttissimo*,[4] and very like it is the *giudizio immediato*,[5] where in undefined circumstances where the *pubblico ministero* feels that there is enough evidence to go to trial without an *indagini preliminari*, he may ask the *gip* to remit the case immediately. The accused may also request this if he does not wish his case to be disclosed before the full *dibattimento*.

In both of these situations, the trial is markedly accusatorial. It is the inquisitorial elements that are omitted. However, in the other exceptions to the ordinary process, it is the inquisitorial element which prevails at the expense of the accusatorial. Thus, in the *giudizio abbreviato*,[6] it is open for the accused to request that the *gip* not only determines whether there is a case to answer but also whether the accused is guilty. The consent of the *pubblico ministero* must be obtained and this request can be made in relation to any offence that does not carry a life sentence, *ergastolo*. The trial is based on the *atti* in true inquisitorial style; appeal is limited but review to *Cassazione* is possible. The trial is not public but secret, and saves the accused publicity. Moreover, in return for saving the court time, the accused's sentence if found guilty will be reduced by a third. There is nothing however to preclude his being acquitted, as he has not agreed to plead guilty.

Under *patteggiamento*[7] however he does confess the crime in return for a reduction of one-third in his sentence, the sentence never being allowed to exceed two years imprisonment. The judge could still acquit the accused, as he is still required to consider the evidence. However, in reality, *patteggiamento* is a bargain between the *pubblico ministero* and the defence, under which time is saved and the accused gets a reduced penalty. It can be made at any time during the process, not only during the *indagini preliminari* but also during the *dibattimento*.

Proceedings which end by decree, *decreto penale*, remain the most common form of summary criminal process.[8] Under the new Code, the *pubblico ministero* can ask the *gip* to issue a *decreto penale*, in effect decreeing that the accused is guilty of the crime in the absence of a trial and without the accused having to be present. This can only be done in relation to offences which are to be proceeded against *ex officio* and which carry only pecuniary penalties. The sentence can be halved under this proceeding, and the accused can challenge the decree within fifteen days. Such methods are regularly used in relation to trials before the *pretore*, where it is also common for the parties to agree to allow the *pretore* in a *dibattimento* to ask all the questions and take all the evidence, thus preserving the inquisitorial nature of the proceedings. The *pubblico ministero* can also in cases involving lesser penalties offer the accused the chance to avoid criminal proceedings by reaching a settlement with the offended party. The payment in settlement is called the *oblazione*.

These exceptions to the ordinary criminal process under the new Code are virtually all aimed at ensuring that criminal justice is speedily administered. Under the pre-1989 law, it was very common for cases to take an inordinate length of time to reach trial, no form of plea bargaining being allowed. Indeed, the back-log was such that periodically a general amnesty for lesser crimes would be issued so as to clear the back-log. Defence counsel regularly dragged out criminal proceedings in the hope of there being an amnesty before a case came to trial. This delay came to be seen as one way in which the old system in effect failed to provide justice - justice delayed, it was said, was not justice at all. Accordingly, a high premium has been placed upon dealing with cases speedily. It is this expedition which the exceptional processes are meant to provide. However, they do this at the expense in many instances of allowing the process to be truly accusatorial, albeit that in such cases the consent of the accused is obtained. Many however believe that this sort of speed is not really commensurate with justice either, and it must be admitted that the end result is that the vast majority of criminal cases in contemporary Italy are being dealt with in processes technically deemed exceptional. From the outset, the ordinary criminal process of the new Code has been in truth the exception, and the exceptional processes the rule, and the exceptional processes contain much that is inquisitorial in nature.

6 Punishment

Once the trial phase has determined that the accused person is guilty of the crime, the convict becomes liable to punishment. According to Italian law, the purpose of punishment is to inflict a just suffering upon the convict. This suffering is due to the convict because he has interfered with the legally protected rights of another subject. His right to liberty or to his property will therefore to some degree, commensurate with the wrong he has been proven to have done, be diminished. To that extent he is outside of the law's protection, but only the State may inflict this harm upon him.

Under Italian law, punishments fall into three categories. The convict may either suffer a penalty, a precautionary measure or an alternative. Penalties are either custodial, patrimonial or accessory. Custodial penalties deprive the convict of his freedom through imprisoning him. If he is guilty of a delict, he will suffer *reclusione*; if a contravention, *arresto*. The institutions in, or the institutional regimes under, which these different types of imprisonment are served are different. Moreover, so is the potential range of the sentence: *arresto* can last from five days up to three years, whereas *reclusione* can last from fifteen days up to twenty-four years. There is also a sentence of life imprisonment, called *ergastolo*.

Pecuniary or patrimonial punishments hit the pocket or property of the convict. Again, they are of two sorts depending upon whether the convict has been found guilty of a delict or a contravention. For a delict, a *multa* of between 10,000 and 10,000,000 lire can be imposed, while for a contravention, an *ammenda* of between 4,000 and 2,000,000 lire is in order. Accessory penalties can be imposed alongside the other types of punishment. They include the right of the court to deprive a person of civic and political rights, such as the right to stand for election to or hold a public office, or the removal of the civic status which allows someone to practise a profession or calling. In other words, lawyers or doctors could find themselves struck off as would be said in Britain; but this does not require a separate hearing before a professional body; the sentence is imposed by the criminal court.

Precautionary measures are imposed as a punishment upon someone who has been found guilty of a crime, but can also be used to restrain those who have conspired to commit crimes, attempted impossible crimes or are established as being dangerous persons because of their criminal tendencies. Such measures are either personal or patrimonial, and if personal are either custodial or non-custodial. Personal custodial measures include the placing of the delinquent in a labour colony or a mental hospital, while personal non-custodial measures encompass such measures as prohibiting a person from frequenting taverns, attending football matches or going to places where there is a high risk of their committing a crime. They may also include ordering a person to stay indoors at certain times, for instance during a carnival, when again the risk of their offending is known to be great. Patrimonial measures can either consist of having the convict deposit a sum of money as security that he be of good behaviour, or of confiscating certain articles which the convict is likely to put to nefarious purposes if they remain in his possession.

Alternative measures are those which are substituted judicially for other punishments which have been imposed. The role of the magistracy in the criminal process does not end with the conviction and sentence of the accused. The magistrates also supervise the punishment, in as much as any decision to release the convict early and on what terms must be taken by them. The whole of the penal process is judicialized. This is a signal application of the principle of the separation of powers. At every *corte d'appello*, there is a *Tribunale de sorveglianza*, chaired by a judge of appeal court status and consisting of one other professional judge of *Tribunale* status and of two social workers. All decisons with regard to the substitution of alternative measures for other punishments are to be taken by this court. It has four possible alternative measures from which to choose. Probation allows them to release a convict before his sentence is completely served into the custody of a social welfare organization or some other such body to help him rehabilitate and get back into the community. It is only available in the case of first offenders who have not been sentenced to lengthy periods of imprisonment and who have not committed serious crimes. Day release permits the convict to leave the place of his incarceration each day to undertake a job of work again clearly to enable rehabilitation within the community to occur. Advance release allows the convict the remission of a proportionate part of his sentence if he has distinguished himself while in gaol by good behaviour, and the measure is forfeit if he reoffends after release. Leave is another rehabilitating measure which allows a convict forty-five days a year out of prison as a further device to get him back into the community usually after a period of day release has proved beneficial.

Prisons are run by the Ministry of Grace and Justice, but their supervision, to ensure that they are run in accordance with the law and meet its requirements, is entrusted to a supervising magistrate, again illustrating the judicialization of the penal process within Italy.

Notes

[1] For instance, offences against the State, offences against the person, offences against property, and so on.

[2] Depending upon whether they are to be dealt with by the police or by administrative process.

[3] The new Code of Criminal Procedure is divided into eleven books. Book I is concerned with the *dramatis personae* of criminal proceedings: the judicial authorities, the *pubblico ministero*, the judicial police, the accused, the party claiming damages for the wrong, the party civilly responsible for the wrong, the party civilly responsible for the fine, the victim and the defence counsel. Book II deals with the compilation of the *atti* or dossier, and Book III with the various kinds of evidence which may be used. Book IV is concerned with precautionary measures, such as remanding in custody. These first four books comprise Part I of the Code.

Part II is concerned with the dynamics of the criminal process. Book V deals with the *indagini preliminari* and the *udienza preliminare*. Book VI deals with the exceptional procedures, and Book VIII with the trial itself. Book IX is concerned with appeals and review, Book X with the process of punishment and Book XI with cases with a foreign element.

[4] *Codice di Procedura Penale*, art. 449-452.

[5] *Cod. Proc. Pen.*, art. 453-458.

[6] *Cod. Proc. Pen.*, art. 438-443.

[7] *Cod. Proc. Pen.*, art. 444-448.

[8] *Cod. Proc. Pen.*, art. 459-464.

10 Administrative Justice

1 Administrative Law

Administrative law is that part of public law which regulates the legal relationships between the State, regional and local organs of public administration, one with another and with the citizens of the State. It differs from constitutional law in that it is not concerned with the rights of the citizens or the mechanisms for carrying those rights into legal effect or adjudicating upon them, but is rather concerned with how policy is implemented in an arena of action where it is bound to affect, beneficially or adversely, the rights and the legitimate interests of those subject to the administration's influence.

Although one could state that administrative law is that body of law which regulates the relations of the public administration with the citizenry, it is much more difficult to define administrative law than constitutional law, criminal law or civil law. This is because it is not concerned solely with one body of rules contained in a single code, but often with measures and indeed individual acts of the public administration carried out under powers given by national, regional or local legislation. Sometimes those acts affect the subjective rights of citizens, that is rights which they enjoy under the ordinary civil law. At other times, those measures or acts, while not affecting subjective rights as such, affect other legitimate interests. The legitimate interest is for some jurists the key element in understanding the nature of Italian administrative law. The whole issue however is probably best understood by making use of some simple hypothetical examples to illustrate the situations in which administrative law comes into play and the distinctions pertaining to it.

X lives in a house which he owns situated on a main road. Although the road is reasonably busy, the noise does not adversely affect X's enjoyment of his property because it is set back from the road. Between X's house and the road, there is a front garden which belongs to X and also a broad grass verge which is in the public domain.

The local authority has powers under the law to authorise the widening of roads. It may exercise this power, but is not bound to do so, if the volume of traffic using a certain road exceeds a certain limit. To exercise this power the Transport Committee of the local authority, which to be properly constituted must have been sworn in by the mayor, must decide that the widening is necessary after having ascertained that the volume of traffic is sufficient to allow the power to authorize the widening to be exercized. In order to widen the road, the local authority has powers to compulsorily purchase land in private ownership adjoining the highway if this is necessary for the widening to take place. If the authority decides that widening is necessary, it must advertise the fact that it is considering this possibility in the local press and invite objections to be made. It must consider those objections and, if it decides to go ahead with the project, the chairman of the Transport Committee must certify in writing that the decision was taken after having considered the objections raised. Thereafter, the authority must inform all residents living within a certain distance of the development of its decision.

The local authority of the town where X lives has decided to widen the road outside his house. If it is intended to purchase compulsorily a part of X's front garden to achieve this, then X's subjective right of ownership is affected by the decision. If it is not intended to purchase a part of his property in order to advance the project, but only to convert the grass verge into part of the highway, X's subjective rights are not affected, but he still has a legitimate interest to be consulted as what is going to occur may affect his enjoyment of his property, or even the value of his property, even though his right of ownership will not in any way be prejudiced.

One can contrast this situation with one where X's neighbour, Y, who owns a similar property, wishes to construct a drive leading to his house. The question for X and Y in this situation will be whether Y has a right to build a drive and whether X has a right ot stop him. The questions turn on what rights the parties have. The local authority has no more right than Y to take a part of X's land for its purposes nor any greater right to interfere with X's rights by conducting activities on its own property which adversely affect X's enjoyment of his. However, the local authority has legal powers under which, if properly exercised, it can acquire the right to take or interfere with X's property. Such rights are given it under administrative law, but in exercizing such powers, the local authority, like any other part of the public administration, must proceed according to the requirements of administrative law and administrative justice so as to ensure that the legitimate interests of persons such as X are respected. X's administrative law remedies are therefore aimed, unlike his private law remedies, not at enforcing his rights or his neighbours' duties, but in establishing whether his legitimate interests have been respected. If they have not, X will be able under administrative law to have the offending measure set aside. This to some is the hallmark of administrative law; it is aimed at invalidating administrative decisions which offend against legitimate interests and not at enforcing rights or duties. The remedy is always the undoing of an administrative decision, not the enforcing of a right or the obtaining of compensation for breach of a duty.

X's recourse therefore in this situation is not to assert that the local authority has no right to widen the road, but rather that because of some defect in the administrative measure utilized, they have failed to give themselves the necessary right. There are several defects which can be established to undermine the validity of the local authority's actions so as to invalidate their right to widen the road.

Firstly, if the Transport Committee, which is the committee authorized to make the decision, has not been properly sworn in by the mayor then the individuals concerned do not constitute the Transport Committee. Their decisions while purporting to constitute the Transport Committee are therefore in law non-existent. If this is the case, no administrative measure will have been made and no right to widen the road obtained by the local authority.

Secondly, if the Transport Committee was properly constituted, it must have followed the correct forms and procedures as demanded by the law upon the basis of which the exercise of its powers is based. Thus, if it is required as stated above that notice of the proposal be advertised in the local press so as to give interested parties an opportunity to object and this has not been done, then the procedure is faulty and can be declared void for failure to conform to the appropriate procedure. Likewise, if, having considered the objections, the Committee's chairman does not, as required, sign a written statement to the effect that the objections were considered and the decision reached, then again the decision is void for lack of use of the proper form. Finally, if it is stipulated as stated above that the decision must be notified to the residents affected by it and this has not been done, then the procedure is again flawed and the measure will be void for illegitimacy.

Thirdly, as well as problems of non-existence, and formal or procedural defects, the measure may be flawed for incompetence. Thus, if the wrong local authority made the decision or issued the measure, the act would be void for incompetence. If the road was one which, for instance, was under the supervision of the provincial, not the communal, council and the latter purported to issue an order for its widening, its decision would be void for incompetence.

Fourthly, the measure may be void for excess of power. This may arise where, for instance, the decision was made for reasons other than those for which the power to make it was given to the local authority. Thus, if, for instance, the motive force was not to ease traffic congestion but to supply a better means of access and egress to a factory owned by a local politician in the neighbourhood, the measure will be voidable for excess of power if this can be proved.

Fifthly, an administrative measure may be challenged as being in violation of the law under which it is made. This problem vitiates the measure when, for instance, the governing law required the existence of some set of facts as a condition precedent for the authority's exercizing its power and the authority wrongly held that these facts existed. In the above example, it will be recalled that the road-widening order could only be made if the volume of traffic had exceeded a certain level. If X can show that the authority is wrong in its belief that the volume of traffic on the road is in excess of that level, then he can have the measure set aside as being in violation of the law under which it was purported to be made.

All of the above issues challenge the legality of the measure. It is also however open to X to challenge the decision on its merits, that is to argue that even though the decision has been properly made in terms of its existence, form, procedure and competence, and even though the volume of traffic does justify the widening and the reasons for widening are proper, nevertheless in all the circumstances of this particular case, the decision to widen the road should not have been taken.

2 Administrative Justice

Civil law systems generally, following the French model, have a set of administrative courts, separate form the ordinary courts, to deal with the administration of administrative justice. Italy, however, has only really gone over to this sytem in the last quarter-century after the Constitutional Court, at the end of the 1960s, ruled that its previous method of dealing with administrative disputes did not conform to the Constitution's requirements with regard to the separation of powers and the independence of the judges taking the decisions in administrative disputes.

In Italy, dividing lines are drawn between various kinds of redress in relation to administrative matters. If the complaint concerns the invasion of a subjective right as a consequence of the making of an administrative measure, then the party prejudiced by the measure must seek his relief in the ordinary courts. For instance, in the example given above, suppose the local authority had issued a compulsory purchase order to acquire a portion of X's front garden in order to widen the road. If X could show that the administrative measure was defective in some way, that is show that it was flawed in terms of its legality rather than wrong on the merits, then proof of that fact would be of use to him, for instance, in a civil action to prevent the local authority invading his property rights by sending their diggers and excavators onto his land. Thus, X could seek an order to prevent feared damage being done to his land by the defendants, the local authority. As this action would be brought in relation to his subjective right of ownership, X would commence his suit in the ordinary civil court with competence to hear his case. He would challenge the council's right to commence the work on the basis that they were interfering with his ownership of the land. The council would doubtless defend their action by seeking to justify it on the basis of their compulsory purchase order made in pursuance of the decision to widen the road. If X could then show that that decision was flawed for illegality in any of the ways outlined above, the council's justification for its actions would fail and X's suit to enforce his rights as owner would succeed. In such a case, the ordinary civil court never declares the administrative measure to be void or illegal. It merely affirms the subjective right of the party, in our example X. The basis of its decision is of course in part the flaw in the legality of the administrative measure, but it is not the concern of the court to make a declaration relating to a public law matter. The ordinary court confines itself to declaring X's right of ownership unaffected by the purported exercise of the local authority's statutory powers. Had the local authority actually entered upon or damaged X's property, he would have been able to sue them for compensation. Had they proceeded against him for blocking their access onto the land in question and he had successfully responded by asserting, on the basis of the illegitimacy of their administrative measure that they had no right to do so, they would have lost their action on their subjective right.

In Italian law, therefore, it is to the ordinary courts that recourse must be had where the matter in dispute concerns subjective rights. However, even if the local authority was not purporting to compulsorily purchase X's land but rather merely to extend the road onto the grass verge outside his property, he would still have a legitimate interest which could be protected through the processes of Italian administrative justice. Today, he could challenge the decision on its merits within the administrative structures of the public administration or challenge it on its legality within either those structures or through the administrative courts created since 1971. Before considering the operation of these procedures however, it is worth sketching in briefly the process by which administrative justice has reached this stage in the almost century and a half since unification.

The Italian States which existed prior to unification had by and large absorbed the doctrine of the separation of powers, so that in virtually all of them it was thought improper that disputes involving the public administration should be settled by the ordinary judiciary. Accordingly, administrative boards of review existed in most of the States with a jurisdiction to hear and determine disputes between citizens and the public administration. After unification, however, in 1865, this approach was challenged in that it allowed matters affecting the subjective rights of the citizen both in public and private law to be settled other than by the courts of ordinary jurisdiction being set up by the first Code of Civil Procedure promulgated in that year to adjudicate upon the subjective rights set out in the first Italian Civil Code also promulgated in 1865. From 1865, all litigation concerning subjective rights, whether involving ordinary citizens or the public administration, had to be heard by the ordinary courts. The erstwhile administrative boards of review were abolished.

This arrangement, whereby the ordinary courts adjudicate over administrative disputes involving subjective rights, continues to apply in Italian law. In the years after 1865 however, it had a considerable defect in that it left the legitimate interests of Italian subjects entirely within the jurisdiction of the administrative structures of the State. There were no administrative courts, only reviews by superior administrators. To remedy this defect, two innovations were made in 1889 and 1890 respectively. In 1889, Section IV of the Council of State was given jurisdiction to hear and determine disputes concerning the legitimacy of administrative measures generally and also in exceptional cases the right to review decisions on their merits. In 1890, *Giunte Provinciali Amministrative* were established to have first instance jurisdiction over local administrative measures. Thus emerged the on-going distinction in Italian law between cases involving subjective rights over which the ordinary courts have jurisdiction and cases involving legitimate interests over which administrative tribunals have jurisdiction. The distinction between subjective rights and legitimate interests was never particularly easy to apply, and in 1923 the administrative tribunals were given exclusive jurisdiction over certain administrative matters, even where subjective rights might be involved. Most notably, the administrative tribunals were given at this time exclusive jurisdiction over the employment disputes of public servants.

Administrative justice remained in this form in Italy until in the late 1960s the Constitutional Court challenged the constitutionality of certain aspects of the structures. It criticized the *Giunte* as being insufficiently independent of the administrative powers of the State to conform with the requirements of the Constitution regarding the independence of the judiciary. The upshot of these criticisms was that in 1971 an entirely new system of administrative justice was introduced into the Italian republic. Each region was allotted a *Tribunale Amministrative Regionale*, a court of first instance to hear and determine disputes regarding the legitimacy of administrative measures. Disputes regarding subjective rights continue to go to the ordinary courts. In addition, the Council of State, sections IV, V and VI, was given appellate jurisdiction over administrative law matters with competence to hear and determine appeals from the *Tribunali Amminstrativi Regionali*, other than the Sicilian TAR from which appeals lie to the Council for Administrative Justice for the Sicilian Region. Questions relating to whether a matter involves a subjective right or a legitimate interest, that is questions of jurisdiction between the ordinary and the administrative courts, are settled by the Court of Cassation sitting as a full court with a bench of nine judges.

The TARs and the Council of State are administrative courts, separate from the jurisdiction of the ordinary courts, thus satisfying the requirements of the doctrine of the separation of powers, but also independent from the public administration itself, in that they are staffed by career judges who are not part of the public administration. These administrative courts are concerned with issues of legality affecting administrative measures. They are not concerned with the merits of administrative decisions. Citizens who wish to challenge administrative decisions on their merits must do so by means of hierarchical review within the structures of the administration itself. This reflects the fact that questions relating to the merits of a decision are questions of policy, not of law.

3 The Administrative Courts and their Procedure

A citizen who wishes to challenge an administrative measure must therefore first of all determine, upon legal advice if necessary, whether it affects his subjective rights or legitimate interests. If the former, his remedies will lie in the ordinary courts. Only very exceptionally are the administrative courts given jurisdiction by law over the subjective rights of citizens. As has been said, since 1923, the administrative courts have full jurisdiction over the employment of public employees. In addition special administrative courts, the Tax Commissions, operate with jurisdiction over revenue matters, the Court of Accounts has jurisdiction over pensions matters and the Tribunals for Public Waterways also have full jurisdiction in their area of operation over subjective rights as well as legitimate interests.

With the exception of these special cases, however, citizens who wish to impugn administrative measures because of their effects upon their subjective rights must do so in the ordinary courts, whether civil or criminal. If however it is their legitimate interests that are affected they must proceed either by seeking administrative review within the public administration itself or by judicial review before the administrative courts. As a rule, the administrative courts are only concerned with the legitimacy of administrative measures, that is whether they are illegitimate because of incompetence, excess of power or violation of law, whereas the former method, by administrative review by the administration itself, allows them also to complain regarding the merits of a particular decision even if it has been made perfectly properly as far as its legality is concerned.

If the citizen opts to proceed initially within the framework of administrative review, this does not preclude a later resort to the administrative courts if the outcome of the administrative review is not to the complainant's satisfaction. However, if the citizen opts to proceed via the courts, either after or instead of administrative review, the outcome of a judicial review in the administrative courts is final, unless the decision is open to revocation for judicial fraud or other good cause.

Administrative review is available wherever an administrative decision is not definitive, that is where it is not final. Definitive decisions can only be challenged with regard to their legitimacy, and usually therefore only through the courts. Non-definitive decisions can however be challenged within the administrative structures regarding either their legality or their expediency. This is done by giving notice within thirty days of the decision being published that one intends to seek an administrative review from the body within the administrative hierarchy which has the competence to review the decision of its administrative inferior body. That hierarchical body then has ninety days in which to hear and determine the challenge. If it allows the challenge, then it may either rescind the earlier measure, or replace it with another. If it upholds the measure, or after ninety days has not determined the issue, the complainant is free to proceed within the administrative courts with a judicial review.

Only one administrative review of administrative decisions is allowed even if the measure originated from a body which had several tiers above it in the hierarchy. Once such a review has been undertaken, the complainant must either let the matter drop or proceed through the administrative courts, unless that is he wishes to avail himself of the technique of extraordinary review by the President of the Republic. Such an extraordinary review is an alternative to proceedings before the administrative courts, and precludes any later resort to them in relation to the matter. Accordingly, it is always open for other parties with an interest at odds with that of the complainant, a counter-interest as it is called, to require that a matter which is to undergo extraordinary review be transferred to the administrative courts for disposal. Extraordinary review is only available against definitive administrative measures, so any opportunity of hierarchical review must be completed first. The request for extraordinary review must be made within 120 days of the decision's being published and extraordinary review is only allowed with regard to the legitimacy of the measure. It takes the form of an application for review to the President of the Republic who seeks the advice of the Council of State, that is sections I, II and III of the Council of State, which are the consultative sections as opposed to sections IV, V and VI which are the judicial sections. The judges of the first three sections meet in General Assembly under the President of the Council of State and advise the President of the Republic as to the legitimacy of the administrative measure in question. His decision on their advice is then embodied in a Presidential Decree which settles the matter. This decree is issued to the Minister of the government department concerned who must abide by it unless he is prepared to seek the support of the Cabinet to challenge it. Otherwise the Decree is final unless subject to revocation for judicial fraud or challenged in the judicial sections of the Council of State for its formal and procedural propriety, this being a matter over which the judicial sections of the Council of State have first instance competence.

The only other form of review permitted within the administrative structures themselves is opposition, which is the right in certain circumstances defined by law to oppose certain definitive administrative decisions before the body which originally made them. This form of review is of very limited application, being only available in a small number of situations defined by the law.

Since 1971, judicial review of administrative decisions is available before the administrative courts set up in that year. In each region, there is a TAR, a *Tribunale Amministrative Regionale*. Its purpose is to hear and determine complaints against the public administration by citizens who believe that their legitimate interests have not been respected and wish to challenge an administrative measure as a consequence regarding its legality. Exceptionally, but only in a limited number of situations defined by law, a TAR may also enquire into the merits of an administrative decision. Generally, however, their jurisdiction is limited to the legality of a measure.

TARs are situated in the regional capitals, although sections may sit at other centres in a region. Each TAR has a President, who is the office superior, assisted by other judges. The courts sit as a collegiate body consisting of three judges. When a matter is brought before it, it proceeds by means of an instruction phase followed by a decision-making phase. The instruction phase is brief in comparison with that of the civil courts, being limited to examining the documentation relevant to the administrative decision, and possibly seeking further clarification of the reasons for the decision, for instance when excess of power has been complained of, and possibly asking that certain facts upon which the decision turned be verified, as when for instance violation of law has been claimed. When the instruction phase is complete, the court may hear the submissions of the parties through their legal representatives and then hand down its reasoned decision. This may either annul the measure for incompetence, excess of power or violation of law, or uphold it. In the few cases in which the TAR has jurisdiction over the merits of a case, it may also substitute an alternative measure for one it finds to be inexpedient. The TAR may also award costs.

One area in which the TAR always has jurisdiction over the merits of a case is where it is asked to enforce a judgement of the ordinary courts against the public administration. This is part of the jursidiction of every TAR. While claims for breach of contract or causing damage by illicit acts will be brought against the public administration in the ordinary courts because such claims involve subjective rights, enforcement proceedings against the public administration now always lie in the administrative courts. This preserves the integrity of the doctrine of the separation of powers in that the judicial arm of the State is not seen to be interfering with the administrative or executive arm. Only the administrative courts may compel the public administration to fulfil its legal obligations.

The TARs are now the administrative courts of first instance. Appeals from them lie to the judicial sections, that is sections IV, V and VI, of the Council of State. Each section has a particular subject-matter remit, the work of each department or ministry of State being allocated to a particular section of the Council of State. Each section is staffed by a President, the office superior, a Vice-President, seven councillors and a number of additional referees who assist the councillors in their work. When a section sits to hear an appeal from a TAR, it sits as a collegiate court of seven magistrates. Appeals form all TARs go to the Council of State, other than from the TAR of Sicily. Appeals from the Sicilian TAR go to the Council of Administrative Justice for the Sicilian Region. From this body, however, a further appeal is possible to the Plenary Assembly of the Council of State. This body consists of the President of the Council of State and four councillors from each of sections IV, V and VI, thus comprising a collegiate court of thirteen judges. Apart from final appeals from Sicily, the Plenary Assembly hears final appeals from the judicial sections of the Council of State in order to resolve any conflicts in the jurisprudence, that is the case law, of the Council of State which may have arisen as between the three judicial sections. Decisions of the Council of State are final, being only impugnable by means of revocation or challengeable before the Court of Cassation on the basis of the Council of State having acted outside its jurisdiction.

The administrative law and administrative justice of modern Italy is a large subject which cannot be dealt with adequately within the scope of one chapter of this work. Nevertheless, an appreciation of its place in the Italian legal order is desirable, and it is hoped that this chapter has provided a broad overview of the Italian system of administrative justice. The remainder of this work will however now be concerned with the basic concepts and structures of Italian civil law as contained in the Italian Civil Code.

11 The Family and the Law

Book One of the Italian Civil Code deals with Persons and the Family. It is concerned with answering the question who may be the subject of rights and duties under Italian law. In terms of sentences of the pattern "A owns X" or "A owes £5 to B", it is concerned with defining who may, according to Italian law, be A or B in these sentences in order that the sentences may be not only grammatically sound but also logical and legally correct.

Legal persons in Italian law are either natural or physical persons, that is human beings once born, or juridical persons. Juridical persons are not human beings but are treated by the law as capable of being the subjects of rights and duties as though they were individual human beings. Juridical persons may be either public or private. Public juridical persons are public entities such as the provinces and communes of the republic, which have their own separate personality in the eyes of the law, but these are the creatures of public rather than private law. Private juridical persons are those which have been granted legal personality by the State, having satisfied certain requirements for the granting of such status. They comprise associations, institutions, foundations and certain *società.* Although their membership may comprise individuals who have legal personality in their own right, the entity formed by them constitutes in law a separate legal person which can, for instance, have its own property or patrimony and be subject to rights and duties in its own name. It is also possible under Italian law for associations which do not have legal personality to have patrimonies controlled by their members for their purposes, rather in the manner that trust property in common law systems forms an identifiable corpus of rights without enjoying legal personality.

Book One of the Civil Code is also concerned with rights and duties which do not have a patrimonial character, that is, which do not have a material or monetary value. These include the rights and duties of married couples, parents and children, and other family relationships. In other words, it answers the legal questions which arise from statements such as "A is the spouse of B" or "A is the parent of C", and addresses issues such as how persons are married, how parental rights are acquired, what is the content of marital and parental rights and duties, how such rights and indeed relationships are terminated, and so on. Much of Book One is concerned therefore with what would be described by an English lawyer as family law, and it is from this perspective that the contents of the first two books of the Civil Code will now be examined, the second book of the Civil Code being concerned with succession, which in part considers family interests in the property of a deceased person and therefore bridges the treatment of the law of persons in Book One and the law of property in Book Three.

1 The Concept of the Family

It is useful to begin by considering the implications of the central concept, the family, from the perspective of someone who has been brought up in the United Kingdom and whose way of thinking reflects the tacit assumptions of life in this country. The word *family* to a native of the United Kingdom conjures up in all probability the notion of a household consisting of a husband and wife and their young or teenage children. It would be tendentious to describe this as an average family, but it is the norm from which divergences, such as single persons, one-parent families and childless couples, are measured. It is also the mean which allows a larger household, consisting perhaps of the parents or brother or sister of one of the spouses, to be described as an extended family. The extension is an extension beyond an assumed norm.

There is a second sense in which the word *family* is used which is wider than the first. This is the sense which is attached to the word when, for instance, it is said that a gathering such as a wedding or a funeral was limited to the family of the couple or of the deceased. In this sense, the concept extends beyond the household to include relatives by blood or marriage, such as uncles, aunts, nephews, nieces and cousins in the first, second, but rarely the third, degree. In the first sense, the word *family* is synonymous with a particular household, while in the second the exact limits of the concept are not defined, there being some persons who are definitely within the family, some who are definitely not, and others whom it is difficult to categorize as being either relatives or non-relatives. In both senses, the exact meaning of the concept will vary from household to household, or from family to family.

This inherent vagueness in the modern concept of the family is in stark contrast to the far more definite meaning attaching to the word in Roman law. The *familia* to the ancient Roman was that group of persons under the control or *potestas* of a particular individual, the *paterfamilias* or head of the household. All the children born to a *paterfamilias* within a lawful, Roman marriage were within his power, as were the children of his sons and their sons if he were still living at the time of their birth. Every Roman was, unless emancipated, within the *potestas* of his or her oldest surviving male ancestor in the male line, until that control was broken by death. Control then passed to the next oldest surviving male ancestor in the male line, for example from grandfather to father, until all such male ancestors were dead, whereupon the Roman man or woman became fully responsible for himself or herself, that is *sui iuris*. At this point, males also became responsible for their descendants in the male line. The limits of the *familia* were those of the power of the *paterfamilias*, and had therefore to be certain. Both the general concept of the family and, as a result, the membership of any particular family, were readily definable.

The same was true of the broader meaning of the family in Roman law. For a large number of purposes, kinship was measured by a system of degrees, reckoned by counting the steps from a particular individual to the common ancestor which linked him to the other person concerned, and then counting the steps down to that other. Thus, one's brother was related to one in the second degree - one step up to the common ancestor, the parent, and one step down to the sibling, while an uncle was related in the third degree - two steps up to the grandparent who was the common ancestor, and one step down to the uncle. Family relationship was acknowledged as far as the sixth degree, and, in the case of second cousins only, as far as the seventh. The limits of the concept of the family in this sense too were therefore clearly set.

One person who was not a member of the Roman family in either of the senses described above was the Roman wife. In the first sense, that of the household, she was not a member as it was exceptional for a Roman woman to move from the *potestas* of her own *pater* upon marriage into that of her husband or of his *pater*. Roman women usually retained their own family connections. This meant that they became independent, *sui iuris*, upon the death of all their male ancestors in the male line, and thus enjoyed far greater independence from their husbands than has generally been the case in western societies. Marriage itself was based upon the combined intention of the spouses to live together as man and wife, and ceased upon the withdrawal of such intention by either partner. No formalities were required for either marriage or divorce.

The family was the basic unit of Roman social life, and in a sense the State was a large-scale model of the family organization. Moreover, the family was seen as a continuing phenomenon, by no means restricted to the generations currently in existence, but extending back in time to include deceased ancestors and forward in time in anticipation of unborn generations. This dimension is discernible in the family cults of the traditional pagan religion of the Roman people and from the law of succession. Piety to the ancient Roman involved the performance of certain rituals with regard to the spirits of the ancestors. Thus, on certain days in the year, the living family would consume a special banquet in the family mausoleum. This building would have been of two storeys, and the meal would be eaten in the upper room. In the lower chamber would have been stored the cremated remains of the deceased ancestors in urns, connected to the upper chamber by tubes. Quantities of food and wine would by passed down the tubes during the course of the meal to include the ancestors in the feast and to provide them with the nourishment necessary for their sustenance in their new existence. Spirits not so nourished were believed to return to haunt the living, in particular the descendants whose neglect had forced the return of the ancestors from the spirit world.

The continuity of the Roman family is perhaps best exemplified by the law of succession. Under the civil law of succession, all of a *paterfamilias*' children succeeded him as his heirs when he died. They were not only described by the Romans as heirs, *heredes*, but as heirs to themselves, *sui heredes*. This emphasized their right to succeed to the control of the family and its property upon the death of the *pater*. While he lived, he controlled the family and its property, but it would be wrong to see this as some form of absolute power. Rather it was a responsibility which he had a duty to discharge, and which responsibility passed to his heirs when he died. From early times, the power of the *paterfamilias* to exclude children from the succession was strictly limited, and even when it became simple and usual for a *pater* to make a will and appoint an heir from outside the family, the *sui heredes* had to be expressly excluded from their heirship and moreover had to be provided for in the will by legacies on pain of the will being declared unduteous and therefore of no effect. The underlying principle is not difficult to discern. The family was seen as a continuing entity, the control of which passed from one person to another over the generations but which institution itself remained in existence. Individual preference mattered less than family duty. Heads of the household came and went, but the family continued. It was the duty of each generation to protect what it had received from the ancestors, and to hand the patrimony on undiminished, and if possible increased, to future generations.

Matrimony was merely an adjunct to this notion of the family, the means by which the end of family continuity was promoted. The tie of affinity between husband and wife was regarded as distinct and less significant than that which bound the family members together. In turn, this meant that the maternal bond linking mother to child was not regarded as being of the same order as that linking the children to their father. The matrimonial bond only acquired pride of place within the family with the conversion of the Romans to Christianity, and from the fourth century onwards the family becomes associated in the popular consciousness with the household and kinship of a particular married couple. Marriage was now to be for life; divorce was restricted and discouraged. However, the idea of the continuing family persisted, with the Christianization of the pagan pieties in the requiem masses which came to mark the anniversaries of the dead. Likewise, the Christian emperors, in particular Justinian, maintained the classical restrictions upon freedom of testation so as to guarantee children's rights of succession.

The order of succession fixed by Justinian was adopted by the mediaeval Catholic Church, and as a part of canon law was enforced by the ecclesiastical courts throughout western Europe during the Middle Ages. Thus, the continuing notion of the family persisted in the West. In England, this system was at odds with the inheritance customs of the royal courts which favoured the claim of the eldest son to the deceased father's lands. From the twelfth century, it was settled that freehold land should descend according to the custom of the King's court, that is the common law with its preference for primogeniture, while other forms of property were to descend in accordance with the canon law. Thus, for all property other than freehold land, the canon law system based on later Roman law governed succession, even in England. The continuing notion of the family, however, frequently affected the settlement of land, as is witnessed in the attempts to devise methods by which land could be kept in the family from generation to generation. The entail is a mediaeval device to achieve this end, and the strict settlement a modern method. The latter, interestingly, was worked out during the later seventeenth and eighteenth centuries, when classical influences were again making themselves felt throughout Europe.

The nineteenth century, however, saw a marked assertion of individualism as against family interest. In part, this was a product of the new wealth of the Industrial Revolution, which had seen individual entrepreneurs make considerable fortunes within one lifetime. This engendered the view that the wealth made by one man was his own to do with as he liked, and that what he had gained by his merit and enterprise was only to descend to his family if he chose to bequeath it to them. This view of wealth as being personal to the individual rejected the notion of his having the responsibility of controlling it for the benefit of his family, some of whom would one day inherit it. Instead, there was asserted the freedom to do as one wished with one's own property. While the next generation might expect or hope to inherit, they had no right to succeed.

The logical outcome of this view was that questions began to be asked concerning the justice of allowing the children and grandchildren of successful businessmen to enjoy great wealth which they themselves had played no part in creating. Individualism was now affecting concepts of social justice, and discounting the claims of the continuing family. The activities of each generation were regarded as discrete, it being questioned whether the merits, privileges and wealth of the father should be visited upon the children. It is against this background that the Finance Act, 1894 introduced a heavy tax upon property inherited, for example, by children from their parents. The imposition of what has since been termed Inheritance Tax was a decisive blow to the continuing notion of the family in this country.

Individualism has continued to triumph for much of the twentieth century. This can be seen in such varied developments as the preference for the creation of life peerages rather than hereditary peerages since the nineteen-sixties, but more importantly in the way in which family life in Britain has changed. It is now common, almost the rule, for children to leave their parents' home on reaching roughly the age of majority, and to choose to make their own way in the world. They remain part of the family in the second sense, but not part of the household. The expectation that children will provide for their parents in their old age has decreased. Even as between husband and wife, individualism has operated, asserting the rights of the wife to her own separate property, her own career and income, and her right to privacy with regard to taxation. Reluctance to limit individual freedom by accepting marriage as a life-long union has led to a significant increase in the number of marriages ending in divorce, as well as to many couples choosing to remain unmarried while cohabiting. Both divorce and cohabitation illustrate the rejection of a long-term family view in favour of a shorter-term individualist approach to life and to 'family' relationships. The relationship of parent and child within one household is for a shorter span, and marriage itself or its equivalent may not be expected to be a life-long union.

The development of English law over the last two centuries manifests the impact of these social changes upon family arrangements. Individuals are free to dispose of their property upon death with scarcely any restriction, apart from the discretion of the courts to intervene on behalf of a very limited category of relatives if adequate provision has not been made. The freedom of testation allowed by English law is markedly different from the rights accorded to a wider circle of relatives to receive a fixed portion of the deceased's property under most civil law systems. Since 1882, married women have not been subject to the control of their husbands with regard to the ownership of any kind of property, and are now always assessed separately for Income Tax purposes. The family or marriage settlement, providing for the husband and wife for life and then for any children born to them, has been superseded, largely for tax reasons, and today the matrimonial home is usually owned jointly by the spouses according to terms worked out by them, which terms can be varied by the courts if the relationship breaks down irretrievably. As a rule, no interest in the property is however given to the children of the marriage by their parents, nor by the courts upon dissolution of the matrimonial tie. In recent years, however, the classical concept of carefully stewarding resources bequeathed by earlier generations so as to leave them undiminished to succeeding generations has staged a revival in the area of environmental issues.

2 The Italian Family

Article 29 of the Italian Constitution provides that :

> La Repubblica riconosce i diritti della famiglia come società naturale fondata sul matrimonio.
>
> The Republic recognizes the rights of the family as a natural association founded upon matrimony.

The article presents the concept of the family in Italian law as being 'a natural association founded upon matrimony'. The word natural in this context carries for the civil lawyer an unmistakeable echo of the definition of natural law given at the beginning of Justinian's Institutes. Natural law is there defined as

> what nature teaches every animal, for this law is not confined to humankind but is for every animal which is born, whether in the sky, on the land or in the sea. From it proceeds the union of male and female which we call matrimony, together with the procreation and upbringing of children.
>
> Justinian, Institutes, I. 2.pr.

The Italian legal concept of the family, therefore, is rooted in the civil law tradition. It is a 'natural association' in the sense of an association taught by nature's laws for natural purposes. The word *società* implies a partnership entered into freely by the parties, on analogy with the consensual contract discussed in Chapter Fourteen. This partnership, freely entered into by the parties in accordance with the natural order of things, is said to be founded on matrimony, that is upon the legal institution of marriage.

This emphasis upon marriage as the foundation of family life reflects the teachings of the Roman Catholic Church and of its canon law, a distinct echo of which is also to be heard in the word *società*, partnership. Canon 1055 of the Code of Canon Law speaks of the marriage covenant being one whereby

> a man and a woman establish between themselves a partnership of their whole life, and which of its own very nature is ordered to the well-being of the spouses and to the procreation and upbringing of children.

This definition again echoes the terminology of the Institutes, thus uniting the streams of civilian and canonical tradition which flow so abundantly through modern Italian law. Interestingly, the canon states that the subject of the partnership is to be the parties' whole life, thus identifying one particular form of the contract of *societas* known to the classical and mediaeval jurists.[1]

The modern Italian concept of the family thus has its roots in civil and canon law. For the Roman lawyer too, the *familia*, the entity within the *potestas* of the *pater*, had its origins in matrimony, albeit it the much less formal, largely consensual, Roman law marriage. Only from a lawful marriage did authority and control over children derive, and it was the *paterfamilias* who had that authority and control. Accordingly, one is led to ask whether Italian law also regards the *paterfamilias* or *padre di famiglia* as the person who has authority within the family.

Paternal rather than parental authority was indeed the case in Italian law until very recently. Only in 1975 was the legal equality of the spouses recognized in Italian law, but it was then given the full force of a constitutional principle. A second limb was introduced to article 29 of the Constitution which reads:

> Il matrimonio è ordinato sull' eguaglianza morale e giuridica dei coniugi, con i limiti stabiliti dalla legge a garanzia dell' unità familiare.
>
> Marriage is ordered upon the moral and juridical equality of the spouses, within the limits established by the law as a guarantee of family unity.

This change has been of considerable legal significance. It has imposed upon the Italian people a principle of equality of the spouses within marriage, ending the undisputed control which Italian fathers hitherto enjoyed both with regard to the upbringing of their children and the management of the family property. Instead, both parents now share responsibility and authority for the upbringing of their children, and the family property has been subjected to a system of communion of goods which is a hallmark of the approach of civil law systems generally. In the absence of an agreement by the spouses to adopt a different regime of family property ownership, the system of communion is imposed by law. It is, however, very significant that any variation from the system of communion must be based upon the agreement of both the parties, which is itself symptomatic of the newly imposed equality. The spouses are not free to vary their equalized responsibilities concerning the upbringing of their children, which rights and duties are the subject of constitutional provision.

The changes introduced in this area of Italian law in 1975 in no way affect the legal doctrine of marriage as a partnership. Indeed, they would appear to highlight the importance of partnership within the institution. In a very important sense, Italian law has rediscovered the partnership element within matrimony which is stressed by most civil law systems and by the canon law. One can legitimately compare the imposition of equality between spouses in Italian law with, for instance, the omission of the traditional vow that a wife 'obey' her husband in modern English marriage rites.

However, the question has to be asked whether the change in the law of Italy reflects a change which has actually occurred in Italian life, or whether the law is anticipating social developments and, indeed, seeking to guide, if not accelerate, them. It may well be the case that in the prosperous urban areas of northern Italy, women are seeking equal status with their menfolk, pursuing their own careers, and demanding an equal say in the upbringing of their children and the management of the family wealth to which they contribute by their earnings. In cosmopolitan centres such as Milan or Rome, support for such ideas may indeed be found among the male population. It would, however, be optimistic in the extreme to expect the changes to have been accepted let alone welcomed in the less-developed, economically poorer, more traditional societies of rural Italy and the South, the *Mezzogiorno*. It is doubtful whether the changes have had much impact upon the settled ways of life in these latter areas, and it may well take a generation or two for them to make much impression. The introduction of equality of the spouses into Italian family law is a legislative intervention which seeks to influence the direction and pace of social change, as was the case with, for example, race relations legislation in Britain in the nineteen-sixties and sex discrimination legislation in the 'seventies. In Italy, however, there is a greater danger of further dividing the already disparate societies of the prosperous North and the poorer South in a nation where regional identities and loyalties have always been a strong counterpoise to the development of a true national consciousness. Much the same is true of the introduction of divorce legislation into Italy at this time. Many see the innovation as a law for the middle classes of the Italian cities, where wives have the economic independence to contemplate the break up of their marriage, whereas in the traditional rural areas such a step would not be seriously contemplated. Likewise, the opposition of the Church to divorce is more powerful among the less well-educated populace of the country and the South, but of less influence among the more highly-educated urban population of the North. While the changes described have been of considerable legal significance, it would be wrong to deduce that they have been of great social significance in all parts of the republic.

The introduction of equality of the spouses within the family is a change to the perception of the family in the first sense discussed earlier, that of the household. The perception of the family as a continuing entity, embracing several generations and involving responsibilities between different generations over and above those owed to young children being brought up by their parents, remains unchanged. This is immediately apparent from two facets of modern Italian law, those of the alimentary obligation and the *riserva*.

The alimentary obligation is regulated by articles 433-448 of the Civil Code. It is concerned with the support of persons who have become needy, and imposes an obligation upon various relatives to support the needy person by relieving his or her need, having regard to the position of that person in society and the means at the disposal of the obligees. The obligation can be discharged either by providing for the support of the needy person through paying him sums of money, or by taking the person into the home of those obligated and discharging the obligation in that way. The extent of those bound by this obligation is, however, likely to surprise those whose notion of the family corresponds to the nuclear model proposed at the start of this chapter. The obligation falls upon the following, the absence of members of any one category causing the obligation to pass to the next. In descending order, these are:

the spouse
the children or remoter issue
the parents or remoter ancestors
sons-in-law and daughters-in-law
father-in-law and mother-in-law
brothers and sisters.

The tenor of these provisions is quite clear. Where one member of a family through age, illness of infirmity is in need of financial or other assistance, in short requires looking after or care, the burden of providing that care, the duty of caring, falls upon other members of the family. Most naturally, given the Italian legal view of marriage outlined above, the obligation rests upon the other spouse. In the absence of a surviving spouse, the obligation passes to the children, or in their absence grandchildren, of the person in need. If there are no descendants, or none capable of providing the care needed, the obligation passes to the parents. This would cover for instance the obligation to look after a young person who has suffered an injury causing incapacity or who suffers from a disability which makes it impossible for him to look after himself. If the parents are not able to provide for such a person, the grandparents are bound to do so. Most surprising perhaps to modern English eyes are the next two categories. If no spouse, descendants or ancestors are living, the obligation falls to the sons-in-law and daughters-in-law of the person concerned, or, if there are none, to the parents-in-law. This obligation ceases if the person in need remarries; in that event there will of course be a spouse to discharge the obligation. It also ceases if the spouse who creates the tie of affinity between the person in need and the in-laws or more usually the children or remoter descendants of the marriage have all died. This instance is worth dwelling on, because it illustrates the importance of the family unit. The in-laws are not allowed to look after their grandchildren, for instance, to the exclusion of the children's father, but once their family interest ceases upon the death of their grandchildren so does their obligation. In the absence of any of the above-mentioned relatives, the brothers and sisters of the person in need have a duty to provide for him. However, their obligation is limited to providing the bare necessities for an adult, but extend to paying for the education of a child.

The alimentary obligation is regarded as a very important element of Italian family law. It is not a legal fossil which has remained upon the statute book long after its relevance and usefulness have ended. It is a living force in Italian family life, and was indeed amended in part but not abrogated by the very legislation which introduced divorce and equality of the spouses in 1975. It confirms that the concept of the family which permeates modern Italian law and society is different from that which subsists in Britain. In this country, one may well find in-laws who care for a widowed son-in-law, but it would be unthinkable to consider imposing upon them a legally enforceable obligation to do so. Yet such is the position in Italy.

The fact that a needy relative can call upon the resources of his family to relieve his want is more understandable if it is remembered that in Italy members of the family have an interest in each others' property which cannot be defeated by the making of a will or *inter vivos* gifts. The Civil Code fixes the portion of the estate of the deceased which cannot be disposed of outside the family according to the composition of that family. It is this portion which is known as the part reserved for the family, the *riserva*, and shares in this are guaranteed to the spouse and any children or remoter issue, as well as to the parents and remoter ancestors if there are no descendants. It must be stressed that the *riserva* belongs to these relatives by right. It is not a question of their applying to the courts for reasonable provision to be made for them because the deceased has failed to do so in his will; it is property to which they have an indefeasible legal right. This is very different from the complete freedom of testation accorded to testators in England and Wales, which freedom can only be curtailed by claims from a more limited class of relatives under the Inheritance (Provision for Family and Dependants) Act 1975, which allows the courts to make reasonable financial provision for an applicant. The English courts are not bound to allocate anything to an applicant, and there is certainly no right to a fixed portion of the estate. Moreover, the class of relatives who may apply is limited to the spouse and children, although a person who was being treated as a dependant at the time of the testator's death may also apply. Parents and other ascendants would only be included if within the last category. Prior to

1938, no restrictions were placed at all upon a testator's right to disinherit his family totally, and from 1938 to 1975, provision could only be made to maintain a surviving spouse, sons who were under 21 and unmarried daughters.[2] Although the current provisions are more generous, they are a still a far cry from the civil law notion of relatives being entitled to a fixed quota of the estate.

The Italian system of succession recognizes the continuity of the family. The family is seen as a unit, to which the individuals who compose it contribute. They all have an interest in it, and this interest does not cease upon children reaching the age of majority or getting married. Thus, family obligations continue over several generations, and so do rights in the patrimony of the family. It is important perhaps to note that much of the difficulty experienced in introducing divorce into Italian society and law stemmed from the incompatibility of the concept of terminating a marriage with the notion of the continuity of the family.

To understand Italian family law, it is necessary first of all to appreciate the Italian idea of the family. Having introduced that concept, it is now possible to proceed to elaborate upon it by an examination of the legal provisions. This is best done by following chronologically the progression of an Italian family from marriage, on which the family is founded, through the birth and upbringing of children to the death of the spouses.

3 Marriage[3]

In Italy, as in England and Wales, marriage ceremonies are of two kinds - civil and ecclesiastical. The ecclesiastical ceremony in Italy is that of the Roman Catholic Church, which is not an established Church like the Church of England. Indeed, following the unification of Italy in the nineteenth century, the first Civil Code provided that all marriages should be solemnized according to a civil ceremony, a Church wedding being an optional extra of no significance to the civil law. The approach of the 1865 Civil Code is the one adopted in the vast majority of civil law countries. Marriages have to be solemnized before a civil magistrate to be valid, and only upon completion of the civil formalities may an ecclesiastical ceremony take place. No distinction is made between the various religious denominations, and it is unlawful, indeed criminal, for a religious ceremony to precede the civil formalities.

In Italy, this standard civil law approach ended in 1929 with the signing of the Lateran Pacts between the Italian State and the Vatican. The second of these pacts was a Concordat settling the question of the relation between the Roman Church and the Italian State. Although this Concordat has now been superseded by another, agreed in 1984, the effect upon the law relating to marriages is unchanged in that the marriage ceremonies of the Roman Church continue to be recognized as valid by the State without need of any civil ceremony either before or after the religious service. Hence, from the standpoint of validity, either an ecclesiastical or a civil ceremony is sufficient to contract a marriage in Italian law. It must however be stressed that only the Roman Catholic rite is accorded this privilege. Other religious bodies must conduct their services following a civil ceremony, although a special law passed immediately after the 1929 Concordat allows what is still in law regarded as a civil ceremony to take place in a recognized place of worship other than a Roman Catholic church in the presence of its minister and a State official. The arrangement is much the same as that permitted to non-Anglican marriages under English law.

The 1929 Concordat allowed the Roman Church wide powers with regard to the regulation of ecclesiastical marriages. These extended, for instance, to questions of capacity to contract a marriage and the circumstances in which marriages might be annulled. In effect, the State abdicated jurisdiction over such matters to the ecclesiastical authorities to decide in accordance with canon rather than civil law. The 1984 Concordat has narrowed these powers quite considerably, demanding that for an ecclesiastical ceremony to be recognized as initiating a valid marriage in civil law, the parties must have capacity according to civil as well as canon law. In addition, the 1984 Concordat has ended the automatic acceptance of ecclesiastical nullity decrees in the civil courts, requiring that for acceptance they must satisfy the general requirements set down by the law of the State for the recognition of foreign judgements.

It is necessary, therefore, if one is to understand the law relating to the contracting of marriage in Italy to consider both civil and ecclesiastical ceremonies. As the civil rules regarding capacity apply to both, it will be convenient to consider the civil marriage first.

Civil Marriage[4]

In order to contract a valid, civil law marriage, the parties must both have attained the age of 18, be of sound mind, unmarried, and not related to each other within certain prohibited degrees. In addition, neither must have been convicted of the actual or attempted killing of the other's spouse, the so-called criminal impediment. The female partner must, moreover, not have been married to any other person within the previous 300 days.

These rules relating to capacity are subject to certain exceptions. Thus, it is possible for the *Tribunale* at the suit of the interested party, and having satisfied itself of the physical and mental maturity of the applicant and having heard the views of the *pubblico ministero* and the parents or guardians of the young person, to decree that a person of sixteen or seventeen may proceed to get married if there are weighty reasons for permitting this. Likewise, the same court may permit a woman to remarry within 300 days of the termination of her previous marriage if it is proved conclusively that she is not pregnant or cannot be pregnant by her previous husband. If she is actually pregnant at the time of the termination of her previous marriage, the term during which she may not remarry automatically ends at the birth of the child or other termination of the pregnancy.

With regard to soundness of mind and the criminal impediment, if, at the time when the parties notify the authorities of their intention to marry, proceedings have been commenced but not concluded which could give rise to either of these impediments, it is open to the *pubblico ministero* to seek a postponement of the wedding until the issue of the existence or otherwise of the impediment has been settled. Again, jurisdiction lies with the court of *Tribunale*.

Marriage in Italy is not permitted between persons related in the following manner: between

> any direct ancestor and a direct descendant;
> brothers and sisters, whether of the full or half blood;
> uncle and niece or aunt and nephew;
> anyone and the spouse of a direct ancestor or descendant;
> anyone and the spouse of a person related in the second degree;
> the adopter and the adoptee or any of the latter's descendants;
> children adopted by the same person;
> the adoptee and a child of the adopter;
> adoptee and adopter's spouse or adopter and adoptee's spouse.

The *Tribunale* again has the right to waive the prohibition between uncle and niece, aunt and nephew or anyone and the spouse of a person to whom they are related in the second degree, and may also waive the prohibition preventing marriage with the spouse of a direct ancestor or descendant, provided in this last instance that the marriage has been declared a nullity.

Persons wishing to marry according to the forms of the civil law are required to publish their intention at the town hall or town halls of the commune or communes where they live. The publication consists of a notice being placed at the entrance of the town hall, stating their names, occupations, places of birth, addresses, whether they are of full age or minors, and the place where they intend to get married. The names of their parents, including the maiden names of their mothers, must also be given. It is sufficient for the parties to request publication in the commune where one or other of them resides, the official of that commune having the responsibility of arranging that it be published in the commune of the other party. Both must usually be present to make the request, unless a special authorization has been given to someone to act in their stead. If either or both have not been resident in the commune where they are currently living for a year, publication must also take place in the commune where they were previously resident. The notice must remain open to public inspection for at least eight days, including two successive Sundays.

When the parties go to the town hall to request publication of their intention to marry, they must supply the State official with a copy of their birth certificates together with a signed declaration that they are not prohibited from marrying as a result af any impediment of kindred or affinity. A false declaration constitutes a serious criminal offence. The official has the power to refuse to proceed to publication, but he must give his reasons for so doing in a written certificate. His refusal can be challenged by the parties in the *Tribunale*.

The purpose of publication is to provide an opportunity for objections to the marriage to be raised. Italian law refers to such objections as oppositions. An opposition on the basis of any impediment to the marriage may be raised by the parents of either party, and in the absence of parents by remoter ascendants or collateral relatives within the third degree. If either party is subject to guardianship of any sort, the guardian is permitted to enter an opposition. Where the impediment alleged is that the party is already married, this may be raised by the spouse of the existing marriage, and where it is the 300 day rule that is being violated, the opposition may be lodged by the previous spouse or his relatives. The *pubblico ministero* is also empowered to enter oppositions on any relevant ground.

The notice of opposition must declare the qualification of the person entering the opposition to do so and the nature of the impediment alleged. Notice of the opposition must be given in the form of a citation to the parties and to the State official of the commune where it was intended to celebrate the marriage. An opposition from a qualified objector which raises a just impediment has the effect of suspending the solemnization of the marriage until a judicial sentence has disposed of the opposition. If the opposition is unsuccessful, the objector, if not an ascendant or the *pubblico ministero*, will be liable to compensate for any loss caused to the parties.

If no opposition to the marriage is registered, the marriage may be celebrated not less than four days and not more than 180 days after the completion of the process of publication. The publication is void after this time has elapsed. The marriage must be solemnized in public at the town hall before the State official to whom the request for publication was made. If the marriage is to be celebrated in a different commune, the State official of that commune must be requested to solemnize the wedding by the official to whom the request for publication was made, and must send the latter a transcript of the marriage certificate mentioning the request. This must be sent the day after the marriage. The marriage is solemnized in the presence of two witnesses, who hear the parties declare in turn that they wish to take one another as husband and wife, following which the official declares them to be married. The marriage certificate is drawn up immediately after the ceremony.

It is possible for the formalities described above, both with regard to publication and solemnization, to be varied in certain circumstances. Where weighty cause has been shown, the *Tribunale* may reduce the period of publication to a shorter time or dispense with it altogether. To dispense with publication, very serious cause must be shown. This is done by four relatives of the parties declaring upon oath before the *pretore* of the *mandamento* where at least one of the parties lives, that the parties are well-known to them and that they know of no impediment to the marriage. The *pretore* then sends the declarations to the *Tribunale* with the reasons for the omission of the period of publication. If permission is forthcoming, the parties must present to the official who will solemnize the marriage the evidence normally required of them to commence the process of publication.

Where one of the parties is in imminent danger of death, the State official may proceed immediately to solemnize the marriage upon the parties swearing that there is no impediment to their marriage. The official must state in the marriage certificate the manner in which he satisfied himself that there was imminent danger of death. Where there is no such danger, but one of the parties is unable to attend the town hall owing to illness or some other similar cause, the official accompanied by a secretary is permitted to solemnize the marriage wherever the incapacitated party is situated, proceeding in the normal fashion but in the presence of four, rather than two, witnesses.

Concordat Marriages[5]

Whereas marriages which are to be solemnized in a place of worship other than a Roman Catholic church must conform to the above requirements in all respects other than the location of the ceremony, Roman Catholic weddings form a distinct class in that the religious ceremony is of itself treated as giving rise to a valid civil law marriage. This is broadly similar to the manner in which ecclesiastical weddings solemnized according to the rites of the Church of England or the Church in Wales are treated in this country. If, however, the Roman Catholic wedding is to give rise to a valid civil law marriage, it is necessary that both parties should have capacity to marry according to the civil law rules discussed above. Thus, for instance, although the canon law regards sixteen and fourteen as being the age at which capacity to marry arises in males and females respectively, Italian law would not accept as valid for example the ecclesiastical marriage of a fifteen year old girl. In fairness, it should be stated that the canon law permits the Episcopal Conference to substitute higher ages within its territories so as to obviate any risk of conflict. However, although the Church cannot dispense with the civil law requirements regarding capacity, it is permitted to insist upon additional qualifications. Thus, the State accepts that the Church may refuse to marry the unbaptised, those who have been ordained into Sacred Orders or who have taken vows of chastity, and those who are perpetually impotent. Generally, the Church also forbids marriage within the fourth degree of collateral relationship, which is two degrees wider than the civil law, although it reserves the right to grant dispensations to those related in the third and fourth degrees. It also recognizes an impediment of public propriety, whereby a relationship within one degree to either of a cohabiting couple is a bar to matrimony with either partner. If either party has been previously married and the spouse of that marriage is still living, the marriage not having been annulled, this too is an impediment to a Concordat marriage.

Prior to an ecclesiastical ceremony, the parties approach the parish priest upon whom the duty rests of inquiring with regard to the existence of these impediments. It is likewise his responsibility to see that banns are published at the church, giving an opportunity to others to raise objections to the marriage. The couple themselves must declare that they know of no impediment to their union and that they are baptized. Following the due publication of banns, which is conducted in the manner designated by the Episcopal Conference, the marriage is generally to be solemnized in the parish church of the ecclesiastical parish where at least one of the parties is domiciled or has been resident for one month prior to the ceremony. The service is usually conducted by the parish priest, and there must be two witnesses present. The ceremony must follow the liturgy of the Roman Catholic Church or a rite approved by the bishop. It must always contain a request for the consent of the parties to marry one another, which consents must be forthcoming. The marriage must be registered as soon as possible after this, and it is in fact customary for the registration to take place immediately after the exchange of vows within the main body of the church before the assembled congregation, prior to the celebration of the nuptial Mass. Special provisions exist to deal with emergency situations, such as where one party is in imminent danger of death, allowing sworn declarations to be taken in lieu of the publication of banns.

Nullity[6]

So far the discussion has turned upon the qualifications which Italian law demands of parties who wish to be married, and the formalities which have to be observed. It has been seen that opportunity is given for objections to be raised to a marriage. However, if a ceremony has taken place, it is still possible for the validity of the marriage celebrated to be challenged. Such challenges after a ceremony allege that the marriage which has been celebrated is a nullity. Nullity decrees relating to marriages celebrated according to the civil law regulations are sought in the civil courts, while those relating to ecclesiastical ceremonies are pursued in the courts of the Church. The grounds of nullity differ in part depending upon the jurisdiction consulted.

Within the jurisdiction of the civil law, no marriage can possibly exist if the parties are of the same sex or if the necessary promises were not exchanged. The promises are regarded as not having been exchanged if either or both parties make them subject to any sort of condition. In other cases, however, a nullity decree has to be sought by a person interested in the marriage. Sometimes the class of person who may contest the validity of the marriage is limited. Where a decree has to be sought for the marriage to be annulled, it is said to be voidable. A marriage may either be absolutely or relatively voidable, the former category being those which any interested party can contest, the latter confined to those expressly allowed to challenge its validity in law. The former class consists of marriages which are marred by the existence of an impediment by reason of a prior marriage, relationship of the parties within the prohibited degrees or the existence of the criminal impediment. However, where the prohibited degrees concerned are those from which the *Tribunale* can grant a dispensation, if the marriage is not challenged within a year of its celebration, it ceases to be voidable.

Where the impediment relates to age, mental infirmity, natural incapacity to understand the nature of marriage or the ceremony, duress, error, impotence or simulation, it may only be challenged by certain persons. In the case of age, the spouses may contest the validity of the marriage within a year of reaching the age of majority, and the parents of the spouses and the *pubblico ministero* may seek to annul the marriage at any time prior to the spouses reaching the age of majority or conceiving a child, the latter event terminating the possibility of objection only if the spouses themselves wish the marriage to continue. Where the objection is that a spouse was judicially interdicted as mentally infirm at the time of the marriage, the guardian or the *pubblico ministero* may seek annulment at any time up to one year after the interdict is lifted. Where the complaint is that a spouse was temporarily incapable of understanding that he or she was getting married at the time of the ceremony or the nature of the promises being made, either spouse may seek annulment unless they have cohabited for a year since the incapacity ended. If one spouse was forced by violence or fear to contract the marriage, that spouse may seek its annulment unless he or she has continued to cohabit with the other for a year since the duress or fear ended. In the case of simulation, that is a pre-marital agreement not to honour the rights and responsibilities which attend matrimony, either spouse may contest the marriage's validity within a year of its celebration, whereupon the possibility of annulment ceases if during that time they have lived together as man and wife. If either spouse was permanently impotent at the time of the marriage, the other may seek annulment at any time thereafter. Error as to the identity of the other party or in relation to certain personal characteristics of the other will permit of a nullity decree. In this last case, however, it must be shown that the party seeking the decree would not have consented to marriage if he or she were aware of the true facts, and the error must relate to a physical or mental condition or sexual proclivity of the other party which impedes the development of married life. Alternatively, the other must have been convicted of a crime and condemned to a prison sentence of at least five years, been declared an habitual or professional criminal, or been convicted for crimes relating to prostitution and sent to prison for at least two years. Error as to a personal quality is also admitted if the wife has, since the marriage, been found to be pregnant with another man's child.

All of the above are causes for the granting of a decree of nullity in the civil courts in relation to a marriage according to the civil regulations. Where the marriage was solemnized by the Roman Catholic Church, the issue of nullity is to be tried by the ecclesiastical courts. A finding of nullity in those courts will only be accepted by the State courts on the same basis that the judgement of a foreign court will be endorsed. Extra grounds of nullity are available in canon law, for instance those deriving from the impediment of being unbaptized, being in Sacred Orders or having undertaken a vow of perpetual chastity. Nullity may also arise from the extended prohibited degrees recognized by canon law and from the concept of prohibiting marriages against public propriety. Although the civil law does not itself recognize these impediments, where the parties have chosen to marry according to the rites, and therefore the law, of the Roman Church, the ecclesiastical nullity decree will be accepted by the civil authorities. If the parties had wished to exclude this possibility of nullity, all they needed to do after all was opt for a civil ceremony.

4 The Spouses and their Children[7]

The formation of a valid marriage between a husband and a wife brings into existence a whole set of predetermined legal obligations. These obligations are now by and large mutual given the principle of equality between the spouses introduced in 1975. Both the husband and the wife therefore are currently subject to the same rights and duties, each spouse having a right to expect that the other will fulfil his or her duties. The duties are those of fidelity, the giving of moral and material assistance, cohabitation and collaboration in the management of the interests of the family.

The fact that these duties are actually expressed in the Civil Code is significant. English lawyers would probably recognize in them standards deviation from which would constitute what was once called a matrimonial offence. Thus, breach of the duty of fidelity constitutes adultery; breach of the duty to cohabit is desertion, and so on. What Italian law has done is to articulate its underlying doctrine of marriage, and the doctrine is manifestly related to that which exists in English law, both being descendants of the canonical concept of matrimony as a partnership of the spouses. The great difference in Italian law since 1975 is that the notion of collaboration has replaced that of the wife's obedience to her husband, a change which brings Italian marriage closer to both its canonical and civilian roots.

Each spouse is bound to discharge the duties described according to the means at his or her disposal, having regard to their capacity to work both in the sense of going out to work and working in the home. By these means, both are required to contribute to the needs of the family. Upon marriage, the wife adds to her own name that of her husband. Thus, for instance, upon marrying Signor Leonardo Bruni, the Signorina Maria Carpanini would become the Signora Maria Carpanini Bruni. Her right to her husband's name would remain if she was widowed, but would be lost upon remarriage. Continued membership of her own family is signalled by her continued formal use of her maiden name, and this membership is of course a real connection given the existence, for example, of the alimentary obligation.

Since 1975, it is for both spouses to decide questions of family life by agreement. Thus, the Civil Code expressly states that they are to agree as to where the family should live. In the event of their being unable to agree, either may informally request the arbitration of the *pretore*, an excellent example of the informality which is a distinctive feature of the Italian courts at local level. The *pretore* listens to both sides of the argument, and very significantly is required to listen to the views of any children who are aged sixteen or over and who are living at home. This last point illustrates neatly that the function of the *pretore* is to settle a family problem, not just a dispute between the spouses. Having listened to the parties, he attempts a compromise solution. If his compromise is not acceptable, and the dispute is about something which has to be determined one way or another, for instance where the family is to live, then the spouses jointly may expressly authorise him to settle the question as he deems best for the unity and life of the family. Again, family interests are uppermost. This provision allowing the *pretore* to settle the question in these circumstances is very significant, for it exemplifies the notion of judicial authority arising from the agreement of the parties, not as the result of the imposition of State power. Such an idea is deeply rooted in the civil law tradition, being the original basis of adjudication in classical Roman law.[8]

Either spouse forfeits the right to moral and material support by leaving the family home without just cause, just cause being in effect an intention to seek the termination of the relationship by annulment, divorce or separation. Where an unjustifiable departure leads to a failure by the departing spouse to honour the obligation to provide moral and material assistance to the deserted spouse, the courts can order sequestration of property sufficient to ensure that the obligation is discharged.

Children[9]

Both spouses are under a duty to maintain, educate and bring up their children, having due regard to the latter's capacity, natural inclination and aspiration. In discharging this obligation, regard must be had to the spouses' means, and their ability to work either professionally or in the home. The Italian notion of the family surfaces once more at this point because the law expressly provides that if the parents do not have sufficient means to discharge their duties to their offspring, other ascendant relatives, according to the nearness of their relationship to the children, must provide the parents with the wherewithal to fulfil their responsibilities. If they do not contribute in this manner, the *Tribunale* can declare the contributions which must be paid by them to either parent. Such a declaration can be appealed against, and the interests of others to whom the persons owe obligations must be borne in mind.

Children in Italian law have duties with regard to their parents also. Thus, it is expressly provided by law that they owe their parents respect, and should contribute according to their means and ability to the maintenance of the family while they are living as part of it. There is no right to leave home prior to reaching the age of majority. Children are subject to the authority, *potestà*, of their parents until they reach the age of majority, which in Italy is eighteen, or are emancipated. Emancipation occurs in the case of a minor who marries before coming of age. Parental authority was once that of the father alone, but since 1975 has been jointly exercised by both parents. The possibility of dispute which this admits is resolved by the provision that such problems shall be resolved by the *Tribunale per i minorenni*,[10] which must decide such issues in the interests of the child and, significantly, family unity. Where either parent is absent from the home or incapacitated, parental authority is exercised by the other. The rights and duties of parenthood do not cease for either spouse upon the termination of the marriage by divorce or separation.

Children have the right to their own property in Italian law, but the parents have both the right and the duty to manage this property and to represent their children's interests in any litigation regarding it. They are not however allowed to perform transactions which could endanger the capital, for instance by sale, gift, mortgage or pledge. The parents have a usufruct of their children's property, that is a right to use it and take the income, but only to provide for the maintenance of the family and the education of the child. In essence, this right of usufruct corresponds to the child's duty, if he or she has an income, to contribute to the family's maintenance. The usufruct does not attach to property which the child has obtained through his or her own labour, nor to property given or bequeathed to the child for the purpose of carrying on a profession, trade or calling, nor to property given or bequeathed to the child against the parents' wishes or subject to an express exclusion of the parental usufruct. Mismanagement of a child's property by the parent can lead to the appointment of a curator to supervise the child's affairs.

Parental authority arises in relation to the legitimate children of the spouses born during their marriage. A child is deemed to be legitimate if conceived during the course of the parents' marriage, Italian law unlike English law making conception not birth the important factor. A child is presumed to have been conceived during the marriage if born more than 180 days after the celebration, and not more than 300 days after the termination of the marriage or the separation of the spouses. If the child is born before 180 days have elapsed since the ceremony, the presumption of legitimacy remains unless challenged by one of the spouses or the child, while if the child is born outside of the 300-day limit, it is for the parents or their heirs to seek a declaration of legitimacy in favour of the child.

A child conceived outside of lawful wedlock is called in Italian law a natural child, an expression which sounds a trifle antiquated to English ears. Such a child can be recognized by either of its parents, that is acknowledged as a child to whom all the rights and duties of parenthood pertain. A child born of an incestuous union may not however be recognized, an incestuous union being for this purpose one in which the parties are related by kindred or affinity in the direct line or within two degrees of collateral relationship, provided in the case of relationships by affinity that the relationship was known to the parties and that the marriage giving rise to it has not been annulled. Either parent may recognize a natural child, but if the child is sixteen years old or over, his or her consent to the recognition must also be obtained. The child takes the surname of the recognizing parent. Recognition does not however legitimate the child. Legitimation can only be achieved by the subsequent marriage of the parents or by decree of the *Tribunale per minorenni*, the latter method being used mainly where one parent is dead so that legitimation by subsequent marriage is impossible. Only children who may be recognized can be legitimated, and legitimation can affect the rights of descendants of a natural child who had died prior to legitimation. The rights of legitimated children and of their descendants are backdated to the time of their parents' marriage, and they are recognized as the children of both parents.

Adoption[11]

In England and Wales, adoption is thought of in terms of two interrelated functions. These are to provide young children for the spouses of a childless marriage, and to provide a home for children who have been orphaned, abandoned or for some other cause deprived of their parents' care. These are not the traditional motives for adoption in civil law jurisdictions. In the latter, it is not the care of orphans or the opportunity for parental fulfilment which provides the context for adoption, but the need to continue the family into the next generation. To die without leaving an heir was traditionally regarded as a disaster, and one way of remedying the lack of a child to fulfil the function of heir was to adopt the child of another who would thereafter continue the otherwise extinct family line. This second form of adoption is not therefore aimed at the upbringing of young children, but is indeed more common in relation to mature adults. This was in fact the only form of adoption known in Italy until 1967, when adoption of the other variety, concerned with the upbringing of infants, was introduced, as it had been in England and Wales in 1926.[12] In Italy, such adoptions are still termed 'special'.

The traditional form of civil law adoption, as has been said, has as its purpose the provision of an heir for a person with no children of his own. It is therefore only available to childless persons. As the possibility of such persons ever having children must be virtually extinct, such adoption is only available for people aged 35 or over, although in exceptional cases the *Tribunale* can consent to adoption by a person who is under 35 but at least 30 years old. In addition, the adopting parents must be 18 years older than the adopted child. Adoption is only open to married couples, and it is not permitted for them to adopt a child of either of them born outside of their marriage. Both spouses must consent to the adoption, as must the adoptee and the adoptee's parents if alive. The *Tribunale* has powers to substitute its consent if the consent of the adoptee's parents is unreasonably withheld or cannot be obtained. The adoptee takes the surname of the adoptor, but retains the greater part of his rights and duties within his original family. No connection is established between the adoptors and the adoptee's family, nor between the adoptee and the families of the adoptors. Special provision is made for the mode of succession by the adoptee from the adoptor, but the latter has no succession rights as against the former. This reflects the fact that the death of the adoptee prior to that of the adoptor defeats the object of the adoption, namely the continuance of the adoptor's line in the person of the adoptee. This having been frustrated, the adoption ends with the death of the adoptee, whereas its purpose would have been fulfilled by the death of the adoptor. Both parties must be worthy of the adoption, and the *Tribunale* can revoke an adoption following either party committing an unworthy act against the other, for example by attempting to take the life of the other or perpetrating a vicious assault upon them.

This traditional form of adoption is geared to the adoption of a person who has already attained the age of majority. The capacity of the adoptee to consent is essential. The adoption is effected by the decree of the *Tribunale*, which has a discretion to approve or disapprove of an adoption of this sort, but must satisfy itself that the consents of the parties have been obtained. Adult consent is of the essence of this type of adoption, which cannot therefore serve to provide for the adoption of young children. The English lawyer is therefore bound to inquire whether Italian law makes provision for the adoption of orphaned children and for adoption by childless couples who wish to bring up a family.

Given the considerable emphasis placed upon family life by Italian law, it is not surprising to discover that the Civil Code expressly asserts the right of children to be brought up within their own families. This is the starting point for considering what can be done, for instance, for the orphaned child. Thus, the law seeks where possible to place such children in the care of relatives who are appointed their guardians, and there is of course an obligation upon certain relatives to maintain the child by virtue of the alimentary obligation. Until quite recently, if a person had raised a foundling child for a period of three years, it was open for them to seek to have the child affiliated into the family. This gave the child the name of the family, and created the obligations of parenthood between the parties.

However, the child got no interest in the family by succession. In other words, the institution of affiliation was geared to the upbringing of the foundling only, and in fact institutionalized neighbourly conduct. In 1983, this institution was swept away by a new regime, which recognized that such affiliation should only be a short-term measure, and that special adoption was preferable for the child who had no family to which to return.

Today, therefore, Italian law provides that if a child is temporarily deprived of a family environment, such child can be affiliated into another family, possibly one with minor children, or even to a single person or to a family-type community. Such affiliation is meant to ensure the continuance of the child's maintenance, education and upbringing in a family atmosphere. If such affiliation is not possible, the child is placed in a public or private institution of assistance, care being taken that the institution should be as near as possible to the child's home. Affiliation with a family is much preferred, and emphasizes again the importance attached by Italian law to the family context, and also here to the preservation of neighbourliness and community responsibility. Where however the child has been abandoned or the loss of moral and material assistance is not of a temporary nature caused by factors outside of the parents' control, the *Tribunale per minorenni* may declare that the child is adoptable. This enables special adoption of the child to take place.

Special adoption is open to married couples of at least three-years standing, who are living with one another. It is open to such a couple to adopt a child who is at least eighteen and no more than forty years younger than the parties. For the adoption to proceed, the child if fourteen or over must consent, must be consulted if twelve, and may be consulted even if younger. In the normal course of things, the *Tribunale per minorenni* authorizes a period of pre-adoptive affiliation following an informal hearing at which the *pubblico ministero*, the child and the child's parents, if living, are heard. The court does not normally allow one child of a larger family to be affiliated alone. After one year, it is open to the same court as declared the child adoptable to decide that the special adoption may proceed, having listened to the views of the *pubblico ministero*, the child, the child's parents if living, the guardian, the *giudice tutelare*, and the welfare services. If the adopting couple have children of their own, those which are aged fourteen and over must also be consulted. The decree when issued grants the child the status of a legitimate child in the new family, the name of which he takes. The child's rights in his original family cease, but the prohibition upon marriage within the prohibited degrees still applies to the original family.

Guardianship[13]

Where a child is orphaned or for some other reason the parents are unable to exercise their parental authority, the *pretore* has the power to appoint a guardian or *tutore*. In each *mandamento* there is indeed a special magistrate to deal with questions of guardianship, called the *giudice tutelare*. The notion of having a special magistrate to perform this function dates back to classical Roman law and the office of the *praetor tutelarius*. The terminology of Italian law guardianship is also redolent of the civil law inheritance.[14]

The *giudice tutelare* must be informed that a child has been orphaned, either by the State official who registered the death of the parent or by the notary who was responsible for the will in which the deceased parent named a *tutore* for the child. It is however the responsibility of the *giudice tutelare* to nominate the *tutore* officially. It is normal to nominate one *tutore* for all the children of the deceased parent who require one. If the interests of the children conflict in relation to some particular matter, a special curator is appointed to deal with that matter. Usually, the *tutore* appointed is the person named to act in that capacity in the deceased parent's will, or in a public deed or an authenticated private writing. If the parent has not provided for a *tutore* for his child, the office falls to the most closely related ascendant or other collateral relative of the child. The person designated should be heard before being officially appointed, and the views of the child if sixteen or more years old should also be taken. It is important that the person appointed should be suitable. The *tutore* is required to take an oath of loyalty and diligence with regard to the guardianship. The law recognizes valid excuses for declining the office. If no person can be found to assume the responsibility, the child may be placed in an institute for assistance.

The *tutore* has the care of the person of the minor, and represents him in all civil acts and property transactions. The minor in return must respect and obey the *tutore*. In short, the relationship is modelled on that of parent and child. Given the patrimonial responsibility which the *tutore* has, he receives an inventory of the child's property prior to assuming office and is required to provide a regular account of his administration. He may be required to provide a sum of money as security against the possibility of loss being suffered by the minor, which sum is called the *cautio*. Following the standard required in classical Roman law, the *tutore* is expected to manage the property in the manner of a good father of the family, a *buon padre di famiglia*, a designation which has remained unaltered so far despite the advent of equality of the spouses with regard to parental authority and the management of family property. The *tutore* is liable for any loss caused by his failure to achieve this standard of diligence. He can however be exonerated from liability for good cause, but equally can be removed or suspended from office if discovered to be guilty of negligence or abuse of power, or is shown to be inept, unworthy or insolvent. At the coming of age of the minor, a final account of the guardianship must be approved by the *giudice tutelare*, although it is open for either party to commence an action on the guardianship within five years of the office terminating.

5 Family Property[15]

As well as creating a new set of rights and duties among the persons who make up the family, the marriage of the spouses affects their rights with regard to their property. Until 1975, the husband as *padre di famiglia* controlled the family property, but the principle of equality between the spouses has caused Italian law to adopt the regime of communion of goods as between the spouses which is typical of civil law jurisdictions generally.

One must begin by noting the significance of the word communion, *comunione*. It is the term employed by Italian law to indicate co-ownership.[16] Its roots lie in the Roman consensual contract of *societas*, which could indicate a sharing of all of the property of the partners. This is exactly, of course, the definition of marriage to be found in canon law, where it is described as an agreement between the spouses to establish 'a partnership of their whole life', and it is noticeable that life is in the singular to indicate the union achieved. The word *communion* comes from the Greek word κοινωνια which was used to translate *societas* in legal texts. The sacramental dimension of the sharing or partnership which this word implies comes down into English in the use of Communion to describe the sacrament of the sharing of the body and blood of Christ.

To say, therefore, that the spouses share a communion of property is to use a phrase which endorses once more the civil and canon law heritage of the Italian legal tradition. The phrase is not arbitrarily chosen, but full of meaning to the Italian lawyer and lay person. Where the English lawyer speaks of the totality of a person's property as that person's estate, the Italian lawyer uses the word patrimony. However, an English lawyer knows nothing of the notion of family property. To him, the husband has an estate and the wife has an estate, but the family is not a legal person and cannot therefore own property. The Italian lawyer, on the other hand, recognizes that the husband may have his own property which constitutes his patrimony and that the wife may have property which constitutes hers, but he also recognizes a third patrimony which comes into existence upon their marriage, namely that of the family. It is this third patrimony which is composed of the property in the communion.

The parties are not however bound to participate in such a communion. Their consent is essential, as one would expect in an institution based upon a consensual contract. However, that consent is implied unless it is expressly withheld. In other words, upon marriage the spouses are presumed to intend that the provisions of the Civil Code relating to the establishment of a communion of property shall govern their affairs unless it is recorded on their marriage certificate or in a notarially authenticated deed that they wish to continue to enjoy separate property rights, or establish an alternative sharing arrangement. If they opt for a communion of some sort, there comes into existence a patrimonial fund, which is in effect that of the family. This fund will consist of the property which the Civil Code provides is to form the communion, unless the spouses provide an alternative arrangement in the form of a public deed. The fund which is established by either method will last until the marriage itself terminates, but if there are children under the age of majority at that time, the fund remains in existence until they have attained full age. Thus, the fund is not just for the spouses, but for the family which their marriage has brought into being, remembering that this is the purpose of the marriage partnership according to the canonical doctrines which have influenced Italian law. Similarly, the property which constitutes the fund cannot be alienated, mortgaged or pledged without the consent of both spouses and, what is again significant, the consent of the court if there are minor children. The final consent indicates clearly that the children have an interest in the family patrimony.

It is important therefore to remember that an Italian lawyer dealing with the affairs of any person will be conscious of the person's interests in his own personal patrimony and that of his family. Thus, if for a moment attention is limited to the affairs of a married couple who as yet have no children, one must contemplate the existence of three possible patrimonies;

that of the husband, that of the wife and that of the family - the family communion.

All the property which the spouses had acquired prior to their marriage will remain part of their respective personal patrimonies. Likewise, any property which they are given or succeed to after their marriage, or which they acquire for their own personal use. If they acquire property as a result of exchange or purchase from their personal funds, then again such property will enter their personal patrimony, as will property acquired for use in their profession trade or calling, or received in compensation for personal injury.

The family patrimony, on the other hand, will consist of all the property acquired by either or both spouses during the marriage, together with the income earned by the spouses during that period. The income from their personal patrimonies also accrues to the family patrimony while the marriage subsists, and if they establish a business venture together this will also be treated as part of the communion. These provisions relate to marriages taking place after 1975; special provisions cover previously existing unions.

Each spouse remains in complete control of his or her personal patrimony, but the management of the communion is shared by them, unless there is express agreement to the contrary. Both spouses must consent to dealings with the property, otherwise the other spouse may avoid a transaction regarding which there was no consultation within a year of its being discovered or, if it involved immovable property or a registrable moveable, within a year of registration or a year of the end of the communion if the transfer had not been registered. If the property cannot be recovered for the communion, the guilty spouse must compensate the communion from his or her personal patrimony.

The purpose which the communion serves is to provide for the needs of the family. It is important to note that it is not meant to provide for the wants of individual members as individuals. This distinction is absent from English law. Thus, creditors of one spouse cannot proceed against the communion while there are assets within that spouse's personal patrimony, and even after that is exhausted can only proceed against the spouse's share in the communion after creditors of the communion - who are regarded as a separate group - have been satisfied. Likewise, creditors of the communion cannot proceed against a spouse's personal patrimony while there remain assets in the communion. The spouses' personal patrimonies can be indebted to one another and to the communion, and vice versa.

The communion of property usually lasts until the marriage itself ends with the death of one of the spouses or its termination by annulment, divorce, or judicial or consensual separation. However, it is open to the spouses to bring the communion to an end by agreeing to change their patrimonial regime from that of communion to that of separate patrimonies or to a differently constituted communion. The bankruptcy of either spouse also terminates the communion. Likewise, if one spouse is unfit to participate in the running of the communion by reason of being judicially interdicted on grounds of insanity, is otherwise incapable or has proved a bad administrator, the other can seek a separation of goods so as to end the communion.

While the communion is in existence, the spouses have undivided shares therein. Usually, the undivided shares are equal shares. However, the question of the quantification of the spouses' shares does not really arise until the communion ends, when quantification must take place. Unlike English law, which in such circumstances carries out elaborate inquiries into contributions made by the spouses to jointly-owned property, the existence of the communion in Italian law obviates this difficulty. All that has to be done is discover what constitutes the communion. Once this has been done, the fund is divided according to the expressly agreed terms of the communion or, otherwise, in equal shares.

It is open to the spouses, as has been indicated, to vary their interests in the communion, but as this has to be done by deed, the difficult problems which attend questions of implied intention with regard to such matters in English law do not arise. The spouses may also choose to vary the items which make up the communion, for example by excluding the income derived from their personal patrimonies. However, they are not allowed to include in the communion compensation payments, personal effects and items which they own in connection with their work. To include the last category would clearly be to the detriment of business creditors. Independently-minded couples can of course opt for complete separation of patrimonies with no communion. Thus, in effect, Italian law currently has as its mean the regime of communion which reflects its inherent attitude to the partnership involved in family life, but provides for individualist variations to be accomplished. This is not a bad indicator of where Italian family law in general stands on the threshold of the twenty-first century: strong on tradition but accommodating current trends.

6 Termination of Marriage : Separation and Divorce

Marriage in Italian law is, as has been shown, a partnership that is meant to be of the whole life of the couple. The natural termination of the institution is therefore the death of one of the parties. Death ends the union, terminates the communion of property and requires that others succeed to the patrimony of the deceased. Provision may have to be made for the guardianship of children and other obligations which the deceased can no longer perform. Interestingly, if there are minor children at the date of the spouse's death, the communion remains in existence until the youngest has reached majority. This rule can be directly referred to the doctrine that one of the functions of matrimony is the upbringing of children, so that the incidents of matrimony, like the communion of property, cannot cease until the purpose has been achieved.

The termination of marriage by death will be considered below together with the law of succession. However, as well as this natural termination of the married state, marriages can also end in Italy as a result of separation and, since 1975, divorce. As with death, termination by virtue of any of these causes ends the communion of property, as the partnership has ended. However, questions have to be settled about the continuing obligations of the parties to provide moral and material assistance, bring up the children and live in the matrimonial home. Again, the existence of minor children can lead to the postponement of the severance of the communion until they have come of age. These methods of terminating matrimony must therefore be considered in turn.

Separation[17]

Italian law recognizes two forms of separation: judicial and consensual. They differ from divorce in that, although the obligation to cohabit ends, the parties do not re-acquire a capacity to marry, as they remain married to each other. Until 1975, when divorce in the sense of terminating not just the obligations of matrimony but the married state itself was introduced, so that the former spouses are free to remarry, such separation was the only method by which some of the obligations of marriage could be terminated during the joint lifetime of the parties.

Judicial separation is granted by the courts at the suit of one of the spouses, upon verification that circumstances render it intolerable for the spouses to continue living together or risk grave prejudice to the bringing up of the children. It is perfectly possible for such states of affairs to exist without any blame attaching to either spouse, such as where one is suffering from a mental illness. However, in granting the decree, the judge may declare that one of the parties is to blame for the situation, addressing himself primarily to breaches of the obligations of matrimony, for instance adultery or desertion. Such a finding obviously influences the orders which the judge will make concerning the continuing rights and obligations of the parties with regard to one another and the children.

In granting a judicial separation, the judge is required to award custody of the children to one of the spouses, and to take such other steps as are necessary for their welfare in the light of their, that is the children's, moral and material interests, in particular making provision for their maintenance, education and upbringing. The spouse who obtains custody usually has parental authority over the children, but major decisions concerning their upbringing continue to be shared. Occupation of the matrimonial home also normally goes to the spouse who is given custody of the children, a provision which mirrors the fact that the communion of property will not have terminated if there are minor children to be brought up. The decisions made by the judge at the time of granting the judicial separation can be varied at the request of the parties in the light of changes in their circumstances. The question of the obligation to maintain each other must be settled in the light of the blame attaching to either spouse for the separation, the law requiring that maintenance be settled to the advantage of the innocent party, while taking into account their circumstances. Security for the honouring of this obligation can be required, and the obligation is open to variation to take account of changing circumstances. The wife can be forbidden to continue using the husband's name, if this is shown to be prejudicial to him. The separation ends upon the reconciliation of the spouses.

Consensual separation differs from judicial separation, as the description suggests, in that the separation is achieved by the consent of the parties. That consent must however be registered, or homologated to use the technical term employed by Italian law, before the separation is officially recognized, rather in the manner that marriage is based on consent but is only recognized if officially registered. The need for registration allows the judge to inspect the terms upon which the parties have agreed and to vary them, particularly when he feels that the terms which the spouses have worked out are disadvantageous to the children. The hearing before the judge is entirely informal. Reconciliation again ends the separation.

Divorce[18]

The canonical basis of marriage in Italian law meant until very recently that the refusal of the Roman Catholic Church to accept that a marriage could be terminated other than by the death of one of the spouses stood as a barrier to the State developing the institution of divorce in civil law. The presence of an ecclesiastical form of marriage, over which the Church courts continue to have jurisdiction, continues to affect the manner in which the new divorce laws are expressed. Thus, civil marriages are ended by divorce, but ecclesiastically solemnized marriages have their civil effects ended by such a decree. Thus does canon law continue to influence the shape of Italian civil law. In fact, the two concepts do not differ substantially, other than that the parties to an ecclesiastically solemnized marriage the civil effects of which have ended in divorce are not free to remarry in an ecclesiastical ceremony. They can of course remarry in a civil registry.[19]

Divorce legislation was passed by the Italian parliament in 1970, but was not brought into operation until 1975, following a referendum instigated as the result of the opposition of the Christian Democratic Party (DC). The DC had hoped that the Church would step into the fray and condemn the introduction of divorce laws into the republic. However, the politicians of the DC failed to appreciate the international stance which the Vatican had adopted under the papacy of Paul VI. Virtually on the eve of the referendum, the Pope signalled his unwillingness to interfere in Italian domestic affairs, considering it incidental that the Holy See was situated in Italy. He was therefore not prepared to interfere in Italian politics any more than in French, American or Japanese politics. The failure of the Papacy to support the DC contributed to the failure of the referendum to stop the introduction of divorce into Italy, as well as the end of the traditional alliance between the Roman Church and the DC in State affairs.

The 1975 legislation on divorce was amended in 1987. Currently, a decree of divorce will be granted if it is shown by the party seeking the divorce that the other spouse has been convicted of a crime for which a sentence of fifteen years imprisonment or more could be imposed, even if, unknown to the spouse, the crime was committed before the marriage. Conviction for certain other crimes, such as incest, indecent assaults involving violence or upon children and rape, is also a ground for divorce, as is the commission of certain crimes while insane. The non-consummation of the marriage is treated as a reason for divorce in Italy, unlike England

and Wales where, despite severe criticism, it is still a ground of nullity. Divorce will also be granted if it is shown that a foreign court has granted the other spouse a divorce and that other spouse has since remarried outside of the Italian jurisdiction.

At the time of the introduction of divorce into Italy in 1975, separation was a ground for divorce provided it had subsisted for at least five years, which period was extended to six years if the other party opposed the divorce and to seven years if the party seeking it had been solely to blame for the separation. In 1987, these distinctions were swept away, so that today a period of three years separation is sufficient to warrant either party seeking the dissolution of the marriage or the civil effects thereof. This seems a sensible change given the conditions which control judicial and consensual separation.

Where a spouse petitions the court for a divorce, the first duty of the judge is to attempt to reconcile the parties. The informal nature of Italian preliminary hearings makes such attempts a living reality rather than the empty formality which they have become in English law. If the court is satisfied that it is not possible to maintain the spiritual and material communion between the parties, a concept again redolent of the canonical background to Italian marriage law, the application can proceed. Following the issue of a divorce decree, the wife must cease to use the husband's name unless it is in the interest of their childen that she should retain it. Maintenance between the spouses is ordered by the court according to the circumstances which led to the divorce - taking into account the economic circumstances of the family, the responsibility of either for the breakdown of the marriage and the manner in which each had previously contributed to the family expenses and patrimony. The duties of the spouses to maintain, educate and bring up their children continue, even if either or both go on to contract new marriages. The court makes orders with regard to custody and maintenance, having regard to the moral and material interests of the children. Parental authority is again usually granted to the former spouse who gets custody, but both are required to participate in the making of major decisions with regard to the children and the former spouse who is not granted custody has both a right and a duty to supervise the education and upbringing of the children. As with judicial separation, the parent with custody normally retains occupation of the matrimonial home. Apart from these factors, maintenance orders favour the former spouse who has the greater need following the breakdown of the marriage. All such provisions made at the time of divorce can be subjected to variation in the light of changed circumstances, and it remains the case that the communion of property is only dissolved when all minor children have attained their respective majorities.

7 Termination of Marriage by Death and Succession[20]

When any person dies, regardless of whether the person is married or not, the patrimony which that person enjoyed in life is left without an owner. It is the question as to who will succeed to the ownership of the patrimony that must now be considered. If the person who has died was married at the time of death, and the marriage was subject to a communion of property, the communion is dissolved and the share of the deceased in it merges with his vacant personal patrimony.

Under the law of England and Wales, when a person dies, the property which he owned in life continues to form a legal entity, called the deceased's estate. This estate is then managed by the deceased's personal representatives, the executors appointed by him in his will or, if he died without making a will, that is intestate, the administrators appointed by the court. These personal representatives have the duty of gathering together the assets of the deceased, paying his debts and then distributing his estate amongst the beneficiaries named in his will or, on an intestacy, those whom the law provides are to inherit. The estate continues, in a sense, the personality of the deceased with regard to the management of his property until it is distributed among the persons entitled to it.

Italian law does not proceed in the same manner. It follows the civilian tradition of looking for a successor rather than distributing an inheritance. The vacancy in ownership must be filled by the deceased's heir. The concept is similar to that which attaches to certain offices upon the death of the incumbent. The continuity of the office is unbroken in the person of the successor. The approach is neatly summed up in the saying: "The King is dead; long live the King".

When the heir enters upon his inheritance in Italian law, he is at once owner of the entire patrimony of the deceased, which patrimony merges with that which he himself owned prior to acquiring that of the deceased. The two patrimonies merge to form one. The heir succeeds to everything of the deceased, debts as well as assets. He is therefore personally liable to pay the deceased's debts, even if these exceed the assets which he inherits, making good the deficit from what was his own patrimony, but which is now just one undifferentiated part of the new patrimony. This is what is meant by universal succession in civil law. In order to avoid becoming personally liable for the debts of the deceased in this way, Italian law allows the heir to accept the inheritance with benefit of inventory, that is to require that an inventory of the deceased's patrimony be taken so as to disclose whether the deceased was solvent. If the heir accepts the inheritance with benefit of inventory, the two patrimonies are not fused but remain separate, with the result that the deceased's debts must be paid from his patrimony alone, without recourse to that of the heir. Likewise, where the deceased was solvent, those expecting to receive legacies under his will may fear that the creditors of an insolvent heir may diminish the deceased's patrimony so that their expectations will be frustrated. In such circumstances, they may demand that the patrimonies remain separate so as to prevent the deceased's patrimony becoming available to satisfy the debts of the heir. However, acceptance with benefit of inventory and separation of patrimonies are exceptions to the far more general rule, namely that the universal succession of the heir fuses his and the deceased's former patrimonies into one new patrimony from which the heir must satisfy his own and the deceased's creditors and distribute the legacies which are due under the will of the deceased.

Thus, the ownership of the patrimony of the deceased continues in the ownership of the heir, who is the universal successor to the deceased's patrimony. This continuity of ownership and universal succession are the hallmarks of the civil law system of inheritance, whereas English law creates a sort of hiatus between the ownership of the deceased and that of the beneficiaries under his will or intestacy by fictitiously continuing his personality in the institution of his estate. The heir is essential to the civil law system of succession.

The importance of the heir points up once more why Italian law regards the childless person as having suffered something of a disaster. There is no one to continue the family, none to succeed to the family patrimony. Moreover, the patrimony is in many respects that of the family. As will be shown, the deceased's family have important rights to the deceased's patrimony which the deceased cannot defeat. Here again the civilian inheritance of Italian law is in stark contrast to the traditional English law emphasis upon freedom of testation, by which the deceased can disinherit his family entirely. The English view of property ownership is markedly individualistic when compared to the Italian insistence upon the interests of the family in the deceased's patrimony.

There is indeed a sense in which the legal rules relating to succession in any nation are a most important source of evidence for that people's attitude to family life. With that in mind, the discussion of succession in Italian law will begin by examining the persons whom the law says shall be the deceased's heirs if he or she dies intestate. This in effect provides the perimeter separating the family from non-relatives. Then, the methods by which the deceased can choose to depart from these arrangements by making a will will be examined, before finally considering the extent to which such individual arrangements are permitted to defeat the interests of the family, and which members are regarded as so closely related to the deceased as to have an interest in his patrimony which he cannot be allowed to defeat.

Intestate Succession[21]

Under the Italian system of intestate succession, the following members of the deceased's family are entitled to share in the patrimony if no will has been made:

the spouse
the children (and, if any are dead, their issue)
the parents (and remoter ancestors who have survived the parents)
brothers and sisters
parents of a natural child
other relatives as far as the sixth degree.

Where there is no-one in any of these categories, the patrimony passes to the State, which takes for want of an heir rather than as an heir, and is therefore not liable for debts beyond the value of the deceased's assets.

If the deceased leaves no spouse, the children take the whole estate to the exclusion of the other categories. If there is neither a spouse nor a child, the remaining categories take, each excluding remoter categories. Among ancestors, the paternal and maternal lines each share one-half of the patrimony among the living members, but brothers and sisters take equally while in the final category those most closely related to the deceased share the patrimony equally.

If the deceased leaves a spouse but no children, the spouse takes two-thirds of the patrimony, the remaining one-third going to the ascendants. If there are no ascendants, the spouse takes all.

If the deceased leaves a spouse and one child, spouse and child share equally, but if there are two or more children, the spouse takes one-third and the children share two-thirds equally among them. The issue of a dead child take among them the entitlement of their deceased parent.

From this it can be concluded that Italian law favours the claims of the surviving spouse and the children as marking the line of continuity of the family. However, if there are no children, then although the spouse takes a share, the continuing interests of the parents are respected. Remoter relatives are only called to the succession, however, in the absence of such near relations.

Testate Succession[22]

Should the owner of property wish specific items of his property to pass to specific beneficiaries upon his death, or should he wish to benefit persons not included in the scheme for intestate succession discussed above, it is open for that person to dispose of all or a part of his property by means of legacies contained in a validly drafted will. Under Italian law, any person eighteen years old or older, who is generally of sound mind, that is not judicially interdicted from dealing with property because of insanity, and actually *compos mentis* at the time of its drafting, may make a will, provided he or she is not serving a prison sentence of five years or more. Unlike English law, which recognizes only the will signed by the testator and witnessed by two persons, Italian law admits of several methods of making a valid will. Ordinary wills are divided into holograph wills and notarial wills. The holograph will is that which is written in the testator's own hand throughout, and dated and signed by him. It need not be deposited in any official place prior to the testator's death. Notarial wills on the other hand involve the participation of a notary and are of two kinds - the public and the secret will. The public will is drafted by the notary in the presence of the testator and of two witnesses. The secret will on the other hand is merely handed to the notary by the testator in the presence of the two witnesses, the testator acknowledging that it is his will but the contents usually being concealed in a sealed envelope which is not opened prior to his death. This variety of methods of making wills again reflects the civil law tradition going back to Roman times. There are also provisions governing the making of special wills not just for the military as in English law, but also at times of natural disaster, epidemic or on a ship or aeroplane. Such wills, unlike the English military will, require a degree of formality and only remain valid for a limited period of three months from the resumption of normal conditions.

Revocation of these wills takes place, for example, by the destruction or cancellation of a holograph will, the withdrawal of a secret will, the drafting of a deed of revocation by a notary in relation to public wills, or the making of a new will which either expressly cancels the older document or is inconsistent with it. In addition, the sentencing of the testator to a term of imprisonment of five years or more automatically revokes any will made by him. The subsequent marriage of the testator, however, does not revoke a pre-existing will, but the birth, adoption, legitimation or recognition of a child does. The testator's ignorance of the existence of a child of his at the time of making the will invalidates it. These remarkably Roman rules illustrate very clearly the attitude of Italian law to testamentary gifts, namely that they should only be made while fully aware of the responsibility owed to one's family. The birth of a child, whose interests could not have been taken into account, therefore invalidates the transaction.

Protection of the Family Interest[23]

Although such wills may be made under Italian law, their validity upon the death of the testator depends on whether they invade the legitimate expectations of certain of his relatives and, if so, whether those relatives are prepared to accept it. It is necessary therefore to consider what those legitimate expectations are, from which will become clear the extent to which the patrimony controlled by the deceased during his lifetime can rightfully be regarded as the patrimony of the family rather than that of the deceased as an individual.

Firstly, the relatives who have a rightful expectation to the patrimony of the deceased form a smaller group than those entitled upon intestacy. The group includes only the spouse, the issue and the ascendants. The issue again are usually the children, but the issue of a dead child share that child's portion. Likewise, the ascendants are usually the parents, but if they are not living and remoter ancestors are, the nearest ancestors take equal shares of the two halves of the ancestral portion allotted to each of the paternal and maternal lines.

Secondly, it is necessary to ask what constitutes the patrimony of the deceased in which these relatives are granted a share which cannot be defeated without their compliance. If the patrimony was merely what the deceased owned at the date of his death, the expectations of the family could be defeated by the making of gifts outside of the family during the deceased's lifetime. However, the patrimony is not taken to be only that which the deceased owned at the date of his death, the *relictum* as it is termed, but includes also the property which he has disposed of by gift during his lifetime, the so-called *donatum*. The interests of the family are in the sum of these two components, although in claiming their shares they are required to bring into account any *inter vivos* gift or legacy which they have received from the deceased. It will be appreciated that this process of investigation into the content of the *donatum* can be a lengthy one, explaining in part why it is that, while the average estate in England and Wales takes roughly six months to administer, the mean time for settling an Italian inheritance is ten years.

Once the value of the deceased's patrimony has been calculated in this way, shares are allocated to the family in the following manner.[24]

> If the deceased left a spouse but no children or ancestors, the spouse is entitled to one-half of the patrimony, while the deceased is entitled to dispose of the other half as he wishes. The two parts are called the *quota legittima* or the *riserva* and the *quota disponibile* respectively.
>
> If the deceased left a spouse and one child, each is entitled to a third, and the deceased may alienate a third.
>
> If the deceased left a spouse and two or more children, the spouse takes a quarter, the children take a half, and the deceased may dispose of a quarter elsewhere.
>
> If the deceased left no spouse but one child, the child takes a half leaving the deceased free to alienate a half.
>
> If the deceased left no spouse and two or more children, then the children share two-thirds, leaving only one-third in the *quota disponibile*.
>
> If the deceased left a spouse and parents, the spouse takes a half, the parents a quarter, and a quarter is disposable.
>
> If the deceased left neither spouse nor descendants, but there are surviving ascendants, they take one-third leaving two-thirds free for alienation.

It must be emphasized that the *riserva* has to be claimed by the relatives concerned, otherwise any excessive alienations are valid. However, if the *riserva* is claimed, and it is discovered that the deceased has invaded the proper share of an entitled relative, then all the legacies and *inter vivos* gifts must be proportionately scaled down until the appropriate share of the *riserva* is restored to the claimant. Where only one or some of those entitled claim, while others assent to the deceased's dispositions, the gifts need not all be scaled down. In such cases, legacies are scaled down first and then *inter vivos* gifts in order, proceeding from the deceased's death back, until the shares of the complainants are restored. A complaint must be brought within ten years of the testator's death. Where those obligated to return property have alienated it, the third parties who received it must restore the property if it is an immovable, but need not restore moveable property received in good faith.

From the above discussion, it is clear that Italian law does not allow a testator anything like the freedom of testation to be found in English law. At times, freedom of testation and of alienation generally is limited to one-third or even one-quarter of a person's patrimony. Greater freedom can only be got through the compliance of the members of the family entitled to the *riserva*. They are not permitted to agree to forego their share during the deceased's lifetime. Nothing perhaps better illustrates the family perspective from which Italian law views the dealings of husbands, wives, parents and children with 'their' property. The property controlled by them is only 'their' property in a limited sense; in another and important sense, it is the patrimony of the family of which the individual members are only a part. Individualist notions of property ownership sit very uneasily within the framework of Italian family law, and this is an indicator of the civilian tradition within which Italian law stands.

Notes

[1] The *societas omnium bonorum*.

[2] See the Inheritance (Family Provision) Act 1938 and the Inheritance (Provision for Family and Dependants) Act 1975.

[3] *Cod. civ.*, art. 79-116.

[4] *Cod. civ.*, art. 84-113.

[5] *Cod. civ.*, art. 82-83.

[6] *Cod. civ.*, art. 117-129.

[7] *Cod. civ.*, art. 143-148; 315-337.

[8] After the praetor had determined the exact issues in dispute between the parties, he encapsulated it in a written formula and sent it to a judge of the parties' choice

for adjudication. The parties swore an oath that they would accept the *iudex*' decision.

[9] *Cod. civ.*, art. 231-290.

[10] The *Tribunale per i minorenni* is a court to be found at each *corte d'appello* consisting of a college of four judges: a judge of appeal court status who acts as president, a judge of *Tribunale* status, and two qualified social workers over 30 years of age. As well as its functions in family law, it serves as a juvenile court to consider criminal charges against those under 18 years of age, 14 being the age of criminal responsibilty.

[11] *Cod. civ.*, art. 291-314; L. 4 May 1983, n. 184.

[12] See the Adoption Act 1926.

[13] *Cod. civ.*, art. 343-387.

[14] Roman law spoke of *tutela* and *cura* as forms of guardianship, with the respective types of guardian called *tutor* and *curator*.

[15] *Cod. civ.*, art. 159-230.

[16] See below, chapter 12, section 8.

[17] *Cod. civ.*, art. 149-158.

[18] L. 1 December 1970, n. 898; L. 6 March 1987, n. 74.

[19] The result is not therefore different from that achieved under the law of England and Wales, by virtue of which clergy of the Church of England and the Church in Wales have a statutory right to refuse to remarry divorced persons. The law of England and Wales does not however go so far as to describe divorce as terminating the civil effects of ecclesiastical marriages in its deference to the doctrines of the established Church.

[20] *Cod. civ.*, art. 456-535 - for the general concepts.

[21] *Cod. civ.*, art. 565-586.

[22] *Cod. civ.*, art. 587-712.

[23] *Cod. civ.*, art. 536-564.

[24] *Cod. civ.*, art. 537-540.

12 The Law of Property

1 Introduction

According to the traditional mode of analysis in Roman law, private law was divided into three departments: the law of persons, the law of things and the law of actions. The law of persons has already been examined in looking at the family and the law, together with some aspects of the law of things, that is those relating to family property and succession. The law of actions is that department concerned with how rights and duties are enforced, and is that part of the law dealt with in the procedural codes, in relation to private law, the Code of Civil Procedure. This leaves therefore only the law of things, which concerns what can be the objects of legal rights and duties. Modern civil law systems recognize that the law of things can be divided into two compartments: the law of property, concerned with owning, and the law of obligations, which is concerned with owing. The law of property is concerned with what is meant by saying that A owns X, while the law of obligations is concerned with what is meant by saying that A owes X to B. The Italian Civil Code deals with property rights in its third book and obligations in its fourth. In splitting the two topics, it marks a development away from the traditional linking of the two areas as the law of things, which is still observed in the French *Code civil*. It has also separated succession issues from the generality of property rules by placing them apart in the second book of the code, bridging the law of persons and the law of property. This recognizes the connection between personal and property rights involved in issues relating to succession.

It is worth pausing at this point to reflect upon the manner in which civil law analyses property and obligations. There is a sense in which the juristic analysis follows what is almost a grammatical methodology. This begins with a sentence describing the typical fact situation of owning.

A owns X.

This statement gives rise, it is submitted to a number of questions:

1. Who or what can be A, that is, who has the capacity to own?
2. What can be X, that is, who or what can be owned?
3. What does it mean to say that A owns X, that is, what is ownership?
4. Can X be owned in different ways, that is, what types of ownership are there?
5. How did A become the owner of X, that is, how is ownership acquired?
6. How might A cease to be the owner of X, that is, how is ownership lost or how does it cease?

These questions are no longer questions of grammar or indeed of logic; these questions are questions of law. It is legal rules that will answer these questions. The legal rules were originally those in the Digest or the native legal systems of the legal scholars. They however saw it as their duty to present these rules as part of a unity, a legal system, and therefore to present them as answers to these questions. The rules had to be set out systematically, and the system adopted reflected the intellectual background and development of the jurists themselves.

The questions posed above will now be examined in turn. It will be seen that the structure of book three of the Italian Civil Code reflects the fact that it has been constructed as one way of setting out the answers to these questions.

2 Capacity to own

The question of who may be the subject of property rights in the sense of who can own property is basically a question for the law of persons. Any person, natural or juristic, is capable of being an owner. Thus, an individual human being can own property as can a legal entity such as a corporation. Associations which do not have a legal identity cannot be owners because they lack legal personality. Equally clearly, there are some individuals who are not of full capacity, in that they are beneath the age of majority or are not of sound mind. These people can still own property, but the law of persons, through the institutions of guardianship such as *tutela* and *cura*, makes special provision to ensure that their incapacity does not lead to their being overreached in relation to property and other legal concerns.

3 What may be owned[1]

In Italian law, property which may be owned is referred to as goods, *beni*. The word *beni* is therefore equivalent to the Roman law concept of *res* and the common law concept of a *chose*. In accordance with the grammatical/logical root of the questions which lie at the heart of the civilian mode of presentation, *beni* are defined as things which can be the objects of rights.

Roman law categorized things in various ways. An important division was that between moveable and immoveable things. This distinction is of less importance at common law, where however the distinction between land, buildings, plants and other immoveable things and the remainder of things which are moveable is in part reflected in the distinction between real and personal property. However, not all interests in land constitute real rights in English law: leases for instance are categorized as personal rather than as real property. Italian law, in common with other civil law systems, emphasizes the distinction between immoveable and moveable property. Immoveables are defined as the ground, things growing out of it, and watercourses, trees, buildings and other constructions, even if joined to the ground impermanently, and all things which are either naturally or artificially fixed to the ground. Mills, swimming pools and floating structures which are permanently moored are also deemed to be immoveables. All other goods are moveable.

While Roman law divided things into moveable and immoveable, it also divided them into two categories according to their social importance or value. In Roman law, this was the distinction between *res mancipi* and *res nec mancipi*. *Res mancipi* were those things which had been of particular importance when Rome was predominantly an agricultural society. Slaves, beasts of draught and burden, rights of way to walk (*iter*), drive animals (*actus*) or even vehicles (*via)* over land and the right to bear water over land (*aqueduct*), together with the land itself if in Italy, were classified as *res mancipi*. In truth, the common law distinction between real and personal property is a similar distinction because only the most important form of property in feudal society, namely freehold land and freehold rights over such land, were classified as real property. Italian law also makes a distinction of this sort which indicates that today other forms of property as well as immoveables are of considerable economic worth. Thus, some moveables are categorized as registrable moveables in that, like immoveables, the creation, transfer or termination of rights in them has to be done by registration.

Roman law also drew a distinction between things which were susceptible of private ownership and those things which were not, technically *res in patrimonio* and *res extra patrimonium.* To express this distinction in terms of the sentence "A owns X", if X is a thing *in patrimonio*, A can be a private citizen, whereas if X is a thing *extra patrimonium*, A, a private citizen, cannot in law be its owner. According to the Digest, things not susceptible of private ownership fell into two categories: those which were under divine law and those which were under human law. If the thing was under divine law, it was dedicated to a god and therefore regarded as being owned by the god. Thus, temples, burial places and the walls and gates of cities were under the protection of divine law not private law. Some things, however, while under the protection of human law, were nevertheless not capable of being privately owned. These were things which were common to all mankind, such as the air, the sea and the shore. There were also things which were common to all the citizens of a particular state, such as its ports, rivers, roads and so on, and things which were common to all the people in a particular community, such as public libraries and baths.

This type of distinction is also carried over into modern Italian law, where certain property is categorized as forming part of the *demanio pubblico*, the public domain, either as pertaining to the State or to individual provinces or communes. These include, the sea shore, beaches, roads, ports, together with rivers, streams, lakes and other public waters so dedicated by law. Also in the public domain are airports, aqueducts, immoveable property decreed to be of historical, archaeological or artistic interest, together with collections in museums, art galleries, archives and libraries. Such goods are all inalienable and cannot be subjected to third-party rights other than as decreed by law. In other words, if in the sentence "A owns X", X is one of the above things, only the State or a province or commune, can be A, the owner. Cemeteries and public markets are in the provincial or communal domain; in Roman law the former had been dedicated to the gods and the latter only had been public.

It will be recalled that in Italian law, as in most civil law systems, wherever the State or a public body is a party to a juristic relationship, the relationship becomes one governed by public rather than private law. That is to say in this context that if in the sentence, "A owns X", A is the State, then regardless of whether X is susceptible of private ownership or not, A's ownership will be governed by public rather than private law. This does not however place such property in the public domain because it is not owned by the State on account of the nature of the thing but because of the identity of the owner. Such property is said to be not part of the *demanio pubblico* but of the patrimony of the State, *il patrimonio dello Stato*. Into this category fall the forests of the State, its mines, quarries and turbaries, together with things of historical, artistic and like value which are found below ground. Gifts to the President, barracks, military aircraft and warships also fall into this category. Public buildings and other things dedicated to public use belong to the patrimony of the region, province or commune concerned. Further, any immoveable property which is not actually owned by anyone falls into the State patrimony. All things in the patrimony of the State are excluded from the provisions of the private law to the extent that that is not consistent with the particular legal regimes which apply to them. The same is true of that part of the property of public entities which are dedicated to a use which is for the public service. Ecclesiastical property is also subject to a special regime under the Lateran Pacts, but in other respects remains governed by the provisions of private law. Ecclesiastical buildings which are places of Roman Catholic worship, even not Church property, cannot suffer a change of use other than in accordance with the special legal rules relating thereto.

4 The Nature of Ownership[2]

It has sometimes been argued that the civilian concept of ownership involves the right of a person to use, abuse and take the fruits of his property - *ius utendi abutendi fruendi*. This has not gone uncontested, and in modern civil law systems, including the Italian, while an owner retains the rights of using and enjoying, clear limits are set to his right to abuse his property where such abuse redounds to the disadvantage of others as individuals or as communities. Indeed, where a particular use is damaging to the interests of others, such use may be checked by law, thus illustrating that the owner's rights are limited to what a common lawyer would probably describe as reasonable user. Thus, according to article 832 of the Civil Code, an owner has the full and exclusive right to enjoy and dispose of his things, but only within the limits and in the manner established by the law.

By using a thing, the owner has the right for instance to live in his house, drive his car, eat his cake and read his books. By enjoying their fruits, he may let his house and take the rent, or hire his car and pocket the profit. If he owns a field, he may cultivate it, and the crops, the fruit of his cultivation, are his. Likewise he may invest his money and the interest paid upon the investment, its fruit, will be his. The offspring of his animals are their fruit and will be his, as will their produce - milk from cows, wool from sheep and so on.

However, Italian law limits the owner to using and enjoying his property in a manner which does not harm others. The owner of a car may not drive it as he pleases; the owner of a house may not develop it or live in it in a way which is prejudicial to others. Moreover, while an owner may not generally be deprived of anything of his against his wishes, this may be done if it is in the public interest, lawfully declared, and a just indemnity paid. Likewise, private property can be requisitioned on the same terms to meet the needs of some military or civil emergency, and restrictions upon the normal use of property may be imposed to meet the needs of similar situations. Restrictions are also imposed upon the manner in which the owners of things which are of artistic, historical, archaeological or ethnographical importance may use and enjoy such items,[3] and the interests of national production entitles the State to amass certain products, and to expropriate property where the owner has abandoned its conservation or cultivation in a manner prejudicial to the national interest, which here is economic rather than political or military.

The owner of land is also the owner of the subsoil and is therefore entitled to excavate or work below ground level, but only while this does not damage neighbouring property, and special laws dictate how mining and such other subterranean operations are to be prosecuted. Owners are also disabled from objecting to underground or aerial activities below or above their property which they have no interest in excluding. An owner may however close his land or house for as long as he wishes, but must not impede hunting activities while his estate is not closed, provided the activity is carried out in accordance with the laws on hunting and does not threaten the particular cultivation to which the owner has put his land. To fish, however, requires the owner's consent. Owners must also allow neighbours reasonable access to their land to effect repairs and the like to their own property and have no right to object to emissions of smoke, fumes, smells and noises from neighbours' lands and buildings, provided these are within the normal limits of tolerability.

One very palpable interference with ownership is that which affects rural land. As was seen in the last chapter, children have indefeasible succession rights to their parents' property, so that where there is more than one child of a marriage, a family farm has almost always to be divided between the surviving issue of a marriage and it is not possible for a parent to select one child to receive the farm by will. Logically, this means that farms would get smaller and smaller generation by generation until the small holdings would become so small that they were no longer able to support those who inherited them and their families. This point was in fact reached during the nineteenth century and was a cause of the very considerable emigrations from rural Italy to more prosperous parts of that country as well as to other parts of Europe and to the United States.[4] As a result, the Civil Code now provides that cultivated rural land is not to be disposed of in any way in such a manner that the resulting parcels are insufficent to support an agricultural tenant and his family. What constitutes a sufficient estate to achieve this is a matter of local definition, but failure to observe these requirements can be remedied by the intervention of the *pubblico ministero*.

Special provisions also exist to allow for the reclamation of land which is suitable to be placed under cultivation where this is not currently the case, as well as to impose plans for drainage and flood prevention so as to avoid natural disasters. It also open to communes to adopt plans which restrict the development of private property within their areas in a manner which is unsuitable given the character of those areas. All such restrictions are governed by appropriate norms as they interfere with the legal rights of the owners.

A further interference with what might be termed the absolute nature of ownership, but one which has a lengthy pedigree in civil law systems, is that owners are prevented by law from developing their property in close proximity to that of their neighbours. Thus, no wall may be built within three metres of a neighbour's land. Where walls exist along the boundary between neighbouring properties, they are assumed to be in joint ownership, and if they are not, the non-owner has a legal right to have them subjected to joint ownership. Likewise, an existing wall within three metres of a boundary can be subjected to a regime of joint ownership if the non-owner so wishes. Restrictions also apply to the opening of ditches and drainage channels near a neighbour's property, as well as to the planting of trees and hedges. The Civil Code also restricts the rights of owners to have windows which overlook a neighbour's land whether placed so as to provide light to the other property or to provide a view. Owners are generally required to ensure that water which runs off their roofs and other structures drains onto their own premises, and restrictions are placed upon draining such water onto a neighbour's property.

It can thus be seen that modern Italian law is very far from permitting owners absolute control over what is theirs, requiring in many instances respect for the interests of neighbours and even in some cases proper care in the management or development of what one owns so that the interests of the community generally are not harmed.

5 Methods of Acquiring Ownership[5]

Given therefore that Italian law recognizes the right of certain persons to own and that certain things may be owned in accordance with the notions of ownership outlined above, the next question which needs to be answered is how do persons who may own property actually become the owners of items of property which may be owned, that is how is ownership acquired.

Italian law recognizes various modes of acquiring ownership. These include taking or occupation, finding, accession, specification, by uniting or mixing, by prescription or *usucapione* as it is termed in Italian law, as well as through the effects of contracts, by succession upon death, or any other method established by law.

These will now be examined in turn.

Occupazione and Invenzione[6]

Occupation is the acquisition of ownership through the taking of a moveable which is not owned by anyone else. Such things include property which has been abandoned by its previous owner and animals which are the objects of hunting or fishing. Special provisions relate to property in certain wild animals which may be kept for profit or pleasure, such as swarms of bees, pigeons, rabbits and fish. The owner of a swarm is allowed to go on to the land of another to retrieve it provided he makes good any damage caused, although if he has not pursued this right within two days, the owner of the land on which the bees have now swarmed may acquire them by occupation. Animals which belong to a species which are naturally tame may also be pursued on to the land of others subject to the provision of compensation for any damage caused, this time the owner being allowed twenty days to pursue his rights. Rabbits and fish which escape to another's land can be immediately acquired by occupation by that other provided he has not enticed them or obtained their presence by any fraudulent means, and the same is true of pigeons subject to the special legal provisions relating to homing pigeons.[7]

Clearly, a person who finds something capable of acquisition and who wants to acquire it faces a problem if he is uncertain as to whether it is abandoned or lost. Italian law recognizes a duty upon a finder to restore property found to its rightful owner, but if the owner is unknown, the property must be handed to the *sindaco* of the *comune* in question who must advertise its finding. If it is not claimed within a year, the finder acquires ownership of the thing itself or its value if its perishable nature, for instance, required that the thing itself be sold. If it is claimed by the rightful owner, he must idemnify the finder with a tenth of the thing's value.

Treasure found on land becomes the property of the landowner, unless it was found on the land of another, in which case its ownership is shared equally by the finder and the landowner. Special provisions apply to objects of historical, archaeological, artistic or palaentological interest, and special rules also apply to things which have been jettisoned from ships or aircraft, or are otherwise found along the seashore.

Accessione, specificazione, unione and commistione[8]

Accession is concerned with the acquisition of ownership through the incorporation of a lesser into a greater thing, the owner of the greater thing becoming owner of the merged lesser item as a result of its incorporation.

One instance of accession is the planting or building of something in or on the land of another. The general principle is that the landowner becomes the owner also of whatever is planted or built on his property. This rule is however subject to certain modifications, depending upon whether the planting or building was done by the landowner, the owner of the materials or some third party. If the landowner built on his own property using another's materials, he must either allow the owner of the materials to reclaim them, by *rivendicazione,* which is permissible within six months of the owner of the materials discovering the situation, or else the landowner must pay the value of the materials to their owner. If, however, it was the owner of the materials who did the building, the landowner is allowed to choose whether to retain the structure upon payment of the value of the materials or the gain in the value to his property, or to require their removal. The latter request must be made within six months of his discovering that the work has been done. Finally, if a third party built on the land of one person using the materials of a second, the owner of the materials can revindicate at the expense of the builder within six months of finding out, provided he does not damage the land. If the materials cannot be revindicated, then the builder and the landowner, if he was aware of what was occurring, will be liable to the owner of the materials for their value.

Sometimes, the problem of building on the land of another arises when one landowner constructs something on his land which encroaches onto the land of a neighbour. Special rules govern this situation. In order to prevent the neighbour acquiring title by the normal rules of accession, it is provided that if the work had been done in good faith and the neighbour does not object within three months, the building and the ground upon which it stands may be adjudged by the competent judicial authority to belong to the constructor, but that he must compensate his neighbour for any damage caused and pay to him double the value of the ground he has lost.

When things belonging to different owners become mixed or united, as where wine or corn belonging to different people are confused, then either owner is entitled to call for the separation of his goods and if this is not feasible to have the total quantity divided up into shares according to the value of the various contributions to the mixture. Where however two things are joined and one is of much greater value than the other or the identity of the lesser is completely lost in that of the greater, then the owner of the greater becomes owner of the whole, but is obligated to give the other the value of the lesser thing unless the mixture occurred without the new owner's consent, in which case, following the general rule of Italian law relating to unjust enrichment, his obligation is to give the party who has lost out the lesser of one of two sums, namely, the value of the lost thing or the increase in value occasioned to the greater thing.

Specificazione is a mode of acquisition which has been problematic since Roman times. It concerns the question of who owns a new thing which has been made out of pre-existing materials owned by another. Does ownership remain with the owner of the raw materials or does it inhere in the maker of the new thing? Italian law favours the manufacturer of the new thing, reflecting the preference for labour expressed in the first article of the Constitution. French law, by contrast, favours the owner of the raw materials. In the compilations of the emperor Justinian, ownership of the new thing depended upon whether the new thing could be reduced to the raw materials out of which it was made: if it could, the owner of the raw materials retained ownership; if it could not, the manufacturer was the owner of the new thing. Italian law acknowledges these two situations, but, very interestingly for the legal historian, it expressly states that it does not matter whether the thing is reducible or not, thus indicating its full awareness and rejection of the civilian heritage relating to the rule. The manufacturer must however recompense the owner of the raw materials for the value of those materials, but if their value is markedly greater than that of the end-product, ownership goes to the owner of the raw materials who must compensate the manufacturer to the value of the new thing. It is also interesting to note that in modern Italian law, unlike ancient Roman law, the specification problem is presented in general terms, whereas its ancient forebear recounted numerous examples of situations in which materials were made into a new thing, corn into flour, olives into olive oil, grapes into wine, and so forth.[9]

Ancient Roman law also concerned itself with several situations in which the action of rivers affected the ownership of their beds and surrounding lands. Modern Italian law also considers these issues, while reaching different results. Material which is deposited by a river and accrues to a river bank becomes the property of the riparian owner by *alluvio*, while a chunk of river bank torn away by the force of a torrent and carried downstream and lodged against the property of another riparian owner also becomes the property of that second owner, who is obliged to compensate the previous owner. However, if a part of the river bed is abandoned by the river, it does not accrue to the riparian owners but forms part of the *demanio pubblico*, as do islands formed in the middle of a river, although since 1994, islands so formed by the tearing off of portions of a riparian property or formed by the encircling of such land by the river, remain the property of the riparian owner. Where a river changes its course completely however, for whatever cause, the old river bed remains part of the *demanio pubblico*.

An owner has at his disposal the *azione de rivendicazione* to recover his property from the hands of whoever else may be in possession of it or detaining it. The very title of this action in Italian reflects its historical origins in the Roman law action *rei vindicatio*. Likewise the Roman action by which an owner could seek a judicial declaration that another had no rights over his property, the *actio negatoria*, has its modern Italian equivalent in the *azione negatoria* by which an owner can claim that another or others have no right to or over his property. Under Italian law owners may also seek a judicial determination of the boundaries between their property and that of neighbours, or, when for whatever reason the boundaries become unclear, to have them declared at their joint expense.

6 Types of Ownership

Roman law spoke of persons having rights over the property of others and called such rights servitudes. The Roman jurists distinguished praedial servitudes, which inhered in a person as owner of a particular plot of land - the dominant tenement - as against the owner of another neighbouring plot of land - the servient tenement - from servitudes which existed solely for the benefit of their owner without being in any way connected with property he owned and which were called personal servitudes. Modern civil law systems have tended to limit the use of the word servitude to the first of these classes, recognizing in personal servitudes limited forms of ownership or situations in which the various elements of full ownership - the rights to use, enjoy and consume property - are shared between two persons or divided among many. It is tempting to refer to them as limited forms of ownership, but as has been shown, modern Italian law recognizes that all forms of ownership are limited in certain ways. Therefore it is best to refer to them as types of ownership, albeit they are in some measure forms of ownership which are less than ownership in its full sense as recognized by Italian law.

The Civil Code recognizes four basic types of such ownership which give rights over the property of which another is the full owner. These are *superficie*, *enfiteusi*, usufruct and *usus*.

Superficie[10]

Superficie is the right of a person to own a building or other construction upon land even though he is not the owner of the land upon which it is built. It is an exception to the principle that whatever is built upon land accedes to it, *superficies solo cedit*. The right must be granted by the landowner to either build on the land or acquire a pre-existing building on the land. The right may be either perpetual or for a fixed term, but on its expiry the building accedes to the land in accordance with the general principle. While the right exists however it is freely alienable. The landowner must not exercise his rights to the subsoil in such wise as to injure the enjoyment of the building which must, in its turn, be properly maintained.

Enfiteusi[11]

Enfiteusi is the grant of a perpetual right or a fixed term of more than twenty years to enjoy the full rights of ownership over another's land subject to the payment of a rent. The owner of the right, the *enfiteuta*, must improve the property, pay his rent, called the *canon*, and avoid any conduct which causes the property to deteriorate. The interest is alienable, but in the event of its proposed sale, the landowner, *il concedente*, has first refusal of the purchase. At the end of the fixed term, the land reverts to the *concedente*, who nowadays may reclaim the property in the event of the *enfiteuta* failing to comply with his obligations, although the *enfiteuta* may now also require the *concedente* to sell him the ownership of the land in question for a sum which is meant to be based upon the capitalisation of the annual rent.

Usufruct[12]

An usufruct can arise by operation of law or by the act of the parties. It is an arrangement whereby one person, the usufructuary, obtains the use and enjoyment of property which is owned by another, the proprietor. The arrangement can and often does last for life, although it can be created for a shorter period and is limited to a maximum duration of thirty years when it is created in favour of a non-human person which does not have a natural life span. It corresponds therefore in civil law to the concept of a life estate in the common law of property, in that one person enjoys the fruits, or in other words the income, of property without having any right to diminish the capital. In Roman law, this was expressed by saying that the substance of the property should not be diminished. Strictly speaking, this is not accurate, as an usufruct in property such as a quarry or a mine is perfectly possible even though by working it, its future productivity is diminished. Accordingly, in modern Italian law the protection of the capital is expressed by saying that the economic end of the thing must be respected.

The usufructuary is entitled to all the fruits, natural or civil, which the thing produces. Therefore, for instance, if he is the usufructuary of cattle, he is entitled to the calves which are born and to the milk produced by the cows; if he is the usufructuary of a flock of sheep, he gets the lambs and the wool from the fleeces. The usufructuary of a house is entitled to live in it with his family, but also to let and take the rent, the civil fruit. The usufructuary of a garden takes the produce; that of an orchard the fruit, of the vineyard, the grapes, of an olive grove, the olives. If the crops for a particular year have already been sown before the usufruct is created or the proprietor has already started dressing the vines or the olive trees in a particular cycle, then he and the usufructuary must share the profits for that cycle in proportion to the length of time during which each was possessor of the property in question. Likewise, the costs of such a divided cycle must be borne by them in the same manner. If, during the usufruct, the usufructuary makes improvements to the property, he will be entitled to an indemnity from the owner when the usufruct comes to an end. This indemnity will be the lesser of the usual two sums used to calculate whether there has been an unjust enrichment, namely the cost to the usufructuary as opposed to the increase in value which has accrued to the property for the benefit of the proprietor. The usufructuary must also keep up the number of vines, trees and so on on the premises, and if he is enjoying the usufruct in a flock or herd, he must keep up its numbers by allocating sufficient numbers of lambs or calves to the herd or flock to replace losses. He is also responsible for the upkeep and repair of property such as machinery. The standard of care he is expected to achieve is due diligence, that is the degree of care that would be taken by the *buon padre di famiglia*, the good father of a family, the reasonable man of the civil law. He is expected to provide the owner with an inventory at the end of the usufruct, and a deposit by way of guarantee is expected in some cases. Normal running expenses, including those of ordinary repairs and maintenance, fall to the usufructuary, while extraordinary expenses are the responsibility of the proprietor.

Use and Habitation[13]

Both use and habitation are lesser rights to a thing than usufruct. Use allows the concessionary to use a thing but only to take its fruits to the extent that they are needed by him and his family, in the sense of his spouse and children. Any further fruits accrue to the benefit of the proprietor. Habitation is the similar right to live with one's family in a particular dwelling, but not to let it at a rent. Both therefore represent a further diminution of the elements of ownership - this time only the *ius utendi* remaining.

Having examined the rights less than full ownership which were once termed personal servitudes, attention must now be given to those rights over the property of another which Italian law still calls praedial servitudes.

7 Praedial Servitudes[14]

Praedial servitudes are those which exist to benefit one plot of land, the dominant tenement, by burdening another plot of land, the servient tenement, which must be sufficiently near the dominant tenement to allow the servitude to be of use. The properties are often, but not necessarily, adjacent to one another. For the servitude to exist, the properties must not be owned by the same person or persons, and the burden imposed upon the servient tenement must be of utility, in the sense of increasing the convenience or amenities, to the dominant tenement. It must be stressed that such servitudes exist for the benefit of the land to which they appertain and cannot be enjoyed therefore other than in conjunction with a property right to the land in question. They cannot exist independently of some interest in the land in question.

The content of such servitudes include such things as rights of way over neighbouring property, the right to draw water from or across a neighbour's land, rights of support for buildings, and the right to have electricity and telephonic lines of communication come to one's property across a neighbour's land. Although the content of some servitudes is explicitly recognized by law, provided the burden it is intended to impose on the servient tenement is of utility to the dominant tenement, there is no finite list of servitudes which are permissible. The owner of the servient tenement however is not obliged to perform any active duties for the benefit of the dominant tenement; his obligation is to permit the owner of the dominant tenement to exercise the servitude in a reasonable manner, that is with as little interference to the enjoyment of the ownership of the servient tenement as is commensurate with the reasonable user of the servitude.

Praedial servitudes can arise by the voluntary acts of the parties, such as the grant of a right by one neighbouring landowner to another, or by their contractual agreement to create such a right for the benefit of one plot of land. They can also arise by long user, where one neighbouring landowner has consistently exercised the right for the period required for *usucapione*.[15] Servitudes can also arise *per destinazione del padre di famiglia*, where an owner divides his property and by implication intends to retain certain rights, that is rights of servitude, for the benefit of the part he retains.

One of the most interesting features of this area of the law however is that servitudes can arise by demand of one owner. Such demands are allowed where it is impossible to secure full enjoyment of one's property without the existence of a servitude. Examples would be where a plot of land is land-locked, that is completely surrounded by neighbouring properties, so that those properties have to be crossed in some way to reach a public road, or where for a property to have water, electricity or a telephone, these have to be brought over the land of another. Those who seek to create such servitudes must do so by seeking a judicial pronouncement that the circumstances requiring their creation exist, although sometimes an administrative act is capable of creating them, and a proper indemnity to the landowner whose land must bear the burden of the servitude must be paid.

Once in existence, a servitude can continue to benefit and burden the properties concerned indefinitely, being ended only if the two properties come into common ownership, their exercise or the ownership of the servient tenement is abandoned or, their exercise prescribed by the owner of the servient tenement blocking their use for the required period, namely twenty years. Where the servitude is created subject to its determination at the end of a certain period or on the fulfilment or occurrence of some condition, the expiry of that period or the satisfaction of the condition terminates the right..

Italian law still speaks of these rights as praedial servitudes even though the term personal servitude to cover such rights as usufruct, use and habitation, is no longer officially used. The term however indicates the historical root of these rights in Roman law, all being rights over the property of another.

8 Co-ownership[16]

Rights over the property of others must be distinguished from the situation in which the complete right of ownership, of whatever sort, is shared among more than one legal person. This is what Italian law means by *comunione*, and the concept has already been encountered in the institution of the family communion described in the preceding chapter by which spouses are joint-owners of their matrimonial patrimony. The rules relating to co-ownership must now be examined in their general application.

Where any thing is owned by more than one person, the legal rules relating to the *comunione* apply. These assume that unless there has been an agreement to the contrary, each owner has an equal share in the property, that is, each is equally owner of the whole. Whatever the respective shares of the parties, the benefits which they obtain from the thing and the burdens which they are expected to bear are proportional to their respective shares in the ownership of it. Each is allowed to use and enjoy the thing for the purpose for which it is owned by them and subject to the duty of respecting the rights of the other co-owners to enjoy the thing similarly. The expenses of its maintenance and proper enjoyment are shared by the co-owners.

Decisions with regard to the common property are to be taken by all the joint owners. Decisions regarding the general administration of the thing may be taken by majority, but all of the co-owners must be informed of any proposal that leads to a decision. The majority is calculated according to the value of the shares of each co-owner in the thing and not just by counting heads. It is open to any co-owner to seek judicial redress if he feels that his rights have been violated in the manner that a decision has been made. The co-owners as a group are permitted by majority decision to appoint from amongst their number, or from outside, an administrator or manager to run the property, and they can also draw up a *regolamento*, a set of regulations, for the good government of the property.

Exceptional, as opposed to general, administrative decisions require a two-thirds majority of the co-owners, while decisions regarding the alienation of the thing or of rights over it require unanimity. If the thing is an immoveable and is to be used as security for a loan by means of hypothec, the majority required for such a decision is two-thirds.

It is open to any one of the co-owners to alienate his interest in the thing at any time or to call for the *comunione* to be ended. Equally, it is possible for the participants to agree that the *comunione* shall last for a certain period of time, but not for more than ten years. An agreement which purports to create a *comunione* for a longer period is shortened to that span of time.

A particularly important kind of *comunione* is the joint-ownership of a building, referred to in Italian law as a *condominio.*[17] As urban residents in Italy tend to live in apartments rather than in houses, the law relating to the joint-ownership of apartment blocks is of considerable importance, and is one of the largest sources of work for Italian lawyers and a major source of litigation before the civil courts. The Civil Code provides that, in the absence of a contrary agreement between the owners, certain parts of such a building are to be in common ownership, including the foundations, the master walls and common areas such as the entrance, the lifts and so on. Certain other parts of the structure are owned in common by those on adjacent floors, for instance the floors and ceilings between floors. Drainage, electricity and other common services are also shared.

The *condomini*, as the co-owners of this sort of property are known, have shares in the building corresponding to the value of the parts they own in the whole. Their rights and duties are proportionate to their shares. They are expected to contribute to the cost of the building's running and upkeep, and must not exploit their part of it in such a way as to prejudice the rights of their co-owners. The totality of the *condomini* meet in what is called an *assemblea*, where decisions relating to its management are to be taken. If there are more than ten *condomini*, it is required by law that they draw up a *regolamento* for the running of the condominium, the day to day management of which must by law be delegated to an *amministratore* if there are more than four *condomini*. The administrator holds office for a year at a time and must account to the *assemblea* on an annual basis. Decisions of the *assemblea* require that there be a quorum of two-thirds of the *condomini*; thereafter, a simple majority suffices for decisions to be taken. It is part of the administrator's duty to implement the decisions of the *assemblea* and to ensure good order within the apartment block. *Condomini* who are unhappy with decisions taken may challenge them on legal grounds before the civil courts. Such litigation is, as has been stated, very common.

9 Usucapione[18]

Usucapione in modern Italian law, as its name suggests, is derived from the Roman law institution of *usucapio*. It is a means of acquiring ownership by possession of a thing for a given length of time. Possession in this context means more than just the physical possession of the thing; it requires also a mental element, the intention to possess as an owner, and therefore it must be distinguished from situations in which a person has physical possession of a thing but in circumstances in which the possession is clearly not equivalent to that of an owner. Examples would be where the possessor has physical possession through the owner's consent, as where for instance the owner has lent or hired the thing to him. Such a person is said to have detention rather than legal possession of the thing. This distinction is of importance, for instance, with regard to the duties of the person to account for and return fruits to the owner when the thing is reclaimed.

For *usucapione* to operate and to allow the legal possessor to convert his possession into ownership, several factors are relevant. These include, the nature of the property - whether it is a moveable or an immoveable, a registrable moveable or not, and whether it is an improved rural property; the manner in which possession was acquired - was it by stealth or violence, in good or bad faith, by virtue of a just title or not; and the length of time the person has had possession and whether or not that possession has been interrupted. If the property is an immoveable and not an improved rural estate, possession for twenty years is required, although this is reduced to ten years where the possessor is in good faith and obtained possession by a method suitable for transferring title and registered the transfer. For improved rural properties, the period is fifteen years, reduced to five in similar circumstances, and for registrable moveables, ten years and three years respectively. Other forms of moveable property can be acquired immediately if the method of transfer is suitable for transferring ownership and the acquirer was in good faith, but if the method of transfer was not suitable, a ten-year term of possession is needed, while if there was no good faith, the period is twenty years.

This can be set out in tabular form:

Type of property	**with *bona fides* & just title**	**without just title**	**without *bona fides***
Immoveable	10 years	20 years	20 years
Improved rural land	5 years	15 years	15 years
Registrable moveable	10 years	3 years	3 years
Other moveables	Immediate	10 years	20 years

Where the property consists of a universality of moveables, such as the estate of a deceased person, and the acquisition by *usucapione* relates to the entirety of the estate, the same periods apply as for immoveables.

Moreover, the period of possession must not be interrupted. An interruption for the purposes of breaking the running of time for acquisition by *usucapione* means an interruption for more than one year . Thus, if possession is lost for more than a year, time has to begin to run again for the acquirer to get title. However, if he can get the thing back within a year, the period for *usucapione* continues unabated. A person in possession, in the legal sense, has at his disposal a special action for recovery of a thing which is taken from his possession by force or stealth. The action is known as the *azione di reintegrazione* and lies for the benefit of a person despoiled of his possession, and is based on the mediaeval canon law remedy of the *actio spolii* itself based on the Roman law interdict, *unde vi*, which protected possession. This action must be brought within a year of the thing being taken or of its taking by stealth being discovered. A person who obtains physical possession of a thing by force or stealth cannot commence a period of *usucapione* to acquire title to it until the force or the stealth are ended.

Notes

[1] *Codice civile*, art. 810-831.
[2] *Cod. civ.*, art. 832-921.
[3] L. 1 June 1939, n. 1089.
[4] See, for instance, Lucio Sponza, *Italian Immigrants in Nineteenth Century Britain: Realities and Images* (Leicester, 1988); Colin Hughes, *Lime, Lemon and Sarsaparilla: The Italian Community in South Wales 1881-1945* (Bridgend, 1991).
[5] *Cod. civ.*, art 922-947.
[6] *Cod. civ.*, art 923-933.
[7] L. 13 December 1928, n. 3086; L. 4 January 1938, n. 28; L. 22 December 1939, n. 2194; L. 3 May 1956, n. 511.
[8] *Cod. civ.*, art. 934-947.
[9] See ante chapter 2.
[10] *Cod. civ.*, art. 952-956.
[11] *Cod. civ.*, art. 957-977.
[12] *Cod. civ.*, art. 978-1020.
[13] *Cod. civ.*, art. 1021-1026.
[14] *Cod. civ.*, art. 1027-1099.
[15] See below, section 9.
[16] *Cod. civ.*, art. 1100-1116.
[17] *Cod. civ.*, art. 1117-1139.
[18] *Cod. civ.*, art. 1158-1167; for possession generally, see art. 1140-1172.

13 The Concept of a Law of Obligations

1 General Theory

The law of obligations was for the Romans a part of the law of things. However, in some modern civil law systems, including the Italian, there is a recognition that things which can be owned form a separate juristic category from those things which are owed. Obligations are those latter things which are owed rather than owned. If the law of property therefore is concerned with the implications of the statement

A owns X,

the law of obligations is concerned with the implications in law of the statement

A owes X to B.

Again, one can begin by recognizing that the analysis of this statement commences with its parsing as a simple sentence, the subject of which is A who owes, the object of which is X, that which is owed, and the indirect object of which is B, to whom the object is owed by the subject. From this grammatical analysis one can again move to certain logical conclusions so as to say that for the sentence to make sense as well as have meaning A must be capable of owing, X must be capable of being owed and B must be capable of having something owed to him. The jurisprudential questions then follow: who may owe; what may be owed; to whom may something be owed? Further juristic questions also follow, such as: what is meant by owing?, how can a situation of owing arise?, how does a situation of owing cease? Possibly, the question of why something is owed must also be entertained. These are the questions to which the law of obligations purports to set out the answers.

Once more, the mediaeval jurists who first posed these theoretical questions were aware from the Roman law texts they studied and their own experience of the communities in which they lived that situations arose in which one person owed something to another. Accepting that the Roman law texts supplied information about law in its most perfect form, it was to these texts that they turned for the raw empirical evidence from which to derive the data to answer their questions. The rules were ultimately those of the Digest; the method of enquiry was that of the mediaeval scholars. Their presentation of their answers was the setting forth of the written reason of the ancient texts according to the mode of exposition most favoured in their time and it is that mode of presentation which has been refined and continues to supply the means by which the law of modern continental countries is set out in their respective civil codes. To understand the structure of the codes, one must understand the questions which the presentation sets out to answer and the underlying methodology employed. There are therefore certain general questions about the law of obligations which are answered before the stuff of actual obligations is put under the microscope.

2 Obligations as a Single Category in Civil Law

Civil law systems of jurisprudence are more familiar with the concept of a law of obligations than their common law counterparts. An English lawyer thinks of contract and tort, for instance, as separate legal categories. While he may acknowledge that they can be seen as sub-divisions of a larger whole, the law of obligations, his thinking generally treats of them as being distinct legal entities. He is conditioned so to view them because in his legal education he will have encountered them as separate legal subjects and will have studied them from different legal treatises. Moreover, he will be able to cite good reasons for so regarding them. The measure of damages in contract and tort, for instance, are based upon different considerations. In tort, damages seek to restore the victim to the position in which he would have been in had he not suffered the injury. In contract, on the other hand, the measure of damages is designed to place the plaintiff in the position he would have been in had the contract been properly performed, and not to compensate him for the loss he has suffered through the contract being broken. It is however somewhat ironic that the common lawyer does so treat contract and tort, for the common law of contract was historically derived from an action, the action on the case for *assumpsit*, which developed during the late fourteenth and early fifteenth century as an action in what would definitely today be accounted tort. Given that the greater part of the modern English law of contract is derived from a form of action with its origins in tort, it is strange to say the least that English lawyers should be wary of recognizing more fully than they do the unity that exists within the law of obligations of which contract and tort are but parts.[1]

Resistant however they are. It is very difficult for common lawyers to adapt their thinking to accommodate the central role which the concept of obligations plays in the civil lawyer's approach to the topics of tort, contract and restitution. It is therefore necessary constantly to remind the common lawyer or student of the common law coming at the civil law of obligations for the first time that the central role of the concept of obligation has to be kept in mind when examining the sub-categories of obligation which contract and tort represent.

It is best to begin by asking what a civil lawyer means by the concept of an obligation. An obligation is something of pecuniary value which is due from one person to another. The fact that the obligation must be of pecuniary value distinguishes such obligations from duties, such as those discussed above in relation to family law - such as the duties of spouses one to another or the respective duties of parents and children - which do not have a monetary value. An obligation is something of monetary value which is owed by one person to another. It is due. In the third century A.D., the classical Roman jurist Ulpian defined justice as the constant and perpetual wish to render unto each his due.[2] If something is due therefore from one to another, it is the duty of the person from whom it is due to render it. It would be an injustice not to render it and there is an imbalance until it is rendered. This notion of justice as requiring that each be given his due is the backdrop to the civil law concept of obligation.

The Roman jurists envisaged four ways in which something could become due in this manner. It could become due because one person had agreed to render it, the thing due, to the other, in which case the obligation was said to arise *ex contractu* and to be a contractual obligation. It could be due because the one party had harmed the other in some way which the law deemed to be unjust, that is an injury - *iniuria*, so that the wrongdoer should render recompense to his victim. Such recompense became due because of the wrong done, that is it arose *ex delicto*, and the obligation is therefore said to be delictual. Further, recompense may be due because one person has conferred a benefit upon another without there being any agreement or antecedent legal obligation to confer that benefit, but in circumstances in which the law nevertheless deems it unjust for the beneficiary not to compensate the benefactor on account of the benefit given. Insofar as it is often claimed that the beneficiary would have agreed to receiving the benefit had he or she known of the circumstances requiring it, such obligations are said to arise as though out of contract, *quasi ex contractu*, and to be quasi-contractual in nature. However, sometimes the beneficiary is fully aware of the circumstances which make it unfair to keep the benefit and that is the very reason for insisting that the recompense be made. More accurately, in such circumstances, the obligation may be said to be one to make restitution, although the term quasi-contract is nevertheless often used to cover such situations as well. Finally, there are circumstances in which someone is obliged to compensate for an injury suffered by another even though they were not themselves the author of that injury, either because they are responsible for a child or employee who caused the injury or because the thing which caused the injury or the premises through which it arose is owned by them. In the sixth century A.D., the compilations of the Emperor Justinian referred to such obligations as arising as though out of delict, *quasi ex delicto*, thus balancing the concept of quasi-contractual obligations with one of quasi-delictual ones. This brings the number of types of obligation up to four: contractual, delictual, quasi-contractual and quasi-delictual. As a matter of aesthetics, this may be pleasing, and it will indeed be seen that four is a recurrent number in the civil law of obligations, perhaps because it was and is regarded as being a natural number, a number regularly found in nature - four seasons, four points of the compass, and so on. However, many modern civil law systems, including the Italian, have not favoured the continuance of the quasi-delictual head. Instead, delict has become a word associated with crimes rather than torts and both obligations arising out of delict and as though out of delict are now referred to as arising out of wrongful acts - *atti illiciti*. While the three-fold division of obligations which thus arises may not be as stylistically acceptable as Justinian's four, it does reflect, with an aesthetically pleasing economy, the manner in which obligations do indeed arise, for both delictual and quasi-delictual obligations rest ultimately upon the notion that the injury suffered ought not to have occurred, that is that it was unjust in that the harm was not due to, in the sense of deserved by, the victim.

3 The Civil Law Analysis of Obligations : An Example

The civil law insistence that obligations are a unity and that the sub-categories of contract, quasi-contract and delict are but sub-divisions of this unified category can give rise to difficulties for those used to the common law methods of dealing with obligations as being either in contract or tort. The civil lawyer grounds his analysis of obligations upon the manner in which the obligation has arisen : if through agreement, contractual; if through, wrongdoing, delictual; and so on. The common lawyer, however, is not trained to examine obligations according to how they arose, but prone to consider why it is that the plaintiff seeks to sue the defendant. It is the cause of action which grounds his analysis. This can give rise to problems, which problems should be educative, for through an appreciation of their nature, the English lawyer should come to an awareness of the difference between the common law and civil law approaches to obligations and that the boundaries between contract and tort are not drawn in the same place as those between contract and delict, because drawn upon a different principle. From that should spring an important jurisprudential awareness - that the drawing of the boundaries is in a sense arbitrary and that there is nothing natural or intrinsic in their positioning.

A simple example should serve to illustrate this.

> A asks B for a loan of his lawnmower. B lends it to A.

What obligations arise as a result of this transaction, and what sort of obligations are they? Remarkable as it may seem, it is likely that a student of English law will have difficulty with these questions, particularly the second of them. It will readily be appreciated that A is under an obligation to return the lawnmower to B, either when he has finished with it, when B asks for it back or at a time which has been pre-arranged. However, the question of what sort of obligation this is - contractual or tortious - will prove more difficult. The student of the common law will probably begin by saying that contractual obligations are those which are grounded on agreement, but will then have difficulty in concluding that the above arrangement is founded on contract in English law. The difficulty will arise because it is difficult to establish that the above facts will support an action for breach of contract. To begin with, although there is an agreement, it is slightly resistant to the conventional analysis of agreement into offer and acceptance. One could say that A offered to borrow B's lawnmower, but that does violence to the language. One does not offer to borrow something; one requests a loan of it. Nevertheless, here is a request and an acceptance of the request by B so that an agreement results. The next problem is however more difficult. In English law, an agreement is only actionable if it is either reduced to writing in a deed, which is not the case here, or if there has been some consideration for the performance. In that B obtains nothing from A in return for his lending him the lawnmower, there is no consideration for the loan. In the absence of consideration, there is no enforceable contract. The student of the common law will almost undoubtedly come to this conclusion and be embarrassed by the suggestion that English law accordingly places no obstacles in the way of A's keeping the lawnmower. Talk of theft will then ensue, and the student will need reminding that the discussion centres on the private law remedies available and not the punishment of the wrongdoer by the State.

The key question is whether A can keep the lawnmower or whether B can make him give it back. English law tackles the question by saying that if B asks for it back and A refuses to return it, A commits a wrong, a tort, as against B. B is then able to sue A for that tort, a tort which used to be called detinue, that is the wrongful detention of a thing which should be returned, but which is now one kind of wrongful interference with goods.[3] There is however no escaping the point that in this case the detention is wrongful because A having borrowed B's lawnmower, he ought to return it to B, that is he is under an obligation to return it. The obligation antecedes the wrong; indeed, there would not be a wrong without it. However, the common law remedy turns on the wrong and not the nature of the obligation. That is where common law and civil law differ on this matter. The common lawyer ends by saying that the relationship between A and B constitutes in common law what is called a bailment, a relationship which is *sui generis*. The remedies for failure to return however lie in tort because by that time a wrong has been committed.

The civil lawyer on the other hand has no difficulty in stating that the obligation to return the lawnmower exists from the time of the loan and that the obligation arises out of contract. A's request to borrow and B's acceding to that request are sufficient agreement, but there still exists the need to identify some factor which will make the contract actionable. The civil lawyer finds this not in the need for writing or some consideration, but rather in the fact that B has actually handed over the lawnmower to A. The handing over of the thing, the lawnmower, clothes the agreement so as to make it actionable. The civil lawyer recognizes the agreement as a type of real contract, one which is actionable on account of the fact that a *res*, a thing, has been handed over from one party to another under the agreement and which then makes the rest of the agreement legally protected. It is the handing over which makes the agreement actionable. The promise to lend on its own would not give rise to any legal remedies. Thus, if A had asked to borrow the lawnmower and B had agreed to lend it, but had then refused to hand it over, A would have no remedy for B's breaking of his promise because the promise was entirely gratuitous, that is, A had given nothing in return. However, once B hands the thing over to A, the agreement becomes actionable because of the transfer of the thing. That is what constitutes a real contract, and the duty to return it arises out of the agreement and the handing over of the thing. It is therefore a contractual obligation.

The civil lawyer would then be able to go further and identify this contract as a particular kind of real contract, that is one in which the loan is made so that the borrower can use the thing. Such a contract was known to the Roman jurists as *commodatum* and in modern Italian law is called *comodato*. Such a typical contract has duties attaching it in addition to the obligation of A to return the thing in due course. A is also required under the terms of a typical *comodato* to look after the thing while it is in his possession, and he will be liable for any failure to take proper care of it. Thus he must use due diligence in looking after it, that is the degree of diligence that a "good father of a family", the *buon padre di famiglia* would exercise in looking after his own property. A failure to exercise such diligence is what constitutes negligence, *culpa*, in civil law; indeed negligence is seen as the opposite of diligence. The *bonus paterfamilias* of Roman civil law is the embodiment of the abstract standard of diligence in the same manner as in the common law the reasonable man embodies the standard of reasonable care which excludes the possibility of an action for negligence succeeding.

However, there is here a noticeable difference from the approach of the common law. In the common law, the question of whether reasonable care has been used or whether there has been negligence is the sort of question that is canvassed in the context of an action sounding in tort. A common lawyer would find it somewhat remarkable that standards of reasonable care should be regarded as relevant in relation to contractual rather than tortious liability. In civil law, however, in that contract and tort are but sub-categories of the larger unity called the law of obligations, the question of care, the standard required and the consequences of its absence are appropriate questions regardless of the type of obligation under discussion. In that obligations form a unity, there is nothing surprising in treating contractual obligations to the same mode of analysis with regard to their breach as would be applied to delictual ones. Thus, deliberate wrongdoing, *dolo*, and negligence, *colpa*, can be as relevant in the context of contracts as in that of illicit acts. Such standards of liability are relevant to obligations generally. Once more, the importance of the unity of obligations as a category to civil lawyers is demonstrated.

Having established the importance of remembering that in Italian law, as in civil law systems generally, obligations form a unified category, the sub-categories of contractual, delictual and quasi-contractual obligations can now be examined.

Notes

[1] See generally A.W.B. Simpson, *A History of the Common Law of Contract: the Rise of the Action of Assumpsit* (Oxford, 1975); J.H. Baker, *An Introduction to English Legal History*, 3rd Ed., (London, 1990), pp. 374-408.
[2] Justinian, Institutes, I.1.pr.
[3] See Torts (Interference with Goods) Act 1977.

14 Contractual Obligations

1 Introduction

Contractual obligations are those which arise through the agreement of the parties to the obligation. This gives rise immediately to the question of whether every agreement made gives rise to a contractual obligation. Putting aside for the moment the capacity of the parties to enter into contractual relations, the question turns upon whether the law is prepared to recognize and enforce any sort of agreement. Certain agreements will not be recognized by the law because they are unlawful, contrary to public morals or the public interest. However, even if there is no such definite reason for refusing to recognize their validity, the law does not necessarily enforce every agreement which is lawful. Some agreements or promises are too trivial for the law to enforce, and sometimes the parties do not require the intervention of the law.

English law has traditionally only enforced two types of agreement: firstly, those made formally in writing in a deed, which until very recently had also to be under seal; secondly, the agreement that is made for consideration. The latter type of agreement is by far the more common and it is often said that the common law doctrine of consideration was devised in order to distinguish those contracts which deserved the protection of the law from those which did not. An agreement which lacks consideration is a bare agreement, a nude pact, and English law borrows the maxim of the civil law to describe its attitude to such agreements: *ex nudo pacto non oritur actio*; an action does not arise out of a bare pact.

The maxim *ex nudo pacto non oritur actio* was devised by the lawyers of ancient Rome to emphasize that simple pacts or agreements would not give rise to legal actions, and the maxim is as influential in civil law systems today as it is in the modern common law of contract. In the last chapter, the example was considered of A requesting the loan of B's lawnmower and B agreeing to lend it. That agreement, that B lend A his lawnmower, did not give rise to a legally enforceable contractual obligation. The agreement alone was not enough; it was at that stage a bare pact which did not give rise to an action. However, when B actually handed over the lawnmower to A, an obligation arose and an action was thenceforward available for its enforcement. The agreement ceased to be a bare pact with the handing over of the thing, the *res* which was the subject-matter of the contract. Because the agreement had until that moment been a bare pact, *nudum pactum*, and from that moment on gave rise to an action and was therefore no longer a bare pact, the mediaeval jurists spoke of the handing over of the thing as clothing the agreement. Agreements, they maintained, to be actionable must not be bare but clothed, and they developed this literary conceit further, by describing the various factors which operated to make agreements actionable as the vestments which clothed them. Naked agreements could not decently be entertained in the courts. Accordingly, the parties must clothe them with a suitable vestment for them to be admitted. One way of clothing an agreement was by handing over the thing which constituted its subject-matter, in which case the agreement was said to be clothed with or by the thing, *re*. Such agreements which were clothed *re*, by the transfer of the thing which was their subject-matter, were called real contracts.

The concept of a real contract had been recognized by the jurists of ancient Rome, although the development of the doctrine of vestments was the work of the civilian lawyers of the Middle Ages. These latter drew on the learning of the civil law of Rome for the fundamentals of their contractual analysis but developed the ideas they found there into a systematic approach which was their own. Roman law had recognized four basic kinds of contract - real, verbal, literal and consensual. The mediaeval lawyers now developed this into the notion that these types depended upon how the agreement in each type of contract was clothed so as to make it actionable. A contract for them could be clothed or vested with a thing - *re*, with formal words - *verbis*, with writing - *litteris*, or by the meeting of the minds of the parties on certain key issues in the contract, that is by consensus - *consensu*. These were the four main types of contract known to Roman law and were to be the four basic types of contract from which mediaeval and modern civil lawyers were to build their framework of contractual theory.

As has been said, four is something of a magic number in the civil law of obligations. Justinian recognized four ways in which obligations generally could arise and the Roman jurists had recognized four basic types of contract. Real contracts were also divided into four categories, all of which continue to be known as separate real contracts in modern civil law systems including the Italian. The four kinds of real contract are *mutuo*, *comodato*, *deposito* and *pegno.*[1] Each of these will now be examined in turn to illustrate some of the basic features of the modern civil law relating to contractual obligations.

The loan of the lawnmower which has already been discussed is an example of *comodato*, a loan for use. Such an agreement as has been seen only becomes actionable when one party actually hands over the thing, in this case the lawnmower, to the other. Immediately it is handed over, an obligation to return it arises, which is the basic obligation of the contract of *comodato*. As has already been seen, however, that is not the only obligation which arises. The borrower must return the thing in the same condition as that in which it was lent to him, and he will be liable for any harm which comes to it as a result of his failure to exercise due diligence, the diligence of the *buon padre di famiglia* with regard to its care. In other words, he will be liable for any negligence or fault, *colpa*, in his care of it. Likewise he must not deliberately damage the lawnmower or damage it through reckless use, *dolo*. These obligations are basic to a contract of *comodato*. The contractual obligations continue until the lawnmower is returned in good condition to the lender, when the obligations are satisfied.

The real contract called *mutuo* differs from *comodato* in several important respects. A typical fact situation, *fattispecie*, for *mutuo* would be:

> A asks B to lend him a pint of milk until the following week. B agrees and gives A the milk.

As with *comodato*, B's agreeing to loan A the milk does not create an obligation. If B then fails to carry out his promise it is not actionable because it is a bare pact. Once, however, B hands over the milk to A, a contractual obligation arises, the agreement having now been clothed by the transfer of the thing.

So far the situation is as in *comodato*, but the nature of the obligation which has arisen in *mutuo* is very different from that in *comodato*. Come the following week, B does not expect A to give him back the exact same pint of milk that he borrowed the previous week. The whole purpose of borrowing a pint of milk, unlike a lawnmower, is to consume it. The milk is unlike the lawnmower in that it is a fungible, a thing which is consumed by being used. A's obligation therefore in *mutuo* is not the same as the obligation in *comodato*; he is not expected to return the selfsame thing but its equivalent in quantity and quality. The obligation will therefore be satisfied the following week if A returns to B another pint of milk.

This also has consequences for the obligations which A owes B with regard to the care of the thing and also to the title which A gets to the thing when B hands it over to him. When B lent A the lawnmower, he expected to get the same lawnmower back. He did not therefore intend to terminate his ownership of the thing by lending it to A. All A got when the mower was transferred to him was detention[2] of it. B remained its owner. However, when B lends A a pint of milk, he does not intend to receive the selfsame pint when the thing is returned. When he gives the milk to A, he knows that A is going to use and therefore consume it. He does not therefore intend to remain the owner of the milk. Ownership passes to A with a loan for consumption. From this it follows that, as B does not expect to get the selfsame thing back, he has no interest in how A looks after it as it is now A's and not his. If, for example, while carrying the milk home, A drops the bottle and it smashes so that the milk is lost, this does not in any way affect his liability to return a pint of milk to B the following week. If A brought back the spilt milk and the fragments of the bottle, B could refuse to accept this as satisfaction of the obligation owed to him and he would be justified in doing so. Regardless of how A uses or abuses the milk, his obligation to return a pint to B remains unaffected. Accordingly, A does not owe B any duty to exercise due diligence or to abstain from deliberately harming the milk as the milk is his, A's, own property. B has no interest in it once it is transferred to A. B is owed, but does not own, a pint that has been lent. There are therefore similarities and dissimilarities between *mutuo* and *comodato*. A loan of money is also an example of *mutuo*, money being a fungible thing so that it is not expected that the very notes or coins lent will be those returned.

The real contract of *deposito* exhibits similarities and dissimilarities from the other two as well. *Deposito* is also a loan, but for safe keeping rather than use or consumption. A typical fact situation, *fattispecie*, would be:

> A asks B to look after his car by allowing it to be parked in his, B's, drive while he, A, is away for a week's holiday. B agrees and allows A to do so.

Once again, B's agreement is not enough of itself to give rise to an enforceable contractual obligation because it is a bare promise. Once, however, A has actually handed over the car into B's detention by parking it in his drive, an obligation has arisen. Once more, the obligation is to hand back the thing when A gets back from his holiday. As with *comodato*, A expects to get back the very thing that was lent and to get it back in good condition. B is not entitled to use the thing; he is not permitted to use the car for his own purposes. It is a loan for safe keeping not for use. B must therefore refrain from doing anything which he foresees could damage or harm the car in any way, that is, he must avoid deliberately or recklessly harming it. He will be liable for *dolo*.

The question of whether he should also be expected to look after the car during A's absence with due diligence is more difficult. B is not gaining any advantage with regard to the loan of the car, the benefit in this type of loan is entirely with A. In Roman civil law, where this contract was called *depositum*, B would not have been liable for failure to use exact diligence in its care; he was liable for *dolus* but not for *culpa*. In modern Italian law, however, a stricter standard applies and B is expected to exercise the diligence of a *buon padre di famiglia* in looking after the car, although the standard is not applied as strictly as where the loan was for his benefit. He will however be liable for serious negligence as well as for intentional and reckless wrongdoing.

The fourth real contract known to Roman law was *pignus*, the loan for security. A *fattispecie* for what Italian law now calls *pegno* would be:

> A asks B for a loan of £50. B agrees to lend A the money, but asks that A give B his, A's, watch as security for the loan. A hands over the watch.

This is neither a loan for use, consumption nor safe keeping. It is for one purpose only, to give B security for the loan of the money. When A repays the £50, B must return the watch. If A fails to repay the money, B will be allowed to retain the watch or to sell it in satisfaction of the debt. While it is in in B's possession as security for the loan, B must look after it with the diligence of a *buon padre di famiglia*, as it is in his detention for his benefit. He will be liable for any harm that befalls the thing as a result of his *colpa* or *dolo*. Italian law calls this *pegno* reflecting its derivation from the real contract of *pignus* in Roman law. However, Italian law now classifies this as a form of real security and not as a real contract, and it is dealt with therefore in the sixth book of the Civil Code dealing with the protection of rights and not in the fourth book where obligations are discussed.

The classification of real contracts has been discussed in some detail at this stage because it reflects in a microcosm the civilian style of dealing with contractual obligations. Different *fattispecie* are carefully distinguished according to the nature of the obligations involved and different degrees of care and liability are imposed. Thus the purpose of the loan - use, consumption, safe keeping - determines whether title passes and the degree of care which is owed by the borrower. All however are united in the category real contracts in that all only become actionable when the thing which is the subject-matter of the agreement is actually handed over by one party to the other. The civil law of contract exemplifies exceptionally well the juristic elegance - *elegantia juris* - for which Civil law systems are famed, and the careful analysis of concepts by *genus* and *differentia* which contributes so much to the logical beauty of the systems.

Roman law also recognized, as has been said, three other basic types of contract - verbal, literal and consensual. The verbal contract is one where the agreement has to be achieved using a set form of words. It is therefore somewhat ritualistic and most definitely formal. The classic Roman law verbal contract was *stipulatio* which required originally that one party expressly ask the other whether that other promised to do a certain thing using the verb *spondere* for the question, and the other had to reply using the exact same verb stating that he did so promise.

Spondes-ne? Spondeo.

It did not matter what the substance of the promise concerned as long as this form was observed. It was the utterance of the words which, in mediaeval parlance, clothed the promise and made it actionable. Later, other verbs of promising were permitted as long as question and response corresponded, and eventually the question and answer could be framed in Greek as well as Latin. Mediaeval law knew many such verbal contracts. Today, it is only really the contract of marriage which requires that the parties use a set form of words to make a valid agreement. The influence of the verbal contract upon the development of canon law can be seen however in that it still permeates the sacraments of baptism, confirmation and ordination, where exactly corresponding questions and answers are still used to elicit promises from godparents or the candidates themselves.

Verbal contracts demand that an agreement be made in solemn form, so that essentially they are formal contracts. In this, they are comparable with the more usual sort of formal contract, the literal contract, where the form required is writing. Oddly enough, the Roman literal contract was not a contract which had had its terms reduced to writing by the parties, but was concerned with family book-keeping and ledger entries. Modern legal systems generally however recognize that the reduction of an agreement to a written instrument is one way of clothing it so that it becomes actionable before the courts of that system. It is that approach to writing as a form with which to clothe an agreement which marks the mediaeval development of the concept. Modern civil law systems, including that of Italy, prefer to classify such contracts as consensual, merely noting that some contracts based on consensus must also be made in solemn form, that is reduced to writing. This reduces the categorization of contracts to two basic types - real and consensual.

The consensual contract was the fourth and final basic type of contract recognized by Roman law. In this type of contract, all that was required for an agreement to be actionable was that the minds of both parties should be at one over certain essential elements of the bargain. Roman law recognized four sorts of consensual contract - sale, hire, association and mandate. In Latin these were termed *emptio/venditio*, *locatio/conductio*, *societas* and *mandatum*, and their modern Italian equivalents reflect this nomenclature - *vendita*, *locazione*, *società* and *mandato*. Roman law emphasized that in these contracts, agreement alone was sufficient to bind the parties, there being no need for the transfer of a thing, or any written or oral formalities. Modern Italian law on the other hand sees agreement as being enough in contradistinction only to the need for a thing to be transferred in a real contract.

The essential elements that had to be agreed upon in the Roman contract of sale were the thing to be sold and the price. In hire, the essential elements were the thing to be let and the remuneration for the hire. Thus, if A offered - and here the word offer is suitable - to hire B's lawnmower for £5, this would be a contract of hire and not of *comodato*. Accordingly, once B agreed to hire the thing for £5, a binding contract would have been completed. The agreement alone would have produced a binding contract of hire. There would be no need for B to hand the thing over to A for obligations to arise. The element of remuneration removes this agreement from the sphere of *comodato* and places it in that of *locazione*, two different types of contract with different rules with regard to their formation and also with regard to the liabilty of the respective parties. As in *comodato*, A would get only detention not title to the thing, and he would likewise have to look after it with the diligence of a *buon padre di famiglia* and return it at the end of the period agreed. However, he would also be bound to pay the remuneration agreed and he would have certain rights against B with regard to the quality of the thing hired. In that both A and B benefit under the contract of hire, unlike *comodato* which is solely for the benefit of the borrower, B must ensure with due diligence that the thing is fit for the purpose for which A intends to use it. If this were a gratuitous *comodato*, B would only be liable for defects of which he was aware and which he did not disclose to A if A or his property were harmed as a result of B's non-disclosure. However, as *locazione* is not a gratuitous contract but an onerous one, B will also be liable for any harm caused to A or his property from defects of which he should have been aware had he exercized the diligence of a *buon padre di famiglia* as well as those of which he actually was aware at the time of the loan. Again, therefore one sees the precise distinctions which separate the various contractual categories and the legal distinctions which flow therefrom.

Likewise, if A offered - again the word is now appropriate - to purchase a pint of milk from B, rather than borrow one and return it the following week, the contract would be one of sale not of *mutuo*. Thus, being consensual not real, once A and B had agreed upon the thing to be sold and the price, a binding contract would exist between them which either party could enforce. The contract would exist from the time of the agreement not the time of the transfer of the thing. Again, the duties of the parties would now be those of buyer and seller, and B's liability for the quality of the merchandise would be higher than in the case of the gratuitous contract of *mutuo*.

The essentials of the contract of sale offers an opportunity to open up the discussion even further. The Roman jurists had disputed whether in a contract of sale the price had to be in money or whether it could consist of some other thing. Could A, for instance offer to buy a pint of milk from B for a loaf of bread? Eventually, the Roman jurists agreed that such an arrangement was not a sale but an exchange, a contract which they called *permutatio* and which has become the Italian consensual contract of *permuta*. *Permuta* was not however a consensual contract to the Romans, for their list of consensual contracts had closed with the four already mentioned. The Romans therefore classified *permutatio*, somewhat anomalously given that it had a specific name, as an innominate contract, that is one which did not fall into one of the accepted contractual categories. Any lawful agreement which did not fit into one of the recognized contractual categories could therefore qualify to be an innominate contract. Such contracts gave rise to obligations as soon as one party had performed his side of the bargain, in other words once they were partly executed. Such performance could be the delivery of a thing or the doing of an act. It might therefore appear that part performance through delivery of a thing would make the contract real in nature. However, this was not the case, as, for the

Roman jurists, the category of real contracts was closed. Innominate contracts were enforceable not because a thing had been delivered but on account of one party's performance. Four such innominate contracts were identified by name: *permutatio, aestimatum* - the contract of sale or return, *transactio* - the agreement to compromise a legal suit, and *precarium* - the permission to occupy land at the will of the owner. The first three of these are now treated as consensual contracts in modern Italian law.

All named contracts are now, with the exception of the remaining three real contracts, treated as consensual, but, as with the supplementary category of innominate contracts in Roman law, modern Italian law recognizes that any agreement which can be accommodated within its general contractual theory will be binding, even though it does not fit into one of the named categories. The named contracts are said to be those with a typical cause, while those which are not named are said to have an atypical cause. It is still the case therefore that the Italian law of contractual obligation is based on the traditional civil law approach of recognizing different types of contract, each with its own distinct rules relating to formation, obligations, liability and the like. It can justifiably therefore be regarded as a law of contracts rather than a law of contract, even though there are general principles that can be discerned among the respective contractual types and which allow atypical contracts to be enforced before the Italian courts.

2 Typical Contracts in Italian Law

What distinguishes the typical contracts one from another in Italian law is the *causa* of the several contracts. *Causa* is one of the essentials of contractual obligations. It is an important feature of all the civil law systems which are derived from French law, but is absent from those derived from German private law. Indeed, as a concept, it is not to be found in the writings of the Roman jurists, but made its way into the civil law tradition through the writings of the mediaeval canonists. Its usefulness in the exposition of contract law has been and is much debated by civilian writers. However, there is no denying that it is recognized as an essential element of the Italian law of contracts. Typical contracts are those with a typical cause. The meaning of the concept is perhaps more easily illustrated than defined.

B hands over his lawnmower to A. Why?

Various reasons for B handing over his lawnmower to A can be suggested. Perhaps, as outlined above in earlier examples, he has agreed that A should borrow it. Perhaps A has agreed to look after it for B. Perhaps B is paying A to repair it. Perhaps A is paying B for the use of it. Perhaps B has sold the lawnmower to A. Perhaps B is making a gift of it to A.

All of these suggestions are possible explanations of the transfer. In any one instance, however, only one can be correct. If B has agreed that A should borrow it, it is a loan for use, *comodato*. If A has agreed to look after it, it is a loan for safe keeping, *deposito*. If B is paying A to repair it, it is a hire of A's skill; if A is paying for the use of it, it is a hire of B's lawnmower. If B has sold it to A, the delivery is explained as part of a contract of sale. If B intends to give it away, it is the transfer of title. Each is a possible answer to the question of why B has handed over his lawnmower to A. Each is a possible *causa* of the transaction.

It is worth pausing here to reflect on the meaning of the word *causa*. The canonists and modern civil law jurists use it as a noun; in classical Latin it was a preposition. As a preposition, it was placed after the noun or phrase it governed to explain why something was being done. The lawnmower was handed over - *comodati causa*, for the sake of a loan for use; *depositi causa*, for the sake of a loan for safe keeping; *locationis causa*, for the sake of hire; *venditionis causa*, for the sake of selling it; *donationis causa*, for the sake of making a gift. Indeed the mediaeval jurists recognized this use, for they identified three types of contract of hire *locatio/conductio*, being hire of a thing - *locatio/conductio rei*; hire of labour - *locatio/conductio operum*, and hire of services, a skill to do a particular job - *locatio/conductio operis faciendi*. This last expression, which in Latin exhibits a syntactical structure called gerundive attraction, can only be justiied on the basis that the word *causa* is understood to follow. The full should read *locatio/conductio operis faciendi causa* if the *operis faciendi* is grammatically correct.

The *causa* of the contract explains its purpose. This can be of importance to the contract's validity. For instance, suppose B were asked "Why are you handing over the lawnmower to A?" and replied " So that he can use it to mow his lawn tomorrow", whereas if A were asked "Why is B handing over his lawnmower to you?" he replied "As a gift". What would be the effect of the transfer? Would A get title, or would he be bound to give it back? Is he bound to return it as B supposes, or would he have to look after it with due diligence in the interim as a borrower for use would, but which as a new owner he would not? If there is no agreement as to the purpose of a transaction, there is no contractual agreement at all. Some therefore see *causa* as essential to there being a valid contract; others however see it merely as a factor upon which there has to be agreement.

However, even if there is agreement as to the purpose of the transaction, the purpose must still be one which is acceptable in law. If the purpose is illicit, then there can be no lawful contract. Likewise if the purpose is to evade legal obligations or if the motive, the reason, of both parties for entering into the agreement is unlawful.[3]

In relation to contracts which have a typical *causa*, Italian law sets out in relation to each category the rights and duties of the respective parties as has already been illustrated in relation to some of the real contracts. Any other contract which has a lawful *causa* will also be enforced. However, the basic terms of contracts with a typical *causa* are generally set by law. There are currently twenty six such contracts recognized in the Italian civil code. These are:

Contract	Typical Fact Situation	Articles
Vendita	sale - the transfer of property in a thing or some other right in return for the payment of a price	1470-1547
Riporto	contango - transfer of title of credit to a specific thing for a price, the transferee undertaking to transfer equivalent title to the thing at the end of a predetermined period for reimbursement of the price subject to any augmentation or diminution	1548-1551
Permuta	exchange - reciprocal transfer of property in things or of other rights between the contracting parties	1552-1555
Estimatorio	sale or return, one party consigning a thing to another who must either pay the price or return the thing within a set time	1556-1558
Somministrazione	whereby one person obligates himself to perform duties for another for a	1559-1570

	periodical or continuous payment	
Locazione	hire - the obligation to allow another enjoyment of property for a given time for an agreed payment	1571-1654
Appalto	one party undertakes at his own risk to do work or a service for payment in money	1655-1677
Trasporto	the obligation to convey people or things from one place to another for payment	1678-1702
Mandato	mandate - one party obligates himself to perform one or more juridical acts for another	1703-1741
Agenzia	agency - one party undertakes in return for payment the regular duty of promoting contractual arrangements in a particular area for the benefit of another	1742-1753
Mediazione	mediation - putting two or more parties in touch with one another to conclude business without any special relationship with or obligation to any of them	1754-1765
Deposito	one party receives a moveable from another to look after it and return it in due course	1766-1797
Sequestro convenzionale	the entrusting of a thing to someone by persons who are in dispute concerning it so that it will be given back to the person deemed to be entitled when the dispute is resolved	1798-1802
Comodato	the consigning of a thing to another for their use for a fixed time and for a defined purpose with an obligation to return it	1803-1812

Mutuo	the consigning of fixed amount of money or some other fungible by one person to another with an obligation to return the equivalent in due course	1813-1822
Conto corrente	current account - whereby the parties are obligated to note in an account the credits derived from reciprocal transactions, the balance remaining in the account until it is closed	1823-1833
Contratti bancari	banking accounts	1834-1860
Rendita perpetua	the periodical payment in perpetuity of a sum of money or some other render derived from an immoveable or a capital sum which was transferred to the obligee	1861-1871
Rendita vitalizia	the payment of a periodical render for the lifetime of the transferor from the property transferred to the transferee	1872-1881
Assicurazione	insurance	1882-1932
Giuoco e scommessa	gaming and wagering contracts	1933-1935
Fideiussone	a personal obligation guaranteeing the performance of an obligation by another	1936-1957
Mandato di credito	whereby one person obligates himself to another to give credit to a third, for which the obligee stands as guarantor	1958-1959
Anticresi	the transfer of an immoveable to a creditor in order that the debt may be satisfied from its fruits, dividends or even capital	1960-1964
Transazione	agreement to compromise litigation	1965-1976
Cessione dei beni ai creditori	agreement to give goods to creditors in satisfaction of their claims	1977-1986

3 Atypical Contracts

The contracts listed in the table at the end of the previous section are those which are specifically dealt with by name in the Civil Code. Other agreements are however accepted as valid contracts by Italian law even though they do not fit into one of these predetermined categories. In that those agreements which correspond to the contractual situations specifically described by the Civil Code do so because their *causa* is one recognized by the law, they are called contracts with a typical cause. Those which do not so correspond, but are nevertheless valid, are called contracts with an atypical cause.

To be valid, contracts with an atypical cause must conform to the basic, general requirements for valid contractual obligations in Italian law. These are listed in the Civil Code as the agreement of the parties, *causa*, object and, where required by law upon pain of nullity, form. Agreement is defined as being achieved when the offeror is aware of the other party's acceptance. *Causa* is the purpose for which the contract is entered into, for instance for sale, hire or whatever, while the object of the contract is the specific matter about which the parties are contracting. Thus, the object may be to purchase and sell a motor vehicle. The *causa* would be sale, but the object would be that one party buys and another sells the car. The object must be possible, lawful, and either determined or determinable. Thus, an agreement to purchase a unicorn from another is made for a good cause, but the object is impossible so that the contract fails for want of a possible object. Likewise, if the object were unlawful, for instance an agreement to sell a thing which can only be bought and sold under State regulation, such as a precious work of art. Although the object must usually be sufficiently certain for the courts to be able to make orders concerning it, it is sufficient if it can be determined with certainty at a future date or subject to the satisfaction of some condition. Thus a contract to sell some wine, or some corn would not be valid, but a contract to sell all the wine to be found in B's cellar or the corn in his barn at midday on a certain date would be perfectly valid.

Generally speaking, contracts in Italian law do not have to be concluded in any particular form. However, some contracts are required to be made in writing either by notarial deed or by private written instrument to be valid. Failure to comply with the law's demands nullifies the agreement. The contracts to which this requirement applies are set out in article 1350 of the Civil Code. They include contracts which transfer ownership in immoveables; contracts which set up, modify or transfer the right of usufruct in immoveables, *superficie*, *concedente* or *enfiteusi*; contracts which establish joint-ownership in any of the foregoing rights; contracts which set up or modify praedial servitudes; the right of use over immoveables or of habitation; deeds which renounce rights in any of the foregoing; contracts which free land from *enfiteusi*; contracts of *anticresi*, contracts of hire relating to immoveables with a duration of more than nine years; contracts of *società* or association which involve the enjoyment of immoveables or other rights over immoveables if their duration is to be more than nine years or for an unspecified period; deeds which establish perpetual or lifetime renders other than those for the State; deeds which divide immoveables or rights over the same; and contracts of *transazione* (that is, which compromise litigation) relating to any of the foregoing rights. In addition, there are a number of contracts and matters which require written form and which are dealt with in the articles of the Civil Code relating to the same.[4]

These requirements of agreement, *causa*, object and form are in truth general, in that they relate to all contracts. However, the contracts which have a typical cause are regulated not only by the general provisions of the Civil Code relating to contractual obligations but also by the specific provisions relating to each type. Thus, it can indeed be claimed that although Italian law has a law of contract in that it has general rules relating to all contractual obligations, the existence of species specific rules for each type of named contract preserves a sense according to which Italian law still has a law of contracts in the plural.

4 *Società* [5]

Of the four consensual contracts recognized by Roman law, only three are today identified as such by Italian law - *vendita*, *locazione* and *mandato*. The fourth, *società*, although it is not listed as a contract with a typical *causa*, remains of considerable importance as a legal institution in modern Italian law. It is defined as the contract whereby two or more persons dedicate property or services to the exercise of a common economic activity with the intention of dividing the profits among themselves.[6]

The Roman law *societas* began in the arrangement whereby the children of a deceased *paterfamilias* chose not to divide their inheritance but to manage it as an undivided whole. They chose to throw in their lot together, and such an arrangement was also known, for that reason, as a *consortium*. By analogy with this institution, other persons not connected by blood or common inheritance, would sometimes agree to live in community one with another sharing all their property, the *societas omnium bonorum*. From this in turn developed more limited forms of the institution, whereby individuals agreed to share certain items of property together, such as that relating to their common business ventures or to one particular business venture. Thus, the *societas*, which began as a family arrangement, was adapted to meet the needs of commerce, and became a major feature of the commercial law landscape in ancient Rome.

The modern Italian *società* continues to be of major commercial importance. While the family is still described as a natural *società* in the Constitution,[7] most modern *società* are commercial in purpose. They are divided into two basic kinds, personal and share-capital *società*. The standard form of personal *società* is the *società in nome collettivo* or *snc*, which allows two or more persons by agreement to pursue a commercial enterprise (*impresa*) together, sharing the profits and the losses. The sharing of risk is a key factor in this sort of enterprise, and in this sort of *società* the partners bear an unlimited liability for the losses of the *società*. In other words, if the *società* becomes insolvent, the partners remain personally liable from their own patrimonies. This personal liability is less in the case of the *società in accomandita semplice* in which the partners are of two sorts: those who actually run the concern and have unlimited liability for its losses, and those who, while they have invested in it, do not participate in its running and are therefore only liable to the extent of their investment. There is also a *società semplice*, which is confined to partnerships for agricultural purposes, for the joint-ownership of other immoveables, and perhaps any arrangement not commercial in purpose. Liability however is unlimited.

Share-capital *società* correspond in the main to the public and private companies of common law systems. The partners in these enterprises are those who have shares (*azioni*) in the enterprise, that is those who have invested in it by this means. The larger variant is the public company, the *società per azioni* or *SpA*.[8] The shareholders have only limited liability for the company and govern it through their membership and voting rights in its *assemblea*, day-to-day running of the concern being the responsibilty of the directors, *amministratori*. The smaller version, the *società a responsibilità limitata* or *SRL*, is more akin to the common law private company, and allows limited liability to be enjoyed by smaller concerns. Mutual benefit or friendly societies can also be formed and organized as *società*.

A whole range of economic activity is carried on in modern Italy under the guise of *società*. An institution the versatility of which was first appreciated by the Roman jurists continues to be of usefulness in a wide variety of situations to this day. Share-capital *società* are recognized as having separate legal personality from their shareholders. Although it was once argued that personal *società* also had legal personality, this view is not as widely held or supported currently in either juristic doctrine or the jurisprudence of the courts.

5 *Pegno* and Real Security[9]

Just as *società* is no longer listed among the consensual contracts in Italian law but is to be found in Book Five of the Civil Code dedicated to labour law, so also one of the four traditonal real contracts, *pegno*, is not dealt with in Book Four on Obligations but is instead to be found in Book Six of the Civil Code which deals with the protection of rights generally.

Pegno,[10] based on the Roman law contract of *pignus*, pawn or pledge, is concerned with the transfer of the detention of a non-registrable moveable thing by one person to another as security for a credit extended by that other to the first person. Its purpose is to secure the credit by leaving it open to the creditor, if the debt is not satisfied, to proceed in the manner laid down by law to sell the thing pledged so as to be able to recover the debt from the proceeds of sale. It is important to note that neither title in the thing pledged nor legal possession of it passes to the pledgee, and that while the thing is in his detention, he must look after it with due diligence, that is the exact diligence of the *buon padre di famiglia*.

Whereas *pegno* is today regarded by Italian law as a form of real security relating to moveable property, real security of immoveables and registrable moveables is achieved by means of the hypothec.[11] Again, this concept derives from Roman law. In modern Italian law, it secures a debt or other obligation by giving the preferred creditor recourse against a particular item of property in the debtor's patrimony. The hypothec must be created by registration with a notary which secures the creditor's priority as against third parties. In the event of default, the hypothecated property can be sold so that the proceeds of sale can be utlized to satisfy the debt. Unlike the situation in *pegno*, the debtor retains the thing, the registration being sufficient to secure the creditor's position. Hypothecs can arise by operation of law, can be imposed by judicial pronouncement and can be created by the voluntary act of one person or by agreement.

Italian law also grants preference by means of privileges[12] to certain creditors. Thus, the patrimony of a deceased person is charged firstly with the payment of his funeral expenses, the expenses of his final illness, and necessaries supplied to him during the last six months of his life, as well as sums he may owe in fulfilment of the alimentary obligation over his final three months. The whole of the patrimony is charged with the preferred payment of these debts, and the privilege accorded to such creditors is therefore said to be general. Where the privilege relates to specific items of property in the patrimony only, the privilege is said to be special. Special privileges accrue for the benefit of, for instance, professional persons who have undertaken work relating to specific items of property which are then charged with what is owing.

Notes

---

[1] *Pegno* is no longer listed as a real contract in the Civil Code, but is treated in Book Six thereof as a form of real security.

[2] The word *detention* is used in preference to *possession* in order to indicate that A does not have possession of the thing in the legal sense of being possessed as an owner, that is the sort of possession that can ripen into full ownership by *usucapione*. See *ante* chapter 12, section 9.

[3] *Cod. civ.*, art. 1325, 1343-1349.

[4] *Cod. civ.*, art. 1350-1352. The additional situations are set out in art. 1350, comma 13.

[5] *Cod. civ.*, art. 2247-2510.

[6] *Cod. civ.*, art. 2247.

> Con il contratto di società due o più persone conferiscono beni o servizi per l'esercizione in comune di un'attività economica allo scopo di dividerne gli utili.

[7] *Costituzione*, art. 29. See *ante* p. 163.

[8] Once known as the *società anonima* or *SA*.

[9] *Cod. civ.*, Book VI.

[10] *Cod. civ.*, art. 2784-2807.

[11] *Cod. civ.*, art. 2808-2899.

[12] *Cod. civ.*, art. 2745-2783.

15 Delicts or Wrongful Acts

1 Introduction : Civil and Common Law Approaches

One of the most striking differences between the civil law and the common law relating to delicts, torts or wrongful acts is the brevity of the provisions in the various civil codes. It is quite usual for the whole of the provisions relating to civil liability for wrongful acts to be contained on one or two pages of a modern civil code. This is in marked contrast to the lengthy tomes on tort law which set out the equivalent provisions in a common law jurisdiction. This capacity to state all the relevant principles in so small a compass is due to the fact that modern civil law systems analyse civil liability for wrongful acts in terms of the manner in which the person who caused the harm acted. In particular, liabilty is presented in terms of the degree of fault attaching to the wrongdoer.

Italian law presents a particularly clear example of this. The basic legal principles relating to civil liability for wrongful acts are contained in their entirety in articles 2043-2059 of the Civil Code. Article 2043 sets out the basic principle. It reads:

Qualcunque fatto doloso o colposo, che cagiona ad altri un danno ingiusto, obbliga colui che ha commesso il fatto a risarcire il danno.	A deliberate or negligent act of any sort, which causes an unjust harm to another, obligates the person who committed it to compensate for the harm.

An unjust harm, that is one which was not due to the victim, which the victim did not deserve, is to be compensated by the person who caused it if that person acted deliberately or negligently. Nothing is said about the type of harm which has been suffered. Centre stage is occupied by the wrongdoer's act and not by the victim's injury.

This stands in sharp contrast to the traditional approach of the common law and goes a long way to explain why the civil law on wrongful acts is so much more concise. The common law approaches liability for wrongful acts or torts primarily according to the nature of the victim's injury rather than the nature of the tortfeasor's act. Thus, a modern textbook on the subject in English law will be divided into chapters on, for instance, defamation, nuisance, trespass to goods, trespass to land, trespass to the person, and so on. Each chapter deals with a specific type or types of harm suffered by the victim - injury to reputation, injury to reasonable enjoyment of one's property, and so on. The rules of liability determining whether the person who is alleged to have caused the injury in question is liable for the harm or damage which results is then worked out according to the nature of the injury suffered. Elsewhere, the author has described this approach as being victim-based.[1] It contrasts with the modern civil law approach which is grounded on how the defendant in the action acted, so that the author has previously termed this approach defendant-based. The major exception to the victim-based approach of the modern common law is the so-called tort of negligence, and this exception will be discussed further below.

The victim-based approach of the common law reflects the manner in which the common law of torts developed from the forms of action, writs which were based upon the type of harm suffered by the plaintiff. Thus, there were until the middle years of the nineteenth century distinct writs relating to nuisance, defamation, detinue, conversion and all the other torts. The rules of liabilty were worked out in relation to each form of action. Thus, there is a deal of accuracy in describing this department of English law as the law of torts in the plural rather than the law of tort in the singular, as there was in truth no general principle governing liabilty for wrongful acts, only rules relating to liability for each type of wrongful act treated severally. Thus, for instance, a plaintiff in an action for defamation, whether slander or libel, did not have to establish that the defendant had been at fault in publishing the defamation, only that the material was defamatory and that the defendant had published it. Nor would the defendant be exonerated if he could establish that he had acted without fault. Fault was irrelevant in an action for defamation. In an action of trespass on the case arising from a road accident, however, fault would have to be established for the plaintiff to succeed. The rules of liability differed according to the type of injury which the plaintiff had suffered and therefore the form of action, the writ, which he employed to obtain redress.

Originally, Roman civil law also proceeded on a victim-based approach. Thus, in the Digest as in the works of earlier jurists, delictual liability is discussed according to the type of harm suffered. The four main categories of delict in Roman law were *furtum* - theft, *rapina* - robbery, *iniuria* - insult and *damnum iniuria datum* - damage to property. All of these categories are based on the type of harm suffered by the victim and the liability of the wrongdoer is worked out under each heading. However, modern civil law, in response to the rationalism of the eighteenth-century Enlightenment and the contemporaneous clamour for there to be no liability without fault, has restated its rules with regard to civil liability for wrongful acts in terms of the fault attaching to the defendant. It is this defendant-based approach which allows the modern civil law systems to be so succinct in their handling of the subject. They no longer have to catalogue the types of harm which a victim may suffer before considering the rules which determine the liability of the defendant for the harm suffered.

Nor has English law escaped this rationalizing tendency. Prior to the abolition of the separate forms of actions by the Common Law Procedure Act, 1852, it had been necessary for a plaintiff to select most carefully which form of action to employ. The selection of the wrong writ would lead to his being nonsuited and having to recommence his cause using the correct writ with all the doubling of expense that that would entail. Dissatisfaction with the consequences of this rigid formalism led to the abolition of the separate writs in 1852 and their replacement by a uniform writ of summons to commence all actions. Henceforth, the cause of action would be set out in the pleadings rather than in the writ, and the pleadings unlike the writ were susceptible to amendment.

This development opened the way for a restating of the principles of liability, for, as the separate actions had been abolished, it was no longer necessary for the rules of liability to be spelt out in terms of the several headings which had previously been of undoubted importance to the processing of claims. Theoretically, at any time after 1852, it has been possible for the common law judges to state general principles of liability for the commission of wrongful acts rather than continuing to state those principles in relation to the now defunct headings imposed by the writ system. To a large extent, of course, this has not happened. A glance at a modern English textbook on torts will confirm that the law is still viewed from a victim-based standpoint, the type of harm suffered by the victim continuing to form the basis of the classification of wrongs and remedies for them. In other words, the potential for development afforded by the abolition of the forms of action in 1852 has not been realized. This is what the great English legal historian Maitland meant when in 1893, a full forty years after the abolition of the forms of action, he said that although the forms had been buried, they continued to rule English lawyers from their graves.[2]

This is not to say that attempts have not been made to restate the law relating to liability for wrongful acts according to the degree of fault attaching to the defendant. The earliest such attempt was perhaps made by Blackburn J very shortly after the abolition of the writ system in the case of *Rylands* v *Fletcher* in 1866.[3] In that case, Blackburn J set out a general principle of strict liability relating to the keeping or collecting of dangerous things.

> The person who for his own purposes brings on his lands and collects and keeps there anything likely to do mischief if it escapes, must keep it in at his peril, and, if he does not do so, is *prima facie* answerable for all the damage which is the natural consequence of its escape.[4]

The principle was clearly meant to cover a range of cases which had previously been attributed to different heads, but which were now susceptible of being treated under one general principle as a result of the different heads having been abolished. The great step forward however did not come until eighty years after the Common Law Procedure Act, when in 1932, Lord Atkin set out in the celebrated case of *Donoghue* v *Stephenson*[5] a general principle of civil liability for negligent acts.

In his speech in the House of Lords in that case, Lord Atkin acknowledged that the concept of negligence already played a significant role in many of the categories within which civil liability for wrongful acts was determined. However, he believed that it was possible to state one general principle of liability for negligence which would cut across the existing boundaries - or more accurately the boundaries that had once existed between the forms of action - and allow for future cases to be decided in relation to that principle alone without a prior need to categorize the cause of action according to which form of action would have been employed four generations earlier. Lord Atkin's conclusion was that reasonable care should be used to ensure that one's acts or omissions did not injure one's neighbour, and he went on to answer the question of who in law was one's neighbour with his formulation of the famous neighbour principle: "persons who are so closely and directly affected by my act that I ought reasonably to have them in contemplation as being so affected when I am directing my mind to the acts or omissions which are called in question".[6] Subject to this limitation upon who can complain of being harmed by negligence, it is evident that Lord Atkin's principle is akin in its generality to that contained in the codes of civil law systems, for instance article 2043 of the Italian Civil Code, for it is not circumscribed by reference to any particular harm or type of harm suffered by a victim but is concerned only with how the wrongdoer caused that harm.

Acceptance of Lord Atkin's statement of a general principle for determining liability for negligence has not been rapid. It is a matter of modern English legal history as to how staggered that acceptance has been, in particular in relation to negligent statements as opposed to acts, and for instance the way in which Parliament has had to provide for its extension to the liability of occupiers for harms caused by their failure to take reasonable care to ensure that their premises are reasonably safe for lawful visitors.

Moreover, it is interesting to note the manner in which the legal profession in England and Wales as well as academic literature on the law of torts has dealt with the development. In most cases, a chapter has been added to existing discussion of the law, headed "The Tort of Negligence", as though Lord Atkin had discovered a new category of wrongful act rather than having revolutionized the approach of English law to wrongful acts generally by approaching them from a different perspective. Only gradually is English law moving towards fulfilling the potential to restate its rules of liability in relation to wrongful acts which the 1852 legislation afforded. One further example of such progress should perhaps be noted.

In the 1964 case of *Letang* v *Cooper*,[7] the Court of Appeal considered the claim of a young woman who had been injured as a result of having a car driven over her legs while she was sunbathing in a field behind the hotel where she was staying on England's south coast, which field doubled as the hotel car park. She brought her action more than three years after the facts occurred, the period then allowed for actions based upon negligence to be brought being three years. Against the defence that her claim was statute barred, she countered that she was not suing on the basis of the driver's negligence but on the basis that he had inflicted a trespass upon her person. Claims other than for negligence were not barred for up to six years. In effect, she sought to establish that her cause of action came under a heading which was not statute barred rather than one which was, even though such categorization of claims had been abolished over a century previously. The Court of Appeal refused to allow the categories to rule its determination from their graves. Henceforth, Diplock LJ said, plaintiffs should confine their statements of claim to a statement of the relevant facts and not seek to place them within any legal category; the court would determine whether the facts disclosed a good cause of action. The court also restated what was now meant by the term trespass to the person. Henceforth, it decreed, negligently caused personal injuries were not to be categorized as trespasses; trespass to the person required deliberate or at least reckless wrongdoing.[8]

In all of these scattered instances - *Rylands* v *Fletcher* in 1866, *Donoghue* v *Stephenson* in 1932 and *Letang* v *Cooper* in 1964 - the common law is moving towards a representation of its rules relating to liability for wrongful acts in terms of the manner in which the defendant acted rather than upon the basis of the type of harm which the victim suffered. The opportunity to do this was afforded by the abolition of the forms of action in 1852, and it can be seen that the realization of that potential is proving a very slow process. The common law is labouring long and hard to reach the positon that the civil law systems of modern Europe reached during the nineteenth century beginning with the French *Code Civil* in 1804 and ending with the German BGB in 1900. Italy's provisions for civil liability for wrongful acts are part of this movement. The change from a victim-based to defendant-based approach to such liability was part of the pan-European acceptance of the view that liability should be grounded on fault and that generally there should be no liability without fault. The expression of this principle in the civil codes of the countries of continental Europe was also the product of the age of reason which had advanced the fault principle of liability. However, in Britain, acceptance of the need to rationalize the legal system led to the abolition of the forms of action, but the conservative bent of the judiciary and the legal profession has slowed the progress of the change over to defendant-based liability which most of the rest of Europe received as part of the codification movement.

The piecemeal nature of codification in England and Wales has also contributed to the slowness with which the change to defendant-based liability has been effected. Although fault is recognized as the key element in liability for civil wrongs, those wrongs have never been reclassified according to the fault principle and are still analyzed and classified according to the nature of the harm suffered. Thus, liability in defamation continues to differ from that in nuisance because of the nature of the harm and not because of the degree of fault attaching to the perpetrator.

2 The Modern Italian Law

The modern Italian law relating to liability for wrongful acts is to be found in articles 2043-2059 of the Civil Code. The basic principle, upon which the other articles only enlarge, is found in article 2043. This states that a deliberate or negligent act which causes an unjust harm to another obligates the perpetrator to compensate for the harm suffered. A deliberate act is one which is carried out intentionally and wilfully, with *dolo*, while a negligent act is one which involves some lesser degree of fault, *colpa*. *Colpa* is of various kinds: *colpa grave* - the deliberate prosecution of an act which it is known may harm another although it is not intended or willed to do so, generally regarded as equivalent to *dolo*; *colpa lieve* - failure to exercise the standard of diligence expected of a *buon padre di famiglia*, the general standard of care required; and *colpa levissima* - a slight degree of fault not amounting to a failure to exercise due diligence but which in certain circumstances will render the blameworthy person liable for the resulting harm. *Colpa levissima* is not relevant to article 2043 but is relevant in some of the other provisions relating to liability for wrongful acts as will be shown. Neither *dolo* nor the different degrees of *colpa* are defined in the Civil Code. The Civil Code uses the concepts in the sense in which they are defined in the *Codice Penale*.[9]

The harm suffered by the victim must to be compensatable be unjust, in the sense that it was not for any lawful reason due to the victim. If it was due, as a punishment or as a confiscation or distraint, then it is not compensatable. However, even if the harm was unjust as against the victim, it is nevertheless possible for the perpetrator to argue that he was justified in doing whatever it was that caused the harm. Two instances are contemplated in the Code. Firstly, the perpetrator may have acted in lawful defence of himself or of another. This will completely exonerate him of liability. Alternatively, the perpetrator may have been forced to commit the act complained of by the necessity of saving either himself or another from a real danger of serious personal injury. In such case, provided the risk was not voluntarily caused by him or was not otherwise avoidable, his liability to the victim will be limited to an indemnity, the amount of which shall be fixed equitably by the judge.

For the perpetrator to be liable for a harm he has caused, the harm must also be imputable to him. In order for the harm to be imputable, the perpetrator must have the necessary capacity both to intend and will the act which caused the harm at the time when the act was performed, although if the perpetrator lacked this capacity at the relevant time due to his own fault he will remain liable. Where a person who is generally incapable of forming the requisite intention or volition, such as a mental patient, causes an unjust harm to another, the person responsible for his supervision must compensate for the harm unless that person is able to show that he was not able prevent the deed. The supervisor will be liable therefore for *colpa levissima*; if he could have prevented the deed he will be liable even though he used due diligence. Where the victim is not able to obtain compensation from the supervisor because he was absolutely unable to prevent the wrong occurring, the judge is given a discretion to fix equitably the amount of damages which the perpetrator should pay to the victim having regard to the respective economic positions of the parties.

The liabilty of the supervisor for the incapacitated person is clearly a form of vicarious liability. The Code provides that generally parents or guardians are to be liable for wrongs committed by the minor children in their care or living with them or affiliated by them. Teachers likewise and craftsmen teaching their art to apprentices are liable for the wrongful acts committed by their charges while under their supervision. Again, this liability is for any failure to prevent the wrong occurring, but is removed if they can show that it was impossible for them to prevent the deed. The other major head of vicarious liability is that of employers for their employees or servants with regard to harms caused in the course of their employment. Such masters cannot excuse themselves in any way if the wrong is imputable to their servants. In a sense therefore, this is true vicarious liability while that of parents, guardians, teachers and the like is in truth a recognition of part responsibilty on the parts of the superiors themselves for failing to prevent the wrong if that was at all possible.

The Civil Code also recognizes forms of strict liability in certain circumstances, or at least liability that is stricter than for lack of due diligence, *colpa lieve*. Thus, the prosecution of a dangerous activity, or the prosecution of any activity in a manner which is dangerous, renders the perpetrator liable for any harm caused unless he can prove that he had taken all measures appropriate to avoid the harm. Likewise, damage caused by anything in one's custody renders one liable to compensate for it regardless of fault unless one can show that it was a pure accident. Owners, or those who have in their care animals of which they are making use, are responsible for harms caused by the creatures regardless of whether the wrong is done while the animal is in their custody or if it has wandered or escaped, unless they can show the damage was the result of an accident for which they are in no wise to blame. Any damage caused through the ruinous condition of a building or other construction renders the owner liable unless he can prove that the damage was not due to a defect in maintaining the structure on his part or to a flaw in its construction.

One particularly interesting provision relates to the liability of drivers and owners of vehicles for damage caused by their movement.

Article 2054 provides that a driver is liable for any harm caused by the circulation of his vehicle to any person or thing unless he can show that he had done everything possible to avoid the harm arising. Where the damage is caused by a collision, there is a rebuttable presumption that each driver has contributed equally to the damage suffered by his particular vehicle. Moreover, the owner of a vehicle, or a person having use and enjoyment of it or a person who has acquired it under a pact reserving ownership to another, is liable as well as the driver for any harm caused by the vehicle unless he can show that the vehicle was being driven without his permission. If it is unclear therefore who was driving a vehicle at the time of an accident, the victim need not worry about whom to sue; he sues the owner. Drivers and owners are also responsible in the same manner as described above for any flaws in the construction of, or defect in maintaining, a vehicle.

Joint wrongdoers are jointly and severally liable for damage they cause, that is each is liable in full for the damage they have caused together. If judgement is given against one joint wrongdoer, he must seek contribution from the others after he has compensated the victim. Contribution is awarded having regard to the respective degrees of fault attaching to the several parties. In the absence of contrary evidence, the degree of fault of joint wrongdoers is presumed to be equal.

Damages are assessed according to the principles set out in articles 1223, 1226 and 1227 of the Civil Code. Loss of profit is assessed by the judge equitably having regard to the circumstances of the case. Where the damage caused to the victim is of a permanent kind, it is open to the court to compensate him by the award of periodical payments. Security for such payments can be ordered. The victim in suitable cases can ask for a specific restitution of property he has lost, if this is possible in whole or in part. The judge may however in appropriate cases order that an equivalent be returned to the victim if the return of the original is thought to be unduly onerous for the defendant.

Italian law does not however compensate for non-pecuniary loss other than in cases specifically provided for by law, which are those in effect where the civil wrong also amounts to a criminal offence. If the wrong is therefore not a crime, the person harmed by it can only recover for the pecuniary loss which he or she has suffered. This means that, unlike English law, there is no possibilty of recovering damages for pain and suffering, loss of amenity or loss of expectation of life, for instance. Such items, although capable of causing much psychological and emotional trauma, have in reality no pecuniary value and attempts to quantify them in money terms are therefore artificial. Italian law recognizes this and refuses to indulge in an arbitrary quantification of such harms. Instead, it limits itself, in the case of purely civil wrongs, to compensating those harms which can actually be quantified in monetary terms. Thus, the actual monetary loss of damage to property will be assessed, as will consequential losses such as the cost of medical treatment for a person, veterinary treatment for an animal, repair bills for items of property. In addition, consequential losses such as loss of earnings or profits as a result of injuries suffered will be quantified.

Notes

[1] See the author's "Hamlet and the Law of Homicide", (1984) 100 *Law Quarterly Review* 282, at 283-295.
[2] F.W. Maitland, *The Forms of Action at Common Law*, (ed. A.H.Chaytor and W.J.W. Whittaker: Cambridge, 1971) p. 1.
[3] (1866) L.R. 1 Ex. 265.
[4] Ibid., at 279-280.
[5] [1932] AC 562.
[6] Ibid., at 580.
[7] [1965] 1 QB 232.
[8] Ibid., at 243.
[9] *Codice Penale*, art. 43.

16 Quasi-Contracts

1 The Underlying Principle

If an obligation to compensate arises where one person inflicts an undeserved harm upon another, it can fairly be asked whether an obligation does not also arise to compensate a person who confers a benefit which is not due upon another. Such a benefaction, conferred without an intention to make a gift, but rather by mistake or to assist at a time when the other is not able to assist himself or herself, can be viewed as the converse situation to that which gives rise to a delictual obligation. Is there an obligation to make restitution of or for the benefit received? Alternatively, as the name quasi-contract suggests, it can be viewed as a situation in which the parties if they were in good faith could be taken to be in agreement that a benefit given which was not due should be returned.

In Italian law, the concept of quasi-contractual obligations is much more developed than in English law. Indeed, it is fair to say that quasi-contracts are more highly developed in civil law systems generally than in those of the common law. The civilian roots of quasi-contract go back to the law of Rome where the idea of obligations arising *quasi ex contractu* was already recognized. Although to maintain the prevalence of the magic number, four, in the law of obligations, four types of quasi-contractual obligation were recognized in the emperor Justinian's compilations, including the pecuniary obligations arising from joint ownership and from the relationship between guardian and ward, the two major headings of quasi-contract were *negotiorum gestio* and *indebiti solutio*. These are two of the three headings under which Italian law currently deals with quasi-contract, the third being enrichment without cause or unjust enrichment. As will be seen, this head of quasi-contract bears some resemblance to some of the principles of equity in English law. It will be convenient however to begin examining the area with *indebiti solutio*, money paid or property handed over under a mistake of fact, as this is an area known to English law and affords a particularly clear illustration of the basic principles underlying this department of the law of obligations.

2 *Indebiti solutio*[1]

The typical fact situation with which this concept deals is that where A wrongly believes that he is under a duty to pay a sum of money to B and pays it, even though in fact it is not due. Article 2033 of the Civil Code provides that a person who has made a payment that was not due has the right to recover what he paid. The provision goes further than this because it also gives the benefactor the right to recover any fruits or other interests which have arisen since the payment was made if the person who received the payment was in bad faith, that is knew the money was not due and still took it, or, if the payee was in good faith, to reclaim the fruits and other interests which have arisen since the request for repayment was made.

If however the reason that the payment is not due is purely a legal reason, for instance that the debt was statute barred, or one which while due was not legally enforceable, such as a debt of honour, no obligation to make restitution arises, unless that is the payment was made by someone suffering from a legal incapacity. Likewise if a payment is made in satisfaction of a debt which the law would not enforce because it was *contra bonos mores*, a claim in restitution will not be entertained.

The *fattispecie* can of course be varied. A may pay a debt that was owed to B by C, in the mistaken belief that he was obligated to pay it. In such a circumstance, A is again entitled to recover the amount paid from B together with fruits from either the date of payment or the date of its being reclaimed depending upon whether B had been in good faith, but there is here an additional complication. It is possible that B, having accepted payment by A in good faith, has destroyed the evidence of C's indebtedness, or perhaps C's debt is now statute barred. Article 2036 therefore provides that A's claim is only valid if there is no prejudice to B's continuing claim against C. If for any reason A cannot get his money back from B, then he is allowed to proceed against C in the same manner that B would have been.

Much the same problem can arise if what has been handed over is not a sum of money but some item of property. Again, there is an obligation to return it, but in this case there is the possibility that the thing will have perished in the interim. If that is the case, even if the thing perished by accident, a person who received it in bad faith will be liable to restore the value of the thing, or if it has deteriorated rather then completely perished, to restore an equivalent thing or the original together with an indemnity to compensate for the loss in value at the transferor's election. If however the thing had been received in good faith, the transferee is not liable for its destruction or deterioration, even if it is his fault, unless the compensation can be taken from any enrichment he has enjoyed.

When A has mistakenly transferred a thing to B, who received it in good faith and passed it on to C, B is required to hand over any consideration for the transfer to A. If the consideration is still owing to B from C, A steps into B's shoes as the person to whom the debt from C is owed. If the thing was transferred by B to C gratuitously, C becomes liable for its return to A to the extent of his enrichment. If B had passed the thing on in bad faith, he is obligated to restore it or its value to A. A can however claim its restitution or its value directly from C, and even if C had received it gratuitously, he must compensate A to the extent that he has been enriched by the transfer.

If the undue payment or transfer was however made to a person who is not of full legal capacity, then even if the payment was received in bad faith, the payee is not bound to make restitution other than to the extent to which the transaction had worked to his advantage. Further, if the person bound to make restitution has incurred expenses in caring for the thing or in improving it while it was in his possession, reimbursement for such expenses and costs must be made by the person reclaiming it.

3 *Negotiorum gestio*[2]

La gestione di affari is the name given by modern Italian law to the concept of one person assuming responsibilty for doing some act or business on behalf of another when there is no legal obligation upon him to assume that responsibilty. A typical *fattispecie* would be that of a person who, when his next-door neighbour is on holiday, noticing that a window in the neighbour's house is broken, either arranges with a glazier to have it repaired or sets about the repair himself. The question then arises as to whether the neighbour is obligated to pay for the repair which has been done in his absence, there clearly being no contract as between the neighbours or between the glazier and the person whose window has been repaired.

Italian law recognizes that there is in such a situation an obligation on the part of the beneficiary to recompense the benefactor. The obligation will only arise if the work was usefully undertaken; unnecessary officious interference is not encouraged. The beneficiary is required to assume responsibilty for any obligations entered into by the gestor on his behalf and also to indemnify the gestor for any obligations which he has entered into in his own name on the other's behalf or for any necessary and useful expenses incurred, together with interest from the day on which such expenses were incurred. Such an obligation cannot however arise in express contravention of the known wishes of the beneficiary, unless his prohibition upon the doing of certain acts is unlawful, or contrary to the public interest or morality.

The gestor on the other hand is treated in the same manner as though he had entered into a contract of *mandato* with the beneficiary. Indeed, *gestione di affari* is very similar to mandate, and can be viewed as an implied contract in which one person without an agreement does for another what, if that other were aware of the situation, he would readily agree should be done on his behalf by the gestor. However, given the circumstances under which the gestor acts, a judge determining his liability is to moderate any damages awarded against him for the manner in which he carried out the business limiting them to those which can actually be said to have arisen as a result of his fault. To be liable, the gestor must have the capacity to contract and, once having commenced the task, must see it through to completion or until the other party can take over for himself. Even if the other party dies, the gestor must see the work through, unless the heir is able to take over its direction.

Finally, if the interested party becomes aware of what the gestor is doing and ratifies the relationship, that is approves of his doing it, the relationship is converted into one of *mandato*, even if the gestor had believed he was doing the work on his own behalf.

4 Unjust Enrichment[3]

In the absence of any other remedy to rectify the situation, Italian law recognizes the possibilty of an action for unjust enrichment, *l'arricchimento senza causa*. The essence of this obligation is that one party has made a gain at the expense of another, which gain was in no way due to him. As it was not due, it is deemed unjust and therefore the person who has gained is liable to make good the loss to the other but only out of the gain which he has made. If the gain consists in having received a specific thing from the other, the thing itself must be restored if it is still in existence at the time of the claim.

The action is used in Italian law where other actions provide no remedy. It has a certain affinity with the manner in which equity in English law relieves the effects of catching bargains and agreements entered into through undue influence. Thus, if an expectant heir agrees to hand over to a moneylender the whole of his inheritance in return for an immediate loan of a much smaller sum, equity in England and Wales will relieve the heir of the effects of his desperate bargain. Italian law would compel the moneylender to restore that part of what he had received which constituted an unjust enrichment at the expense of the heir.

Likewise, equity in England and Wales will prevent one person taking advantage of a relationship with another which means that the persons are not on equal bargaining terms. Where one person is not really a free agent in his dealings with another, equity insists that the person disadvantaged have independent advice or else any bargain made will be set aside for undue influence, so-called fraud in equity. Italian law would also insist that where the parties are not in equal bargaining positions as a result of their relationship, if one makes a gain at the expense of the other which gain is not due to a just cause, the loss to the person in the weaker bargaining position must be compensated out of the other's gain as an unjust enrichment. The particular strength of the Italian provision is that it is not limited to certain situations but is expressed in general terms. It thus has a wider ambit than its English counterpart.

Notes

---

[1] *Cod. civ.*, art. 2033-2040.
[2] *Cod. civ.*, art. 2028-2032.
[3] *Cod. civ.*, art. 2041-2042.

Select Bibliography

The Bibliography which follows is intended to supply readers with a list of works which will serve to deepen their appreciation of the historical and social context within which modern Italian law operates. In addition, the material listed under primary sources consists of popular editions of the main law codes, most of which are published annually, and which are readily and cheaply available in Italy. The Constitution and other fundamental laws are generally set out at the beginning of every edition of the codes. The texts listed under secondary sources are recommended for a detailed study of their respective subjects. Where no year of publication is given, this indicates that the texts are updated very frequently and that the most recent edition should be sought.

Primary Sources

Costituzione della repubblica italiana. Rome. Buffetti Editore.
I nuovi quattro codici. Francesco Bartolini (a cura di). Piacenza. Casa Editrice La Tribuna.
I quattro codici. Fausto Izzo, Marcello Iacobellis, Raffaele Marino e Giustino Gatti (a cura di). Naples. Edizioni Simone.
Il codice civile. Francesco Bartolini (a cura di). Piacenza. Casa Editrice La Tribuna.
Il codice di procedura civile. Francesco Bartolini (a cura di). Piacenza. Casa Editrice La Tribuna.
Il codice di procedura penale. Giulio Ubertis (a cura di). Milan. Raffaello Cortina Editore.
Il codice penale. Luigi Alibrandi (a cura di). Piacenza. Casa Editrice La Tribuna.
Il codice penale. Roland Riz. (a cura di). Bolzano. AER Edizioni.
Il nuovo codice di procedura penale. Piermaria Corso (a cura di). Piacenza. Casa Editrice La Tribuna.

Secondary Sources

Albisetti, A. *Il diritto ecclesiastico nella giurisprudenza della Corte costituzionale*. Giuffrè. Milan. 1992.
Amato, G. and Barbera, B. *Manuale di diritto pubblico*. Il Mulino. Bologna. 1994.
Antolisei, F. *Manuale di diritto penale*. Giuffrè. Milan.
Attardi, A. *Diritto processuale civile.* Cedam. Padua. 1994.

Bartoli, S., Mastragostino, F., Vandelli, L. *Le autonomie territoriali.* (3a Ed) Il Mulino. Bologna. 1991.
Bassi, F. *Lezioni di diritto amministrativo.* (4a ed). Giuffrè. Milan. 1995.
Biscaretti di Ruffia, P. *Diritto costituzionale. Istituzioni di diritto pubblico.* Jovene. Naples.
Biscaretti di Ruffia, P. *Introduzione al diritto costituzionale italiano e comparato.* Giuffrè. Milan. 1988.
Biscaretti di Ruffia, P. *Un triennio di profonde trasformazioni costituzionali.* Giuffrè. Milan.
Bonsignori, A. *L'esecuzione forzata.* Giappichelli. Turin. 1991.
Cassarino, S. *Manuale di diritto processuale amministrativo.* Giuffrè. Milan. 1995.
Cordero, F. *Procedura penale.* Giuffrè. Milan. 1993.
Cordini, G. *Elementi di diritto ambientale.* Istituto di Studi Politico-Giuridici. Pavia.
Cottino, G. *Diritto commerciale.* Cedam. Padua. 1993.
Diritto Processuale Penale. Giuffrè. Milan. 1994-1995.
Finocchiaro, F. *Diritto ecclesiastico.* Zanichelli. Bologna.
Finocchiaro, F. *Il matrimonio nel diritto canonico.* Il Mulino. Bologna.
Galgano, F. *Diritto privato.* Cedam. Padua.
Lozzi, G. *Lezioni di procedura penale.* Giappichelli. Turin. 1994.
Mandrioli, C. *Corso di diritto processuale civile.* Giappichelli. Turin. 1993.
Mantovani, F. *Diritto Penale.* Cedam. Padua.
Martines, T. *Diritto costituzionale.* Giuffrè. Milan.
Niccolini, G. *Diritto del lavoro.* Giuffrè. Milan. 1992.
Occhiocupo, N. *Liberazione e promozione umana nella Costituzione.* Giuffrè. Milan.
Rescigno, P. *Manuale del diritto privato italiano.* Jovene. Naples.
Tesauro, F. *Istituzioni di diritto tributario.* UTET. Turin.
Trabucchi, A. *Istituzioni di diritto civile.* Cedam. Padua.
Virga, P. *Manuale di diritto amministrativo.* Giuffrè. Milan.

Other works

Arlacchi, P. *Mafia Business.* Oxford University Press. 1988.
Arlacchi, P. *Mafia, Peasants and Great Estates.* Cambridge University Press. 1983.
Barbalich, R. *Italy: Practical Commercial Law.* Longman. London. 1991.
Barzini, L. *The Italians.* Hamish Hamilton. London. 1987.
Bedani, G. "The Concept of the Secular State" in (1996) 1 *Modern Italy: Journal of the Association for the Study of Modern Italy*, 3-22.
Bellamy, R. *Beccaria: On Crimes and Punishments and Other Writings.* Cambridge University Press. 1995.

Bellomo, M. *The Common Legal Past of Europe, 1000-1800*. Catholic University of America Press. Washington DC. 1995.

Blok, A. *The Mafia of a Sicilian Village, 1860-1960*. Polity. Cambridge. 1974.

Bono, P. and Kemp, S. (ed) *Italian Feminist Thought*. Blackwell. Oxford. 1991.

Borkowski, A. *Textbook on Roman Law*. Blackstone. London. 1994.

Brundage, J.A. *Medieval Canon Law*. Longman. London. 1995.

Cappelletti, M., Merryman J.H. and Perillo J.M. *The Italian Legal System.* Stanford University Press. 1967.

Certoma, G.L. *The Italian Legal System*. Butterworths. London. 1985.

Clark, M. *Modern Italy, 1871-1982*. Longman. London. 1984.

Cole, D. *Law Profile of Italy.* The British Council. London. 1995.

Corso, P. "Italy", in Van Den Wyngaert, C. (ed) *Criminal Procedure Systems in the European Community*. Butterworths. London. 1993.

David, R. and Brierley, J.E.C. *Major Legal Systems in the World Today*. (2nd Ed.) Stevens and Sons. London. 1978.

Davis, J.A. *Conflict and Control: Law and Order in Nineteenth-Century Italy*. Macmillan. London. 1988.

Dickie, J. "The South as Other : From Liberal Italy to the *Lega Nord*" in (1994) 14 *The Italianist (Supplement)*, 124-140.

Ginsborg, P. *A History of Contemporary Italy*. Penguin. London. 1990.

Halperin, S.W. *The Separation of Church and State in Italian Thought from Cavour to Mussolini*. University of Chicago Press. 1937. (Reprinted Octagon Books, New York. 1971).

Hearder, H. *Italy in the Age of the Risorgimento, 1790-1870*. Longman. London. 1983.

Hearder, H. *Italy: A Short History*. Cambridge University Press. 1990.

Hine, D. "The New Italian Electoral System" in (1993) 24 *Association for the Study of Modern Italy: Newsletter*, 27-34.

Hine, D. *Governing Italy*. Clarendon Press. Oxford. 1993.

Kelly, J.M. *A Short History of Western Legal Theory*. Clarendon Press. Oxford. 1992.

Kertzer, D.L. and Saller, R.P. (ed) *The Family in Italy from Antiquity to the Present*. Yale University Press. New Haven and London. 1991.

LaPalombara, J. *Democracy Italian Style*. Yale University Press. New Haven and London. 1987.

Mack Smith, D. *Cavour*. Knopf. New York. 1985.

Mack Smith, D. *Italy and its Monarchy*. Yale University Pres. New Haven and London. 1989.

Mack Smith, D. *Mussolini.* Weidenfeld and Nicolson. London. 1981.

Novak, B.C. *Trieste: 1941-1954*. University of Chicago Press. 1970.

Parker, S. "The March 1994 Parliamentary Elections: An Overview" in (1994) 25 *Association for the Study of Modern Italy: Newsletter*, 28-35.

Pugsley, D. and Criscuoli, G. *The Italian Law of Contract.* Jovene. Naples. 1991.
Radding, C.M. *The Origins of Medieval Jurisprudence*. Yale University Press. New Haven and London. 1988.
Robinson, O.F., Fergus, T.D. and Gordon, W.M. *European Legal History*. Butterworths. London. 1994.
Sassoon, D. *Contemporary Italy*. (3rd Ed) Longman. London. 1986.
The Italian Crisis, 1989-1994 in (1995) 1 *Modern Italy: Journal of the Association for the Study of Modern Italy*.
Van Caenegem, R.C. *An Historical Introduction to Private Law*. Cambridge University Press. 1992.
Vinogradoff, P. *Roman Law in Medieval Europe*. Clarendon Press. Oxford. 1929.
Zimmermann, R. *The Law of Obligations : Roman Foundations of the Civilian Tradition*. Juta. Cape Town. 1990./ Oxford University Press. 1996.

Index

References from Notes indicated by 'n' after page reference

Appendix

The structure of the Italian legal profession described on pages 113-115 has undergone considerable modification since the manuscript of this work was completed. *Legge 2 febbraio 1997, n. 27* has abolished the distinction between procurators and advocates within the practising profession. Existing procurators, who had not yet qualified as advocates, were automatically given the higher status, and were moreover deemed to have enjoyed that status from the time when they were first admitted as procurators. What were previously the qualifications for admission as a procurator now become the qualifications for admission as an advocate, although the qualifications for admission as an advocate entitled to practise before the superior courts - *cassazione*, the *Consiglio di Stato*, the Court of Accounts and the Constitutional Court - remain unchanged.

Now that practitioners begin their career as advocates, the time during which they must serve in that capacity before progressing to the status of *avvocati cassazionisti* is increased to twelve years, although this is taken to have included any period during which aspirants practised as procurators under the old structure. However, if it is more favourable to them, this period is reduced to seven years for existing advocates who had progressed to that status by means of taking examinations. Further, those who take the special examinations in the work of the superior courts may progress to practise before those courts after only five years from admission as advocates in the new sense. Those who have qualified as procurators only or have been advocates for less than a year are allowed to reckon their time practising as procurators as part of the five years, and those who have qualified as advocates in the old sense may still progress to practise before the superior courts after only one year if they proceed by examination.

Advocates now perform all the functions which were performed previously either by their branch of the profession or by procurators. In effect, given that the vast majority of Italian procurators went on to qualify as advocates, a somewhat artificial and unnecessary distinction has been removed by the new law, the profession of procurator having been swallowed up by that of advocate, as it always was in reality once a procurator proceeded to the higher status.

The new law came into force and effect on 28 February 1997.

DATE DUE

APR 2 1 2009

APR 1 6 REC'D

SEP 1 4 2009

SEP 1 4 REC'D

NOV 0 4 2009

NOV 0 2 REC'D

DISCARDED
BOWLING GREEN STATE UNIVERSITY LIBRARY

GAYLORD

PRINTED IN U.S.A.

KKH 68 .W38 1997

Watkin, Thomas Glyn, 1952-

The Italian legal tradition